I, Rigoberta Menchú

An Indian woman in Guatemala

Edited and Introduced by Elisabeth Burgos-Debray

Translated by Ann Wright

VERSO

London • New York

First English-language edition published by Verso 1984
Second English-language edition published by Verso 2009
Translation © Verso 1984
First published as *Me Llamo Rigoberta Menchú Y Asi Me Nació La Concienca*
© Editions Gallimard and Elisabeth Burgos 1983
All rights reserved

The moral rights of the author have been asserted

1 3 5 7 9 10 8 6 4 2

Verso
UK: 6 Meard Street, London W1F 0EG
US: 20 Jay Street, Suite 1010, Brooklyn, NY 11201
www.versobooks.com

Verso is the imprint of New Left Books

ISBN-13: 978-1-84467-445-9 (hbk)
ISBN-13: 978-1-84467-418-3 (pbk)

British Library Cataloguing in Publication Data
A catalogue record for this book is available from the British Library

Library of Congress Cataloging-in-Publication Data
A catalog record for this book is available from the Library of Congress

Typeset by Hewer Text UK Ltd, Edinburgh
Printed and bound in the US by Maple Vail

I, Rigoberta Menchú

CONTENTS

TRANSLATOR'S NOTE

Rigoberta's narration reflects the different influences on her life. It is a mixture of Spanish learned from nuns and full of biblical associations; of Spanish learned in the political struggle replete with revolutionary terms; and, most of all, Spanish which is heavily coloured by the linguistic constructions of her native Quiché and full of the imagery of nature and community traditions.

She has learned the language of the culture which oppresses her in order to fight it – to fight for her people – and to help us understand her own world. In doing so, she has created a form of expression which is full of passion, poetry and wisdom. Sometimes, however, the wealth of memories and associations which come tumbling out in this spontaneous narrative leave the reader a little confused as to chronology and details of events.

The problem of translation was how to retain the vitality, and often beautiful simplicity, of Rigoberta's words, but aim for clarity at the same time. I have tried, as far as possible, to stay with Rigoberta's original phrasing; changing and reordering only where I thought the meaning could not be readily understood. Hence, I've left the repetitions, tense irregularities, and sometimes convoluted sentences which come from Rigoberta's search to find the right expression in Spanish. Words have been left in Spanish or Quiché, where they are objects or concepts for which we have no precise equivalent.

The two most obvious words in this category are *ladino* and *compañero*. Although ladino ostensibly means a person of mixed race or a Spanish-speaking Indian, in this context it also implies someone who represents a system which oppresses the Indian – first under Spanish rule and then under the succession of brutal governments of the landed oligarchy. So a word like 'half-caste' would be inadequate. Hence Rigoberta's father's invention *'ladinizar'* (to *ladinize*, or become like a *ladino*) which is a mixture of *ladino* and *latinizar* (to latinize), and has both racial and religious connotations. I think it is clear that the word *compañero*, which literally means companion, changes its meaning during the book. Rigoberta initially uses it for her friends, and her neighbours in the community. But as the political commitment of both Rigoberta and her village grows, it becomes 'comrade', a fellow fighter in the struggle. She uses it for the militants in the trade unions, the CUC and the political organisations. The *compañeros de la montana* are the guerrillas. From these two words comes the rather unwieldy *compañero ladino*.

Rigoberta has a mission. Her words want us to understand and react. I only hope that I have been able to do justice to the power of their message. I will have done that if I can convey the impact they had on me when first I read them.

Ann Wright

INTRODUCTION

This book tells the life story of Rigoberta Menchú, a Quiché Indian woman and a member of one of the largest of the twenty-two ethnic groups in Guatemala. She was born in the hamlet of Chimel, near San Miguel de Uspantán, which is the capital of the north-western province of El Quiché.

Rigoberta Menchú is twenty-three years old. She tells her story in Spanish, a language which she has spoken for only three years. Her life story is an account of contemporary history rather than of Guatemala itself. It is in that sense that it is exemplary: she speaks for all the Indians of the American continent. What she tells us of her relationship with nature, life, death and her community has already been said by the Indians of North America, those of Central America and those of South America. The cultural discrimination she has suffered is something that all the continent's Indians have been suffering ever since the Spanish conquest. The voice of Rigoberta Menchú allows the defeated to speak. She is a privileged witness: she has survived the genocide that destroyed her family and community and is stubbornly determined to break the silence and to confront the systematic extermination of her people. She refuses to let us forget. Words are her only weapons. That is why she resolved to learn Spanish and break out of the linguistic isolation into which the Indians retreated in order to preserve their culture.

Rigoberta learned the language of her oppressors in order to use it against them. For her, appropriating the Spanish language is an act which can change the course of history because it is the result of a decision: Spanish was a language which was forced upon her, but it has become a weapon in her struggle. She decided to speak in order to tell of the oppression her people have been suffering for almost five hundred years, so that the sacrifices made by her community and her family will not have been made in vain.

She will not let us forget and insists on showing us what we have always refused to see. We Latin Americans are only too ready to denounce the unequal relations that exist between ourselves and North America, but we tend to forget that we too are oppressors and that we too are involved in relations that can only be described as *colonial*. Without any fear of exaggeration, it could be said that, especially in countries with a large Indian population, there is an internal colonialism which works to the detriment of the indigenous population. The ease with which North America dominates so-called 'Latin' America is to a large extent a result of the collusion afforded it by this internal colonialism. So long as these relations persist, the countries of Latin America will not be countries in any real sense of the word, and they will therefore remain vulnerable. That is why we have to listen to Rigoberta Menchú's appeal and allow ourselves to be guided by a voice whose inner cadences are so pregnant with meaning that we actually seem to hear her speaking and can almost hear her breathing. Her voice is so heart-rendingly beautiful because it speaks to us of every facet of the life of a people and their oppressed culture. But Rigoberta Menchú's story does not consist solely of heart-rending moments. Quietly, but proudly, she leads us into her own cultural world, a world in which the sacred and the profane constantly mingle, in which worship and domestic life are one and the same, in which every gesture has a pre-established purpose and in which everything has a meaning. Within that culture, everything is determined in advance;

everything that occurs in the present can be explained in terms of the past and has to be ritualized so as to be integrated into everyday life, which is itself a ritual. As we listen to her voice, we have to look deep into our own souls for it awakens sensations and feelings which we, caught up as we are in an inhuman and artificial world, thought were lost for ever. Her story is overwhelming because what she has to say is simple and true. As she speaks, we enter a strikingly different world which is poetic and often tragic, a world which has forged the thought of a great popular leader. In telling the story of her life, Rigoberta Menchú is also issuing a manifesto on behalf of an ethnic group. She proclaims her allegiance to that group, but she also asserts her determination to subordinate her life to one thing. As a popular leader, her one ambition is to devote her life to overthrowing the relations of domination and exclusion which characterize internal colonialism. She and her people are taken into account only when their labour power is needed; culturally, they are discriminated against and rejected. Rigoberta Menchú's struggle is a struggle to modify and break the bonds that link her and her people to the *ladinos*, and that inevitably implies changing the world. She is in no sense advocating a racial struggle, much less refusing to accept the irreversible fact of the existence of the *ladinos*. She is fighting for the recognition of her culture, for acceptance of the fact that it is different and for her people's rightful share of power.

In Guatemala and certain other countries of Latin America, the Indians are in the majority. The situation there is, *mutatis mutandis*, comparable to that in South Africa, where a white minority has absolute power over the black majority. In other Latin American countries, where the Indians are in a minority, they do not even have the most elementary rights which every human being should enjoy. Indeed, the so-called forest Indians are being systematically exterminated in the name of progress. But unlike the Indian rebels of the past, who wanted to go back to pre-Columbian times, Rigoberta Menchú is not fighting in the name of an idealized or mythical past. On the contrary, she obviously wants to play an active part in history and it is that which makes her thought so modern. She and her comrades have given their historical ambitions an organic expression in the shape of the Peasant Unity Committee (CUC) and their decision to join the '31 January Popular Front', which was founded to commemorate the massacre on that date of a group of Quiché Indians who occupied the Spanish embassy Ciudad-Guatemala in order to draw attention to their plight. The group which occupied the embassy was led by Rigoberta's father, Vicente Menchú, who has since become a national hero for the Indians of Guatemala. The Popular Front, which consists of six mass organizations and was founded in January 1981, took the name '31 January' in memory of the massacre.

Early in January 1982, Rigoberta Menchú was invited to Europe by a number of solidarity groups as a representative of the 31 January Popular Front. It was then that I met her in Paris. The idea of turning her life story into a book came from a Canadian woman friend who is very sympathetic to the cause of the Guatemalan Indians. Never having met Rigoberta, I was at first somewhat reluctant, as I realized that such projects depend to a large extent on the quality of the relationship between interviewer and interviewee. Such work has far-reaching psychological implications, and the revival of the past can resuscitate affects and zones of the memory which had apparently been forgotten for ever and can lead to anxiety and stress situations.

As soon as we met, however, I knew that we were going to get along toegether. The admiration her courage and dignity aroused in me did much to ease our relationship.

She came to my home one evening in January 1982. She was wearing traditional costume, including a multicoloured *huipil* with rich and varied embroidery; the patterns were not symmetrical and one could have been forgiven for assuming that they were random. She was also wearing an

ankle-length skirt; this too was multicoloured and the thick
material was obviously hand-woven. I later learned that
it was called a *corte*. She had a broad, brightly coloured
sash around her waist. On her head, she wore a fuchsia and
red scarf knotted behind her neck. When she left Paris, she
gave it to me, telling me that it had taken her three months
to weave the cloth. Around her neck she had an enormous
necklace of red beads and old silver coins with a heavy solid
silver cross dangling from it. I remember it as being a partic-
ularly cold night; in fact I think it was snowing. Rigoberta
was wearing no stockings and no coat. Beneath her *huipil*,
her arms were bare. Her only protection against the cold
was a short cape made from imitation traditional fabric;
it barely came to her waist. The first thing that struck me
about her was her open, almost childlike smile. Her face
was round and moon-shaped. Her expression was as guile-
less as that of a child and a smile hovered permanently on
her lips. She looked astonishingly young. I later discovered
that her youthful air soon faded when she had to talk about
the dramatic events that had overtaken her family. When
she talked about that, you could see the suffering in her
eyes; they lost their youthful sparkle and became the eyes of
a mature woman who has known what it means to suffer.
What at first looked like shyness was in fact a politeness
based upon reserve and gentleness. Her gestures were grace-
ful and delicate. According to Rigoberta, Indian children
learn that delicacy from a very early age; they begin to pick
coffee when they are still very young and the berries have
to be plucked with great care if the branches are not to be
damaged.

I very soon became aware of her desire to talk and of her
ability to express herself verbally.

Rigoberta spent a week in Paris. In order to make things
easier and to make the best possible use of her time, she came
to stay with me. Every day for a week, we began to record her
story at nine in the morning, broke for lunch at about one,
and then continued until six in the evening. We often worked

after dinner too, either making more recordings or preparing questions for the next day. At the end of the week I had twenty-four hours of conversation on tape. For the whole of that week, I lived in Rigoberta's world. We practically cut ourselves off from the outside world. We established an excellent rapport immediately and, as the days passed and as she confided in me and told me the story of her life, her family and her community, our relationship gradually became more intense. As time went by, she became more self-assured and even began to seem contented. One day she told me that until then she had never been able to sleep all night without waking up in a panic because she had dreamed that the army was coming to arrest her.

But I think it was mainly the fact of living together under the same roof for a week that won me her trust; it certainly brought us closer together. I have to admit that this was partly an accident. A woman friend had brought me some maize flour and black beans back from Venezuela. Maize and beans are the staple diet in both Venezuela and Guatemala. I cannot describe how happy that made Rigoberta. It made me happy too, as the smell of *tortillas* and refried beans brought back my childhood in Venezuela, where the women get up early to cook *arepas** for breakfast. *Arepas* are much thicker than Guatemalan *tortillas*, but the ingredients are the same, as are the methods of cooking and preparing them. The first thing Rigoberta did when she got up in the morning was make dough and cook *tortillas* for breakfast; it was a reflex that was thousands of years old. She did the same at noon and in the evening. It was a pleasure to watch her. Within seconds, perfectly round, paper-thin *tortillas* would materialize in her hands, as though by miracle. The women I had watched in my childhood made *arepas* by patting the dough flat between the palms of their hands, but Rigoberta made her *tortillas* by patting it between her fingers, holding them straight and together and

---

* A kind of bread made from maize in Venezuela, normally eaten hot.

constantly passing the dough from one hand to the other. It is much more difficult to make perfectly shaped *tortillas* like that. The pot of black beans lasted us for several days and made up the rest of our daily menu. By chance, I had pickled some hot peppers in oil shortly before Rigoberta's arrival. She sprinkled her beans with the oil, which almost set one's mouth on fire. 'We only trust people who eat what we eat', she told me one day as she tried to explain the relationship between the guerrillas and the Indian communities. I suddenly realized that she had begun to trust me. A relationship based upon food proves that there are areas where Indians and non-Indians can meet and share things: the *tortillas* and black beans brought us together because they gave us the same pleasure and awakened the same drives in both of us. In terms of *ladino*-Indian relations, it would be foolish to deny that the *ladinos* have borrowed certain cultural traits from the Indians. As Linto points out, some features of the culture of the defeated always tend to be incorporated into the culture of the conqueror, usually via the economic-based slavery and concubinage that result from the exploitation of the defeated. The *ladinos* have adopted many features of the indigenous culture and those features have become what George Devereux calls the 'ethnic unconscious'. The *ladinos* of Latin America make a point of exaggerating such features in order to set themselves apart from their original European culture: it is the only way they can proclaim their ethnic individuality. They too feel the need to be different and therefore have to differentiate themselves from the Europe that gave them their world-vision, their language and their religion. They inevitably use the native cultures of Latin America to proclaim their otherness and have always tended to adopt the great monuments of the Aztec, Mayan and Incan pre-Columbian civilizations as their own, without ever establishing any connection between the splendours of the past and the poor exploited Indians they despise and treat as slaves. Then there are the 'indigenists' who want to recover the lost world of their ancestors and cut themselves off completely from European culture. In order to do so, however, they use notions and techniques borrowed from that very culture. Thus, they promote the notion of an Indian nation. Indigenism is, then, itself a product of what Devereux calls 'disassociative acculturation': an attempt to revive the past by using techniques borrowed from the very culture one wishes to reject and free oneself from.* The indigenist meetings held in Paris – with Indian participation – are a perfect example of what he means. Just like the avant-garde groups which still take up arms in various Latin American countries – and these groups should not be confused with resistance groups fighting military dictatorships, like the Guatemalan guerrillas, the associations of the families of the 'disappeared ones', the countless trade union and other oppositional groups which are springing up in Chile and other countries, or the 'Plaza de Mayo Mothers' movement in Argentina – the indigenist groups also want to publicize their struggles in Paris. Paris is their sound box. Whatever happens in Paris has repercussions through the world, even in Latin America. Just as the groups which are or were engaged in armed struggle in America have supporters who adopt their political line, the Indians too have their European supporters, many of whom are anthropologists. I do not want to start a polemic and I do not want to devalue any one form of action; I am simply stating the facts.

The mechanism of acculturation is basic to any culture; all cultures live in a state of permanent acculturation. But there is a world of difference between acculturation and an attempt to impose one culture in order to destroy another. I would say that Rigoberta Menchú is a successful product of acculturation in that her resistance to *ladina* culture provides the basis for an antagonistic form of acculturation. By resisting *ladina* culture, she is simply asserting her desire for ethnic individuality and cultural autonomy. Resistance can,

---

* George Devereux, *Essais d'ethropsychanalyse complémentariste*, Paris 1972.

for instance, take the form of rejecting the advantages that could result from adopting techniques from another culture. Rigoberta's refusal to use a mill to grind her maize is one example. Indian women have to get up very early to grind the pre-cooked maize with a stone if the *tortillas* are to be ready when they leave for work in the fields. Some people might argue that this is nothing more than conservatism, and that indeed is what it is: a way of preserving the practices connected with preparing *tortillas* and therefore a way to prevent a whole social structure from collapsing. The practices surrounding the cultivation, harvesting and cooking of maize are the very basis of the social structure of the community. But when Rigoberta adopts political forms of action (the CUC, the 31 January Popular Front and the Vicente Menchú Organization of Christian Revolutionaries) she is adopting techniques from another culture in order to strengthen her own techniques, and in order to resist and protect her own culture more effectively. Devereux describes such practices as adopting new means in order to support existing means. Rigoberta borrows such things as the Bible, trade union organization and the Spanish language in order to use them against their original owners. For her the Bible is a sort of ersatz which she uses precisely because there is nothing like it in her culture. She says that 'The Bible is written, and that gives us one more weapon.' Her people need to base their actions on a prophecy, on a law that comes down to them from the past. When I pointed out the contradiction between her defence of her own culture and her use of the Bible, which was after all one of the weapons of colonialism, she replied without any hesitation whatsoever: 'The Bible says that there is one God and we too have one God: the sun, the heart of the sky.' But the Bible also teaches us that violence can be justified, as in the story of Judith, who cut off the head of a king to save her people. That confirms the need for a prophecy to justify action. Similarly, Moses led his people out of Egypt and his example justifies the decision to transgress the law and leave the community. The example of David shows that children too can take part in the struggle. Men, women and children can all justify their actions by identifying with biblical characters. The native peoples of Latin America have gone beyond the stage of introspection. It is true that their advances have sometimes been blocked, that their rebellions have been drowned in blood and that they have sometimes lost the will to go on. But they are now finding new weapons and new ways to adapt to their socio-economic situation.

Rigoberta has chosen words as her weapon and I have tried to give her words the permanency of print.

I must first warn the reader that, although I did train as an ethnographer, I have never studied Maya-Quiché culture and have never done fieldwork in Guatemala. Initially, I thought that knowing nothing about Rigoberta's culture would be a handicap, but it soon proved to be a positive advantage. I was able to adopt the position of someone who is learning. Rigoberta soon realized this: that is why her descriptions of ceremonies and rituals are so detailed. Similarly, if we had been in her home in El Quiché, her descriptions of the landscape would not have been so realistic.

When we began to use the tape recorder, I initially gave her a schematic outline, a chronology: childhood, adolescence, family, involvement in the struggle . . . As we continued, Rigoberta made more and more digressions, introduced descriptions of cultural practices into her story and generally upset my chronology. I therefore let her talk freely and tried to ask as few questions as possible. If anything remained unclear, I made a note of it and we would spend the last part of the working day going over anything I was uncertain about. Rigoberta took an obvious pleasure in explaining things, helping me understand and introducing me to her world. As she told me her life story, she travelled back in time, reliving dreadful moments like the day the army burned her twelve-year-old brother alive in front of the family, and the weeks of martyrdom her mother underwent at the hands of the army before they finally let her die. As I listened to her detailed account of the customs and rituals of her culture, I made a list which included customs relating to death. Rigoberta read my list. I had decided to leave the theme of death until last, but when we met for the last time, something stopped me from asking her about the rituals associated with death. I had the feeling that if I asked about them my questions would become a prophecy, so deeply marked by death was her life. The day after she left, a mutual friend brought me a cassette on which Rigoberta had recorded a description of funeral ceremonies, 'because we forgot to record this.' That gesture was the final proof that Rigoberta is a truly exceptional woman; culturally, it also proved that she is a woman of complete integrity and was letting me know that she had not been taken in. In her culture, death is an integral part of life and is accepted as such.

In order to transform the spoken word into a book, I worked as follows.

I began by transcribing all the tapes. By that I mean that nothing was left out, not a word, even if it was used incorrectly or was later changed. I altered neither the style nor the sentence structure. The Spanish original covers almost five hundred pages of typescript.

I then read through the transcript carefully. During a second reading, I established a thematic card index, first identifying the major themes (father, mother, childhood, education) and then those which occurred most frequently (work, relations with *ladinos*, linguistic problems). This was to provide the basis of the division of the material into chapters. I soon reached the decision to give the manuscript the form of a monologue: that was how it came back to me as I re-read it. I therefore decided to delete all my questions. By doing so I became what I really was: Rigoberta's listener. I allowed her to speak and then became her instrument, her double, by allowing her to make the transition from the spoken to the written word. I have to admit that this decision made my task more difficult, as I had to insert linking passages if the manuscript was to read like a monologue, like one continuous narrative. I then divided it into chapters organized around the themes I had already identified. I followed my original chronological outline, even though our conversations had not done so, so as to make the text more accessible to the reader. The chapters describing ceremonies relating to birth, marriage and harvests did cause some problems, as I somehow had to integrate them into the narrative. I inserted them at a number of different points, but eventually went back to my original transcript and followed the order of Rigoberta's spontaneous associations. It was pointed out to me that placing the chapter dealing with birth ceremonies at the beginning of the book might bore the reader. I was also advised simply to cut it or include it in an appendix. I ignored all these suggestions. Perhaps I was wrong, in that the reader might find it somewhat off-putting. But I could not leave it out, simply out of respect for Rigoberta. She talked to me not only because she wanted to tell us about her sufferings but also – or perhaps mainly – because she wanted us to hear about a culture of which she is extremely proud and which she wants to have recognized. Once the manuscript was in its final form, I was able to cut a number of points that are repeated in more than one chapter. Some of the repetitions have been left as they stand as they lead in to other themes. That is simply Rigoberta's way of talking. I also decided to correct the gender mistakes which inevitably occur when someone has just learned to speak a foreign language. It would have been artificial to leave them uncorrected and it would have made Rigoberta look 'picturesque', which is the last thing I wanted.

It remains for me to thank Rigoberta for having granted me the privilege of meeting her and sharing her life with me. She allowed me to discover another self. Thanks to her, my American self is no longer something 'uncanny'. To conclude, I would like to dedicate these lines from Miguel Angel Asturias's 'Barefoot Meditations' to Rigoberta Menchú:

Rise and demand; you are a burning flame.
You are sure to conquer there where the final horizon
Becomes a drop of blood, a drop of life,
Where you will carry the universe on your shoulders,
Where the universe will bear your hope.

Elisabeth Burgos-Debray
Montreux-Paris
December 1982.

I

THE FAMILY

'We have always lived here: we have the right to go on living where we are happy and where we want to die. Only here can we feel whole; nowhere else would we ever feel complete and our pain would be eternal.'

—Popol Vuh

My name is Rigoberta Menchú. I am twenty-three years old. This is my testimony. I didn't learn it from a book and I didn't learn it alone. I'd like to stress that it's not only *my* life, it's also the testimony of my people. It's hard for me to remember everything that's happened to me in my life since there have been many very bad times but, yes, moments of joy as well. The important thing is that what has happened to me has happened to many other people too: my story is the story of all poor Guatemalans. My personal experience is the reality of a whole people.

I must say before I start that I never went to school, and so I find speaking Spanish very difficult. I didn't have the chance to move outside my own world and only learned Spanish three years ago. It's difficult when you learn just by listening, without any books. And, well, yes, I find it a bit difficult. I'd like to start from when I was a little girl, or go back even further to when I was in my mother's womb, because my mother told me how I was born and our customs say that a child begins life on the first day of his mother's pregnancy. There are twenty-two indigenous ethnic groups in Guatemala, twenty-three including the *mestizos*, or *ladinos* as we call them. Twenty-three groups and twenty-three languages. I belong to one of them – the Quiché people – and I practise Quiché customs, but I also know most of the other groups very well through my work organizing the people. I come from San Miguel Uspantán,* in the north-western province of El Quiché. I live near Chajul† in the north of El Quiché. The towns there all have long histories of struggle. I have to walk six leagues, or twenty-four kilometres, from my house to the town of Uspantán. The village is called Chimel,‡ I was born there. Where I live is practically a paradise, the country is so beautiful. There are no big roads, and no cars. Only people can reach it. Everything is taken down the mountainside on horseback or else we carry it ourselves. So, you can see, I live right up in the mountains.

My parents moved there in 1960 and began cultivating the land. No-one had lived up there before because it's so mountainous. But they settled there and were determined not to leave no matter how hard the life was. They'd first been up there collecting the *mimbre* that's found in those parts, and had liked it. They'd started clearing the land for a house, and had wanted to settle there a year later but they didn't have the means. Then they were thrown out of the small house they had in the town and had no alternative but to go up into the mountains. And they stayed there. Now it's a village with five or six *caballerias* of cultivated land.

They'd been forced to leave the town because some *ladino* families came to settle there. They weren't exactly evicted but the *ladinos* just gradually took over. My parents spent everything they earned and they incurred so many debts with these

---

* Municipality and administrative centre of the province of El Quiché.
† Municipality and administrative centre of the province of El Quiché.
‡ Centre of the Ixil people. The word also means 'ocote', in the Quiché language.

people that they had to leave the house to pay them. The rich are always like that. When people owe them money they take a bit of land or some of their belongings and slowly end up with everything. That's what happened to my parents.

My father was an orphan, and had a very hard life as a child. He was born in Santa Rosa Chucuyub,* a village in El Quiché. His father died when he was a small boy, leaving the family with a small patch of maize. But when that was finished, my grandmother took her three sons to Uspantán. She got work as a servant to the town's only rich people. Her boys did jobs around the house like carrying wood and water and tending animals. But as they got bigger, her employer said she didn't work enough for him to go on feeding such big boys. She had to give away her eldest son, my father, to another man so he wouldn't go hungry. By then he could do heavy work like chopping wood or working in the fields but he wasn't paid anything because he'd been given away. He lived with these *ladinos* for nine years but learned no Spanish because he wasn't allowed in the house. He was just there to run errands and work, and was kept totally apart from the family. They found him repulsive because he had no clothes and was very dirty. When my father was fourteen he started looking around for some way out. His brothers were also growing up but they weren't earning anything either. My grandmother earned barely enough to feed them. So my father went off to find work on the *fincas* near the coast. He was already a man and started earning enough money to send to my grandmother and he got her away from that family as soon as he could. She'd sort of become her employer's mistress although he had a wife. She had to agree because she'd nowhere else to go. She did it out of necessity and anyway there were plenty more waiting to take her place. She left to join her eldest son in the coastal estates and the other boys started working there as well.

We grew up on those *fincas* too. They are on the south coast, part of Escuintla, Suchitepequez, Retalhuleu, Santa Rosa, Jutiapa,

---

* Hybrid Hispano-Quiché word meaning 'Santa Rosa before the Hill'.

where coffee, cotton, cardamom and sugar are grown. Cutting cane was usually men's work and the pay was a little higher. But at certain times of the year, both men and women were needed to cut cane. At the beginning things were very hard. They had only wild plants to eat, there wasn't even any maize. But gradually, by working very hard, they managed to get themselves a place up in the *Altiplano*. Nobody had worked the land there before. My father was eighteen by this time and was my grandmother's right arm. He had to work day and night to provide for my grandmother and his brothers. Unfortunately that was just when they were rounding young men up for military service and they took my father off, leaving my grandmother on her own again with her two sons. My father learnt a lot of bad things in the army, but he also learnt to be a man. He said they treated you like an object and taught you everything by brute force. But he did learn how to fight. He was in the army for a long, hard year and when he got back home he found my grandmother was dying. She had a fever. This is very common among people who come from the coast where it's very hot straight to the *Altiplano* where it's very cold. The change is too abrupt for them. There was no money to buy medicine or to care for my grandmother and she died. My father and his brothers were left without parents or any other relatives to help them. My father told me that they had a little house made of straw, very humble, but with their mother dead, there was no point in staying there. So they split up and got work in different parts of the coast. My father found work in a monastery but he hardly earned anything there either. In those days a worker earned thirty to forty *centavos* a day, both in the *fincas* and elsewhere.

That's when my father met my mother and they got married. They went through very difficult times together. They met in the *Altiplano* since my mother was from a very poor family too. Her parents were very poor and used to travel around looking for work. They were hardly ever at home in the *Altiplano*.

That's how they came to settle up in the mountains. There was no town there. There was no-one. They founded a village up there. My village has a long history – a long and painful history. The land up there belonged to the government and you had to get permission to settle there. When you'd got permission, you had to pay a fee so that you could clear the land and then build your house. Through all my parents' efforts in the *fincas*, they managed to get enough money together to pay the fee, and they cleared the land. Of course, it's not very easy to make things grow on land that's just been cleared. You don't get a good yield for at least eight or nine years. So my parents cultivated the land and eight years later, it started to produce. We were growing up during this period. I had five older brothers and sisters. I saw my two eldest brothers die from lack of food when we were down in the *fincas*. Most Indian families suffer from malnutrition. Most of them don't even reach fifteen years old. When children are growing and don't get enough to eat, they're often ill, and this . . . well . . . it complicates the situation.

So my parents stayed there. My mother found the trees and our amazing mountains so beautiful. She said that they'd get lost sometimes because the mountains were so high and not a single ray of light fell through the plants. It's very dense. Well, that's where we grew up. We loved our land very, very much, even if we did have to walk for a long time to get to our nearest neighbour. But, little by little, my parents got more and more people to come up and cultivate the land so there would be more of us to ward off the animals that came down from the mountains to eat our maize when it was ripe or when the ears were still green. These animals would come and eat everything. My father said that one of them was what they call a racoon. Soon my mother started keeping hens and a few sheep because there was plenty of room but she didn't have the time to look after them properly so they'd wander off to find other food and not come back. The mountain animals ate some of them, or they just got lost. So they lived there, but unfortunately it was many years before our land really produced anything and my parents still had to go down and work in the *fincas*. They told us what it was like when they first settled there, but when we children were growing up and could spend four or five months of the year there, we were very happy. There were big rivers rushing down the mountainside below our house. We didn't actually have much time for playing, but even working was fun – clearing the undergrowth while my father cut down trees. Well, you could hear so many different types of birds singing and there were lots of snakes to frighten us as well. We were happy even though it was very cold because of the mountains. And it's a damp sort of cold.

I was born there. My mother already had five children, I think. Yes, I had five brothers and sisters and I'm the sixth. My mother said that she was working down on a *finca* until a month before I was born. She had just twenty days to go when she went up to the mountains, and she gave birth to me all on her own. My father wasn't there because he had to work the month out on the *finca*.

Most of what I remember is after I was five. We spent four months in our little house in the *Altiplano* and the rest of the year we had to go down to the coast, either in the *Boca Costa** where there's coffee picking and also weeding out the coffee plants, or further down the south coast where there's cotton. That was the work we did mostly, and I went from when I was very little. A very few families owned the vast areas of land which produce these crops for sale abroad. These landowners are the lords of vast extensions of land, then. So we'd work in the *fincas* for eight months and in January we'd go back up to the *Altiplano* to sow our crops. Where we live in the mountains – that is, where the land isn't fertile – you can barely grow maize and beans. The land isn't fertile enough for anything else. But on the coast the land is rich and you can grow anything. After we'd sown our crops, we'd go down to the coast again until it was time to harvest them, and then we'd make the journey back again. But the maize would soon run out, and we'd be back down again to earn some money. From what my parents said, they lived this harsh life for many years and they were always poor.

---

* Name given to the western slope of the Sierra Madre going down to the Pacific Ocean.

II

BIRTH CEREMONIES

'Whoever may ask where we are, tell them what you know of us and nothing more.'
—Popol Vuh

'Learn to protect yourselves, by keeping our secret.'
—Popol Vuh

In our community there is an elected representative, someone who is highly respected. He's not a king but someone whom the community looks up to like a father. In our village, my father and mother were the representatives. Well, then the whole community becomes the children of the woman who's elected. So, a mother, on her first day of pregnancy goes with her husband to tell these elected leaders that she's going to have a child, because the child will not only belong to them but to the whole community, and must follow as far as he can our ancestors' traditions. The leaders then pledge the support of the community and say: 'We will help you, we will be the child's second parents.' They are known as *abuelos*, 'grandparents' or 'forefathers'. The parents then ask the 'grandparents' to help them find the child some godparents, so that if he's orphaned, he shouldn't be tempted by any of the bad habits our people sometimes fall into. So the 'grandparents' and the parents choose the godparents together. It's also the custom for the pregnant mother's neighbours to visit her every day and take her little things, no matter how simple. They stay and talk to her, and she'll tell them all her problems.

Later, when she's in her seventh month, the mother introduces her baby to the natural world, as our customs tell her to. She goes out in the fields or walks over the hills. She also has to show her baby the kind of life she leads, so that if she gets up at three in the morning, does her chores and tends the animals, she does it all the more so when she's pregnant, conscious that the child is taking all this in. She talks to the child continuously from the first moment he's in her stomach, telling him how hard his life will be. It's as if the mother were a guide explaining things to a tourist. She'll say, for instance; 'You must never abuse nature and you must live your life as honestly as I do.' As she works in the fields, she tells her child all the little things about her work. It's a duty to her child that a mother must fulfil. And then, she also has to think of a way of hiding the baby's birth from her other children.

When her baby is born, the mother mustn't have her other children round her. The people present should be the husband, the village leaders, and the couple's parents. Three couples. The parents are often away in other places, so if they can't be there, the husband's father and the wife's mother can perhaps make up one pair. If one of the village leaders can't come, one of them should be there to make up a couple with one of the parents. If none of the parents can come, some aunts and uncles should come to represent the family on both sides, because the child is to be part of the community. The birth of a new member is very significant for the community, as it belongs to the community not just to the parents, and that's why three couples (but not just anybody) must be there to receive it. They explain that this child is the fruit of communal love. If the village leader is not a midwife as well, another midwife is called (it might be a grandmother) to receive the child. Our customs don't allow single women to see a birth. But it does happen in times of need. For instance, I was with my sister when she went into labour. Nobody else was

at home. This was when we were being heavily persecuted.
Well, I didn't exactly see, but I was there when the baby was
born. My mother was a midwife from when she was sixteen right
up to her death at forty-three. She used to say that a woman
hadn't the strength to push the baby out when she's lying
down. So what she did with my sister was to hang a rope
from the roof and pull her up, because my brother wasn't
there to lift her up. My mother helped the baby out with my
sister in that position. It's a scandal if an Indian woman goes
to hospital and gives birth there. None of our women would
agree to that. Our ancestors would be shocked at many of the
things which go on today. Family planning, for example. It's
an insult to our culture and a way of swindling the people, to
get money out of them.

This is part of the reserve that we've maintained to defend
our customs and our culture. Indians have been very careful not to disclose any details of their communities, and the
community does not allow them to talk about Indian things.
I too must abide by this. This is because many religious people have come among us and drawn a false impression of the
Indian world. We also find a *ladino* using Indian clothes very
offensive. All this has meant that we keep a lot of things to
ourselves and the community doesn't like us telling its secrets.
This applies to all our customs. When the Catholic Action*
arrived, for instance, everyone started going to mass, and
praying, but it's not their only religion, not the only way they
have of expressing themselves. Anyway, when a baby is born,
he's always baptized within the community before he's taken
to church. Our people have taken Catholicism as just another
channel of expression, not our one and only belief. Our people do the same with other religions. The priests, monks and
nuns haven't gained the people's confidence because so many
of their things contradict our own customs. For instance, they

---

* Association created in 1945 by Monsignor Rafael Gonzalez, to try and
control the Indian fraternities of the *Altiplano*.

say: 'You have too much trust in your elected leaders.' But the village elects them *because* they trust them, don't they? The priests say: 'The trouble is you follow those sorcerers,' and speak badly of them. But for our people this is like speaking ill of their own fathers, and they lose faith in the priests. They say: 'Well, they're not from here, they can't understand our world.' So there's not much hope of winning our people's hearts.

To come back to the children, they aren't to know how the baby is born. He's born somewhere hidden away and only the parents know about it. They are told that a baby has arrived and that they can't see their mother for eight days. Later on, the baby's companion, the placenta that is, has to be burned at a special time. If the baby is born at night, the placenta is burned at eight in the morning, and if he's born in the afternoon, it'll be burned at five o'clock. This is out of respect for both the baby and his companion. The placenta is not buried, because the earth is the mother and the father of the child and mustn't be abused by having the placenta buried in it. All these reasons are very important for us. Either the placenta is burned on a log and the ashes left there, or else it is put in the *temascal*. This is a stove which our people use to make vapour baths. It's a small hut made of adobe and inside this hut is another one made of stone, and when we want to have a bath, we light a fire to heat the stones, close the door, and throw water on the stones to produce steam. Well, when the woman is about four months pregnant, she starts taking these baths infused with evergreens, pure natural aromas. There are many plants the community uses for pregnant women, colds, headaches, and things like that. So the pregnant mother takes baths with plants prescribed for her by the midwife or the village leader. The fields are full of plants whose names I don't know in Spanish. Pregnant women use orange and peach leaves a lot for bathing and there's another one we call Saint Mary's leaf which they use. The mother needs these leaves and herbs to relax because she won't be able to rest while she's pregnant since our women go on working just as hard in the fields. So, after work, she takes this calming bath so that she can sleep well, and the baby won't be harmed by her working hard. She's given medicines to take as well. And leaves to feed the child. I believe that in practice (even if this isn't a scientific recommendation) these leaves work very well, because many of them contain vitamins. How else would women who endure hunger and hard work give birth to healthy babies? I think that these plants have helped our people survive.

The purity with which the child comes into the world is protected for eight days. Our customs say that the newborn baby should be alone with his mother in a special place for eight days, without any of her other children. Her only visitors are the people who bring her food. This is the baby's period of integration into the family; he very slowly becomes a member of it. When the child is born, they kill a sheep and there's a little fiesta just for the family. Then the neighbours start coming to visit, and bring presents. They either bring food for the mother, or something for the baby. The mother has to taste all the food her neighbours bring to show her appreciation for their kindness. After the eight days are over, the family counts up how many visitors the mother had, and how many presents were received; things like eggs or food apart from what was brought for the mother, or clothing, small animals, and wood for the fire, or services like carrying water and chopping wood. If, during the eight days, most of the community has called, this is very important, because it means that this child will have a lot of responsibility towards his community when he grows up. The community takes over all the household expenses for these eight days and the family spends nothing.

After eight days everything has been received, and another animal is killed as recognition that the child's right to be alone with his mother is over. All the mother's clothes, bedclothes, and everything she used during the birth, are taken away by our elected leader and washed. She can't wash them in the well, so no matter how far away the river is, they must be carried and washed there. The baby's purity is washed away and he's ready to learn the ways of humanity. The mother's bed is moved to a part of the house which has first been washed with water and lime. Lime is sacred. It strengthens the child's bones. I believe this really is true. It gives a child strength to face the world. The mother has a bath in the *temascal* and puts on clean clothes. Then, the whole house is cleaned. The child is also washed and dressed and put into the new bed. Four candles are placed on the corners of the bed to represent the four corners of the house and show him that this will be his home. They symbolize the respect the child must have for his community, and the responsibility he must feel towards it as a member of a household. The candles are lit and give off an incense which incorporates the child into the world he must live in. When the baby is born, his hands and feet are bound to show him that they are sacred and must only be used to work or do whatever nature meant them to do. They must never steal or abuse the natural world, or show disrespect for any living thing.

After the eight days, his hands and feet are untied and he's now with his mother in the new bed. This means he opens the doors to the other members of the community, because neither the family or the community know him yet. Or rather, they weren't shown the baby when he was born. Now they can all come and kiss him. The neighbours bring another animal, and there's a big lunch in the new baby's house for all the community. This is to celebrate his integration 'in the universe', as our parents used to say. Candles will be lit for him and his candle becomes part of the candle of the whole community, which now has one more person, one more member. The whole community is at the ceremony, or at least, if not all of it, then some of it. Candles are lit to represent all the things which belong to the universe – earth, water, sun and man – and the child's candle is put with them, together with incense (what we call *pom*) and lime – our sacred lime. Then, the parents tell the baby of the suffering of the family he will be joining. With great feeling, they express their sorrow at bringing a child into the world to suffer. To us, suffering is our fate, and the child must be introduced to sorrows and hardship, but he must learn that despite his suffering, he will be respectful and live through his pain. The child is then entrusted with the responsibility for his community and told to abide by its rules. After the ceremony comes the lunch, and then the neighbours go home. Now, there is only the baptism to come.

When the baby is born, he's given a little bag with garlic, a bit of lime, salt and tobacco in it, to hang round his neck. Tobacco is important because it is a sacred plant for Indians. This all means that the child can ward off all the evil things in life. For us, bad things are like spirits, which exist only in our imagination. Something bad, for instance, would be if the child were to turn out to be a gossip – not sincere, truthful and respectful, as a child should be. It also helps him collect together and preserve all our ancestors' things. That's more or less the idea of the bag – to keep him pure. The bag is put inside the four candles as well, and this represents the promise of the child when he grows up.

When the child is forty days old, there are more speeches, more promises on his behalf, and he becomes a full member of the community. This is his baptism. All the important people of the village are invited and they speak. The parents make a commitment. They promise to teach the child to keep the secrets of our people, so that our culture and customs will be preserved. The village leaders come and offer their experience, their example, and their knowledge of our ancestors. They explain how to preserve our traditions. Then, they promise to be responsible for the child, teach him as he grows up, and see that he follows in their ways. It's also something of a criticism of humanity, and of the many people who have forsaken their traditions. They say almost a prayer, asking that our traditions again enter the spirits of those who have forsaken them. Then, they evoke the names of our ancestors, like Tecun Umán and others who form part of the ceremony, as a kind of chant. They must be remembered as heroes of the Indian peoples. And then they say (I analyse all this later): 'Let no landowner extinguish all this, nor any rich man wipe out our customs. Let our children, be they workers or servants, respect and keep their secrets.' The child is present for all of this, although he's all wrapped up and can scarcely be seen. He is told that he will eat maize and that, naturally, he is already made of maize because his mother ate it while he was forming in her stomach. He must respect the maize; even the grain of maize which has been thrown away, he must pick up. The child will multiply our race, he will replace all those who have died. From this moment, he takes on this responsibility, and is told to live as his 'grandparents' have lived. The parents then reply that their child promises to accomplish all this. So, the village leaders and the parents all make promises on behalf of the child. It's his initiation into the community.

The ceremony is very important. It is also when the child is considered a child of God, our one father. We don't actually have the word God but that is what it is, because the one father is the only one we have. To reach this one father, the child must love beans, maize, the earth. The one father is the heart of the sky; that is, the sun. The sun is the father and our mother is the moon. She is a gentle mother. And she lights our way. Our people have many notions about the moon, and about the sun. They are the pillars of the universe.

When children reach ten years old, that's the moment when their parents and the village leaders talk to them again. They tell them that they will be young men and women and that one day they will be fathers and mothers. This is actually when they tell the child that he must never abuse his dignity, in the same way his ancestors never abused their dignity. It's also when they remind them that our ancestors were dishonoured by the white man, by colonization. But they don't tell them the way that it's written down in books, because the majority of Indians can't read or write, and don't even know that they have their own texts. No, they learn it through oral recommendations, the way it has been handed down through the generations. They are told that the Spaniards dishonoured our ancestors' finest sons, and the most humble of them. And it is to honour these humble people that we must keep our secrets. And no-one except we Indians must know. They talk a lot about our ancestors. And the ten-years ceremony is also when our children are reminded that they must respect their elders, even though this is something their parents have been telling them ever since they were little. For example, if an old person is walking along the street, children should cross over to allow him to pass by. If any of us sees an elderly person, we are obliged to bow and greet them. Everyone does this, even the very youngest. We also show respect to pregnant women. Whenever we make food, we always keep some for any of our neighbours who are pregnant.

When little girls are born, the midwives pierce their ears at the same time as they tie their umbilical cords. The little bags round their necks and the thread used to tie their umbilical cord are both red. Red is very significant for us. It means heat, strength, all living things. It's linked to the sun, which for us is the channel to the one God, the heart of everything, of the universe. So red gives off heat and fire and red things are supposed to give life to the child. At the same time, it asks him to respect living things too. There are no special clothes for the baby. We don't buy anything special beforehand but just use pieces of *corte* to wrap him in.

When a male child is born, there are special celebrations, not because he's male but because of all the hard work and responsibility he'll have as a man. It's not that *machismo* doesn't exist among our people, but it doesn't present a problem for the community because it's so much part of our way of life. The male child is given an extra day alone with his mother. The usual custom is to celebrate a male child by killing a sheep or some chickens. Boys are given more, they get more food because their work is harder and they have more responsibility. At the same time, he is head of the household, not in the bad sense of the word, but because he is responsible for so many things. This doesn't mean girls aren't valued.

Their work is hard too and there are other things that are due to them as mothers. Girls are valued because they are part of the earth, which gives us maize, beans, plants and everything we live on. The earth is like a mother which multiplies life. So the girl child will multiply the life of our generation and of our ancestors whom we must respect. The girl and the boy are both integrated into the community in equally important ways, the two are inter-related and compatible. Nevertheless, the community is always happier when a male child is born and the men feel much prouder. The customs, like the tying of the hands and feet, apply to both boys and girls.

Babies are breastfed. It's much better than any other sort of food. But the important thing is the sense of community. It's something we all share. From the very first day, the baby belongs to the community, not only to the parents, and the baby must learn from all of us . . . in fact, we behave just like bourgeois families, in that, as soon as the baby is born, we're thinking of his education, of his well-being. But our people feel that the baby's school must be the community itself, that he must learn to live like all the rest of us. The tying of the hands at birth also symbolizes this; that no-one should accumulate things the rest of the community does not have and he must know how to share, to have open hands. The mother must teach the baby to be generous. This way of thinking comes from poverty and suffering. Each child is taught to live like the fellow members of his community.

We never eat in front of pregnant women. You can only eat in front of a pregnant woman if you can offer something as well. The fear is that, otherwise, she might abort the baby or that the baby could suffer if she didn't have enough to eat. It doesn't matter whether you know her or not. The important thing is sharing. You have to treat a pregnant woman differently from other women because she is two people. You must treat her with respect so that she recognizes it and conveys this to the baby inside her. You instinctively think she's the image of the baby about to be born. So you love her. Another reason why you must stop and talk to a pregnant woman is because she doesn't have much chance to rest or enjoy herself. She's always worried and depressed. So when she stops and chats a bit, she can relax and feel some relief. When the baby joins the community, with him in the circle of candles – together with his little red bag – he will have his hoe, his machete, his axe and all the tools he will need in life. These will be his playthings. A little girl will have her washing board and all the things she will need when she grows up. She must learn the things of the house; to clean, to wash and sew her brothers' trousers, for example. The little boy must begin to live like a man, to be responsible and learn to love the work in the fields. The learning is done as a kind of game. When the parents do anything they always explain what it means. This includes learning prayers. This is very important to our people. The mother may say a prayer at any time. Before getting up in the morning, for instance, she thanks the day which is dawning because it might be a very important one for the family. Before lighting the fire, she blesses the wood because that fire is going to cook food for the whole family. Since it's the little girl who is closest to her mother, she learns all of this. Before washing the *nixtamal*, the woman blows on her hands and puts them in the *nixtamal*. She takes everything out and washes it well. She blows on her hands so that her work will bear fruit. She does it before she does the wash as well. She explains all these little details to her daughter, who learns by copying her. With the men it's the same. Before they start work every day, whatever hour of the morning it is, they greet the sun. They remove their hats and talk to the sun before starting work. Their sons learn to do it too, taking off their little hats to talk to the sun. Naturally, each ethnic group has its own forms of expression. Other groups have different customs from ours. The meaning of their weaving patterns, for example. We realize the others are different in some things, but the one thing we have in common is our culture. Our people are mainly peasants, but there are some people who buy and sell as well. They go into this after they've worked on the land. Sometimes when they come back from working in the *finca*, instead of tending a little plot of land, they'll start a shop and look for a different sort of life. But if they're used to greeting the sun every morning, they still go on doing it. And they keep all their old customs. Every part of our culture comes from the earth. Our religion comes from the maize and bean harvests which are so vital to our community. So even if a man goes to try and make some money, he never forgets his culture springs from the earth.

As we grow up we have a series of obligations. Our parents teach us to be responsible; just as they have been responsible. The eldest son is responsible for the house. Whatever the father cannot correct is up to the eldest son to correct. He is like a second father to us all and is responsible for our upbringing. The mother is the one who is responsible for keeping an account of what the family eats, and what she has to buy. When a child is ill, she has to get medicine. But the father has to solve a lot of problems too. And each one of us, as we grow up, has our own small area of responsibility. This comes from the promises made for the child when he is born, and from the continuity of our customs. The child can make the promise for himself when his parents have taught him to do it. The mother, who is closest to the children, does this, or sometimes the father. They talk to their children, explaining what they have to do and what our ancestors used to do. They don't impose it as a law, but just give the example of what our ancestors have always done. This is how we all learn our own small responsibilities. For example, the little girl begins by carrying water, and the little boy begins by tying up the dogs when the animals are brought into the yard at night, or by fetching a horse which has wandered off. Both girls and boys have their tasks and are told the reasons for doing them. They learn responsibility because if they don't do their little jobs, well, their father has the right to scold them, or even beat them. So, they are very careful about learning to do their jobs well, but the parents are also very careful to explain exactly why the jobs have to be done. The little girl understands the reasons for everything her mother does. For example, when she puts a new earthenware pot on the fire for the first time, she hits it five times with a branch, so that it knows its job is to cook and so that it lasts. When the little girl asks, 'Why did you do that?', her mother says, 'So that it knows what its job is and does it well.' When it's her turn to cook, the little girl does as her mother does. Again this is all bound up with our commitment to maintain our customs and pass on the secrets of our ancestors. The elected fathers of the community explain to us that all these things come down to us from our grandfathers and we must conserve them. Nearly everything we do today is based on what our ancestors did. This is the main purpose of our elected leader – to embody all the values handed down from our ancestors. He is the leader of the community, a father to all our children, and he must lead an exemplary life. Above all, he has a commitment to the whole community. Everything that is done today, is done in memory of those who have passed on.

III

THE NAHUAL

'That night he spent howling like a coyote while he slept as a person.
To become animal, without ceasing to be a person.
Animal and person coexist in them through the will of their progenitors at birth.'
            —Miguel Angel Asturias, *Men of Maize.*

Every child is born with a *nahual*. The *nahual* is like a shadow, his protective spirit who will go through life with him. The *nahual* is the representative of the earth, the animal world, the sun and water, and in this way the child communicates with nature. The *nahual* is our double, something very important to us. We conjure up an image of what our *nahual* is like. It is usually an animal. The child is taught that if he kills an animal, that animal's human double will be very angry with him because he is killing his *nahual*. Every animal has its human counterpart and if you hurt him, you hurt the animal too.

Our days are divided into dogs, cats, bulls, birds, etc. There is a *nahual* for every day. If a child is born on a Wednesday, his *nahual* is a sheep. The day of his birth decides his *nahual*. So for a Wednesday child, every Wednesday is special. Parents know what a child's behaviour will be from the day of the week he is born. Tuesday is a bad day to be born because the child will grow up bad-tempered. That is because Tuesday's *nahual* is a bull and bulls are always angry. The child whose *nahual* is a cat will like fighting with his brothers and sisters. We have ten sacred days, as our ancestors have always had. These ten days have their *nahual*. They can be dogs, cats, horses, bulls, but they can also be wild animals, like lions. Trees can be *nahual* too: trees chosen by our ancestors many centuries ago. A *nahual* is not always only one animal. With dogs, for example, nine dogs represent a *nahual*. Or in the case of horses, three. It can vary a lot. You don't know how many in fact, or rather, only the parents know the number of animals which go to make the *nahuals* of these ten special days. For us the meekest days are Wednesday, Monday, Saturday and Sunday. Their *nahuals* are sheep, or birds or animals which don't harm other animals.

All this is explained to young people before they get married so that when they have children they know which animal represents each day. One very important thing they have to remember is not to tell the child what his *nahual* is until he is grown up. We are only told what our *nahual* is when our personalities are formed and our parents see what our behaviour is normally. Otherwise a child might take advantage of his *nahual*. For example, if his *nahual* is a bull, he might like fighting and could say: 'I behave like this because I'm such and such an animal and you must put up with me.' If a child doesn't know his *nahual* he cannot use it as an excuse. He may be compared to the animal, but that is not identifying him with his *nahual*. Younger children don't know the *nahual* of their elder brothers and sisters. They are only told all this when they are mature enough and this could be at any age between ten and twelve. When this happens the animal which is his *nahual* is given to him as a present. If it is a lion, however, it is replaced by something else. Only our parents, or perhaps other members of the community who were there when we were born, know the day of our birth. People from other villages don't know and they are only told if they become close friends.

A day only has a special meaning if a child is born on it. If no baby is born on any one Tuesday, it is of no interest to anyone. That is, there is no celebration. We often come to love the animal which is our *nahual* even before we know what it is. Although we love all the natural world, we are often drawn to one particular animal more than to others. We grow to love it. Then one day we are told that it is our *nahual*. All the kingdoms which exist on this earth are related to man. Man is part of the natural world. There is not one world for man and one for animals, they are part of the same one and lead parallel lives. We can see this in our surnames. Many of us have surnames which are the names of animals. *Quej*, meaning horse, for example.

We Indians have always hidden our identity and kept our secrets to ourselves. This is why we are discriminated against. We often find it hard to talk about ourselves because we know we must hide so much in order to preserve our Indian culture and prevent it being taken away from us. So I can only tell you very general things about the *nahual*. I can't tell you what my *nahual* is because that is one of our secrets.

IV

FIRST VISIT TO THE FINCA. LIFE IN THE FINCA

'This is why there is no hope of winning the hearts of our people.'

—Rigoberta Menchú

After forty days, when the child is fully integrated into the community, the routine of going down to the *fincas* begins.

From when I was very tiny, my mother used to take me down to the *finca*, wrapped in a shawl on her back. She told me that when I was about two, I had to be carried screaming onto the lorry because I didn't want to go. I was so frightened I didn't stop crying until we were about half-way there. I remember the journey by lorry very well. I didn't even know what it was, but I knew I hated it because I hate things that smell horrible. The lorry holds about forty people. But in with the people go the animals (dogs, cats, chickens) which the people from the *Altiplano* take with them while they are in the *finca*. We have to take our animals. It sometimes took two nights and a day from my village to the coast. During the trip the animals and the small children used to dirty the lorry and you'd get people vomiting and wetting themselves. By the end of the journey, the smell – the filth of people and animals – was unbearable.

The lorry is covered with a tarpaulin so you can't see the countryside you're passing through. Most of the journey is spent sleeping because it's so tedious. The stuffiness inside the lorry with the cover on, and the smell of urine and vomit, make you want to be sick yourself just from being in there. By the time we got to the *finca*, we were totally stupefied; we were like chickens coming out of a pot. We were in such a state, we could hardly walk to the *finca*. I made many trips from the *Altiplano* to the coast, but I never saw the countryside we passed through. We heard other lorries and cars, but we didn't ever see them. We never saw any other villages on the way. I saw the wonderful scenery and places for the first time when we were thrown out of the *finca* and had to pay our own way back on the bus.

I remember that from when I was about eight to when I was about ten, we worked in the coffee crop. And after that I worked on the cotton plantations further down the coast where it was very, very hot. After my first day picking cotton, I woke up at midnight and lit a candle. I saw the faces of my brothers and sisters covered with mosquitos. I touched my own face, and I was covered too. They were everywhere; in people's mouths and everywhere. Just looking at these insects and thinking about being bitten set me scratching. That was our world. I felt that it would always be the same, always the same. It hadn't ever changed.

None of the drivers liked taking us because, naturally, we were filthy and burned from the sun. No-one wanted to drive us. The lorries belonged to the *fincas*, but they were driven by the recruiting agents, the *caporales*. These *caporales* are in charge of about forty people, or more or less what the lorry holds. When they get to the finca, the *caporal* becomes the overseer of this group. They are usually men from our villages too, but they've been in the army or have left the community. They start behaving like the landowners, and treat their own people badly. They shout at them and insult them. The *finca* offers them opportunities to get on, if they do what the landowners want. They get better wages and they have a steady job. It's their job to order us around and keep us in line, I'd say. They've learned Spanish so they can act as go-betweens for the landowner and his workers, because our people don't speak Spanish. They often take advantage of us because of this, but we can't complain because we never see the landowner and don't know where he lives. We see only the contracting agents and the overseers. The contracting agents fetch and carry the people from the *Altiplano*. The overseers stay on the *fincas*. One group of workers arrives, another leaves and the overseer carries on giving orders. They are in charge. When you're working, for example, and you take a little rest, he comes and insults you. 'Keep working, that's what you're paid for,' he says. They also punish the slow workers. Sometimes we're paid by the day, and sometimes for the amount of work done. It's when we work by the day that we get the worst treatment. The *caporal* stands over you every minute to see how hard you're working. At other times, you're paid for what you pick. If you don't manage to finish the amount set in a day, you have to continue the next day, but at least you can rest a bit without the overseer coming down on you. But the work is still hard whether you work by the day or by the amount.

Before we get into the lorry in our village, the labour contractor tells us to bring with us everything we'll need for the month on the *finca*; that is, plates and cups, for example. Every worker carries his plate, his cup, and his water bottle in a bag on his back so he can go and get his *tortilla* at mealtimes. Children who don't work don't earn, and so are not fed. They don't need plates. They share with their parents. The little ones who *do* earn also have plates for their ration of *tortilla*. When I wasn't earning anything, my mother used to give me half her ration. All the mothers did the same. We get *tortilla* and beans free, but they are often rotten. If the food varies a bit and we get an egg about every two months, then it is deducted from our pay. Any change in the food is deducted.

The same goes for anything we get from the *cantina*. As well as alcohol, the *cantina* in the *finca* also sells things that children like: sweets, cakes and soft drinks. It's all in the shop.

The children, who are hot and tired and hungry, are always asking their parents for treats and it makes parents sad to see their children asking for things they can't give. But everything they buy is marked up on an account, and at the end when you get your pay, you always owe so much for food, so much at the shop, so much at the pharmacy. You end up owing a lot. For example, if a child unintentionally breaks a branch of a coffee bush, you have to work to make it up. They deduct for everything and you end up having to pay debts before you can leave.

Every *finca* in Guatemala has a *cantina*, owned by the landowner, where the workers get drunk on alcohol and all kinds of *guaro*, and pile up debts. They often spend most of their wages. They drink to get happy and to forget the bitterness they feel at having to leave their villages in the *Altiplano* and come and work so brutally hard on the *fincas* for so little. I remember my father and mother going to the *cantina* out of despair. It was sometimes terrible for us. My mother and my brothers and sisters often had to bear all our household costs when the month on the *finca* was over because my father owed all his wages to the *cantina*. He was a very sensitive man. When anything went wrong or when times were very hard for us, he used to drink to forget. But he hurt himself twice over because his money went back to the landowner. That's why the landowner set up the *cantina* anyway. Once I remember my father working the whole day picking cotton but somehow didn't pick the required amount. He was so angry that he just wanted to forget everything and spent the whole night in the *cantina*. When the month was up, he owed nearly all his wage to the *cantina*. We honestly don't know if he really drank all that rum or not, but it was awful to see such a huge debt chalked up against him after a whole month's work. You get into debt for every little thing. This taught us to be very careful. My mother used to say: 'Don't touch anything or we'll have to pay for it.' My mother used to see that we all behaved ourselves and didn't get her into debt.

This is what happened that time we were thrown out of the *finca*. (We were told by one of our neighbours who stayed on there.) When they came to get paid at the end of the month, the overseer included my mother and my brother and me, and a neighbour who was thrown out with us, in the list of workers to be paid, just as if we were finishing the month and collecting our wages. Of course, he collected the pay due to us himself. That's what they do. With what they earn and what they steal from our people, the overseers buy lovely houses in the *Altiplano* and have houses in other places too. They can live wherever they want to, in the places they like best.

Many of them are *ladinos* from Oriente.* But there are also many of our people from the *Altiplano* among them. My father used to call them 'ladinized Indians'. When we say 'ladinized' we mean they act like *ladinos*, bad *ladinos*, because afterwards we realized that not all *ladinos* are bad. A bad *ladino* is one who knows how to talk and steal from the people. He is a small-scale picture of the landowner.

I remember going along in the lorry and wanting to set it on fire so that we would be allowed to rest. What bothered me most was travelling on and on and on, wanting to urinate and not being able to because the lorry wouldn't stop. The drivers were sometimes drunk, boozed. They stopped a lot on the way but they didn't let us get out. This enraged us; we hated the drivers because they wouldn't let us get out although they used to drink on the way. It made me very angry and I used to ask my mother: 'Why do we go to the *finca*?'. And my mother used to say: 'Because we have to. When you're older you'll understand why we need to come.' I did understand, but the thing was I was fed up with it all. When I was older, I didn't find it strange any more. Slowly I began to see what we had to do and why things were like that. I realised we weren't alone in our sorrow and suffering, but that a lot of people, in many different regions, shared it with us.

---

* The eastern part of Guatemala which includes the provinces of Zacapa, Chiquimula, Jalapa, Jutiapa and Santa Rosa. It is mainly populated by *ladinos*.

When we worked down on the cotton plantation (I think I was about twelve) I was already big and did the work of a grown woman. I remember the first time I saw a *finca* land-owner, I was frightened of him because he was very fat. I'd never seen a *ladino* like that. He was very fat, well dressed and even had a watch. We didn't know about watches then. I didn't have any shoes although many of our people wore *caitos*; but nothing which compared to the shoes this landowner had. At dawn the overseer told us: 'Listen, you're going to work one more day at the end of the month.' Whenever anything like this happened, they'd just announce they were adding another day on to the month. If the month had thirty-one days, we had to work the first day of the next month, or if there were rest days for any reason, we'd have to make up the day. So the overseer told us: 'The owner is coming today to thank you for your work and wants to spend some time talking to you, so nobody leave because we have to wait for him.' So we stayed in our camp, in the workers' barracks where we lived and they divided us into groups. Then, when the great landowner arrived, we saw he was accompanied by about fifteen soldiers. This seemed really stupid to me, because I thought they were pointing their rifles at the landowner, so I asked my mother: 'Why are they forcing the landowner to come and see us?' But it was really to protect him. There were about fifteen soldiers and they found a suitable place for the owner to sit. The overseer said: 'Some of you have to dance for the owner.' My mother said no, and hid us. They wanted the children to prepare a sort of welcome for the owner. But none of us dared even go near him because he had so many bodyguards with guns. When the owner began to speak, he spoke in Spanish. My mother understood a little Spanish and afterwards she told us he was talking about the elections. But we didn't even understand what our parents told us – that the *ladinos* had a government. That is, the President who had been in power all this time, was, for my parents, for all of us, President of the *ladinos'* government. It wasn't the government of *our* country. That's what we always thought. So my mother said that he was talking about the government of the *ladinos*. What was it he was saying? The landowner was speaking, and the overseer started translating what he was saying. They told us he said we all had to go and make a mark on a piece of paper. That would be a vote, I imagine that it was a vote. We all went to make our mark on the paper. They gave my father one and my mother and showed them the place to put their mark. I remember that the paper had some squares with three or four drawings on it. So my parents and my older brothers and sisters marked the paper in the place the owner told them. He warned us that anyone who didn't mark the paper would be thrown out of work at the end of the month. Anyone who was thrown out would not be paid. The workers were forced to mark the paper. So that was another day of rest, and it meant we would have to work the second day of the next month as well. The land-owner left, but afterwards . . . I dreamed about him over and over again . . . it must have been the fear, the impression made on me by that man's face. I remember telling mother: 'I dreamed about that old *ladino* who came here.' And mother said: 'Don't be silly, he's only a man, don't be afraid.' That's what she said. But all the children there ran away from their parents and cried when they saw that *ladino*, and even more at the soldiers and their weapons. They thought they were going to kill their parents. I thought so, too. I thought they were going to kill everybody, because they were carrying guns.

We didn't even know what the name on the paper was. My father sometimes used to tell us names because of the things he remembered. In the defeat of 1954, he said they captured men from our region, and from other regions. They took our men off to the barracks. My father was one of those caught. He has very black memories of those days. He says many, many of our people died and we only escaped because of our own quick wits. That's how we survived, my father said. His memories of this period are very bad. He always talked about the President there was then, but we didn't know any of the others. We didn't know the rest, not their names or what they were like. We knew nothing about them. Then the landowner came to congratulate us. We saw him a second time. He came with his wife and one of his sons. They were nearly as fat as he was. They came to the *finca* and told us that our President had won, the one we had voted for. We didn't even know that they were votes they'd taken away. My parents laughed when they heard them say 'our President', because for us he was the President of the *ladinos*, not ours at all. This was my impression as a small girl and I thought a lot about what the President would be like. I thought he was an even bigger man than the landowner. The landowner was very big and tall, and we didn't have big men like that in our village. So I thought that the President was even taller than the landowner. When I was older, I met the landowner again and he asked my parents for me. That was when I was sent to the capital. That's another stage in my life.

V

FIRST VISIT TO GUATEMALA CITY

'When I went to the city for the first time, I saw it as a monster, something alien, different.'

—Rigoberta Menchú

I felt grown-up for the first time when at the age of seven I got lost in the mountains. That was the time when we came back from the *finca* to the *Altiplano* and my brothers and sisters and I all fell ill. We'd got back from the *finca* in an awful state. When our money ran out, my father said if we went back down to the *finca* with sick children, he'd be left alone to bury his children there. So he said: 'The only thing to do is to go up into the mountains and collect *mimbre*.' My elder brothers and sisters, my father and myself. In fact, we children often went up to collect *mimbre* when we had some spare time because it grows near where we live. My father also went whenever he had a moment, or a week without other work. So we all went to cut *mimbre*. In a week, between the lot of us, we collected a *quintal* (a hundredweight) of *mimbre*. Then it was dried. We pulled it along with ropes and collected it together. Some of us stripped the bark off and some rolled it up. We'd gone further up into the mountains that time and up there if you're not careful you can get lost. We had a dog with us as a guide. He used to look out for animals and knew the way. That dog used to guide us everywhere in the mountains. Anyway, the blessed dog saw we didn't have any food; we'd finished the food because we'd been in the mountains for over eight days. The poor dog was hungry, so one night he went back home. He'd gone before we realized it. We'd no idea where we were. It was the rainy season: June or July, if I remember right. So there were lots of black clouds and we couldn't get our bearings. My father was very worried because if we stayed in the mountains, we could be attacked by wild animals. How were we going to find the path? So we started walking and walking, on and on. We didn't know if we were going further into the mountains or out of them. We couldn't hear the noise of animals from any of the villages. We couldn't hear any dogs barking. Usually when dogs bark in any village, the sound carries a long way in the mountains. But there was nothing. And then, the others were so busy looking for the path, they forgot about me and I was left behind. I didn't know which way to go and my father was almost in tears looking for me. In the mountains, it's the one furthest ahead who decides the path: he opens the way for the others to pass, and that's how we were going along, in a line. Since I was the smallest, and my brothers and sisters were so tired and annoyed from having to walk so much, they didn't want to be bothered with me and so I dropped back and got further and further behind. I started shouting but no-one heard me, they just went walking on. I had to follow the trail they made, but there came a moment when I just couldn't see the way they had gone. My father turned back to find me but he couldn't find the same path back and so they lost me for seven hours. I was crying, shouting, but no-one heard me. That was the first time I felt what it must be like to be an adult; I felt I had to be more responsible, more like my brothers and sisters. When they found me, they all started telling me off, that it was my fault, that I didn't even know how to walk. So we were walking like this for three days without anything to eat. We cut *bojónes* and ate the tender part of the plant, as if we were chewing meat. We were getting weaker and weaker, and still had to carry all the *mimbre* we'd cut.

And that's when that damned dog – perhaps because he realized we were near the village – came to meet us. He came to meet us so happily, but we could have killed him, we were so angry. My mother and all our neighbours were very worried. They didn't know what to do because they knew that if we got lost in the mountains, a lot of them would have to go out and look for us. Of course, with the dog they would have found us, but they were still waiting in the village, all very angry. It's something I've never forgotten, because of the anger I felt at the way we live. After all the work we put into cutting the *mimbre*, we couldn't carry it all, especially when it rained. We had to throw away some of what we'd cut and got back to the village with only some of it. In those days, in the capital they used to pay us fifty *quetzals* for each *quintal* of *mimbre*. So for five or six members of the family working the whole week, all day long, up the mountains, we got fifty *quetzals* the *quintal*. On top of that we had to meet all the costs of transport from our village to the town and from the town to the capital.

So we set off for the capital. My father loved me very much and I was very fond of him, so it always fell to me to travel with him and share his suffering with him. We arrived in the capital. In those days it made me really angry that I couldn't understand what my father and the man he wanted to sell the *mimbre* to were saying to each other. The man was telling him he had no money and wouldn't buy the *mimbre*. He was a carpenter, an old man. In Guatemala they still use *mimbre* for furniture and it's usually the carpenters, especially carpenters in Antigua,* who buy the *mimbre* to make their special kind of open wickerwork. So we went there and I could see the gestures the men were making to my father but I didn't know what they were saying. Afterwards my father was very worried because they wouldn't buy the *mimbre*. We went looking for other buyers but for us the capital is like another

---

* Capital of the Captaincy General of Guatemala under Spanish rule (1542–1773), now capital of the province of Sacatépequez.

world: one we don't know, because we live in the mountains. In the end, my father had to leave the *mimbre* with the first man who only paid him half what he asked. And we went back home with only 25 *quetzals*. After so much work! We returned home and it was awful because we found my mother had been really counting on our work and thought we were coming back with a lot of money. And we had hardly any. My poor mother nearly died of anger and rage at the fact that after all our suffering we hadn't any money. She felt sorry for all us children because she knew the hunger and cold we'd gone through collecting the *mimbre*. In the end, we were forced to go back to the *finca* to get a bit of money together.

Sometimes we took mountain mushrooms and herbs from the fields to town as well. We sold them and came back with a few *centavos* in our hands. But for us children, our work was mainly collecting *mimbre*.

My first visit to the capital was a big step in my life. I was my father's favourite; I went with him everywhere. It was the first time that I'd been in a truck with windows. We were used to travelling in closed lorries, as if we were in an oven with all the people and animals. It was the first time I'd ever sat on a seat in a truck – *and* one with windows. I didn't want to get in at first, because it wasn't like the trucks I knew. So my father said: 'I'll hold you tight, don't worry. We'll get there all right.' He gave me a sweet so I'd get into the truck. And so we set off. I remember the truck starting up . . . I hardly slept at all looking at the countryside we passed through from Uspantán to the capital. It impressed me very much, it was wonderful to see everything along the way – towns, mountains, houses very different from our own. It made me very happy, but also a bit frightened because I thought, as the truck pulled away, that we would go over into the ravine. When we reached the capital, I saw cars for the first time. I thought they were animals just going along. It didn't occur to me they were cars. I asked my father: 'What are they?' 'They're the same as the big lorries, only smaller,' he said, 'and they're for people who only want to carry small loads.' 'What we go to the *finca* in, what the workers ride in, is a lorry for our people,' my father said, 'and what we're travelling in now is what people go to the capital in, just to travel, not to work. And those little ones, they belong to rich people to use just for themselves. They don't have things to carry.' When I first saw them, I thought that the cars would all bump into each other, but they hardly did at all. When one stopped, they all had to stop. It was all so amazing for me. I remember when I got home telling my brothers and sisters what the cars were like, how they were driven, and that they didn't crash into one another or kill anyone, and a whole load of other things as well. I had a long tale to tell at home.

My father told me: 'When you're old enough, you must travel, you must go around the country. You know that you must do what I do.' That's what he used to say. After we sold the *mimbre* and got so little money for it, my father went to the office of the INTA.* My father went to the Agrarian Transformation offices, as they call it, for twenty-two years. When people have problems with land, when they're sold land, or when the government wants to settle peasants in other areas, they go through the Agrarian Transformation Institute. They give you a certain day on which you have to turn up and anyone who doesn't keep his appointment is punished, or fined. My father explained to me that there was a prison for the poor people and if you didn't go to that office, that's where they put you. I didn't even know what a prison was. My father said the people there didn't let you in unless you showed them respect. 'When you go in, keep still, don't speak,' he said. We went in and I saw my father take off his hat and give a sort of bow to the man sitting at a big table writing something on a typewriter. That's something else I used to dream about – that typewriter. How was it possible for paper to come out with things written on it? I didn't know what to think of all those people but I thought they were

---

* Instituto Nacional de Transformación Agraria de Guatemala (Guatemalan National Institute for Agriarian Transformation).

important people because my father took off his hat and spoke to them in a very humble way. Then we went home, but after that, every time my father went to the capital I wanted to go with him, but he didn't have the money to take me. There were so many interesting things, but also things that I didn't want to see, that frightened me. I thought, 'If I were alone, I'd die here.' The city for me was a monster, something alien, different. 'Those houses, those people,' I thought, 'this is the world of the *ladinos*.' For me it was the world of the *ladinos*. We were different. Afterwards I went to the capital a lot, and it became more familiar. But my first impression stayed with me. I remember that my father and I were very hungry. We didn't have anything to eat. My father said: 'We're not going to eat because we've got to go here and go there.' We went all over the city. But I was very hungry and asked my father: 'Aren't you hungry?' 'Yes,' he said, 'but we've still got so many things to do.' And instead of food, he bought me a sweet to suck. That impression stayed with me as well – that every time my father went to the capital I thought of him going hungry. I'd never had an ice cream, a *nieve* as they call it, so my father once bought me one for five *centavos*. I ate it and it tasted very good.

We spent three days in the capital. My father had a friend there who was from our region, he used to be a neighbour of ours. But he'd started buying and selling things and moved to the capital. He had a house on the outskirts of the city, a tiny shack made of cardboard. We stayed with him. I was very sad to see the man's children, because before they moved away we used to play together in the countryside and go to the river. I cried when I saw them because they asked me: 'How are the animals, the rivers; how are the plants?' They wanted to go back and I was very sad for them. They hardly had any food to eat in the house. They couldn't give us anything to eat because they had hardly any food. Anyway, that's where we stayed.

VI

AN EIGHT-YEAR-OLD AGRICULTURAL WORKER

'And that's when my consciousness was born.'
—Rigoberta Menchú

I worked from when I was very small, but I didn't earn anything. I was really helping my mother because she always had to carry a baby, my little brother, on her back as she picked coffee. It made me very sad to see my mother's face covered in sweat as she tried to finish her workload, and I wanted to help her. But my work wasn't paid, it just contributed to my mother's work. I either picked coffee with her or looked after my little brother, so she could work faster. My brother was two at the time. Indian women prefer to breastfeed their babies rather than give them food because, when the child eats and the mother eats, that's duplicating the food needed. So my brother was still feeding at the breast and my mother had to spend time feeding him and everything.

I remember that, at that time, my mother's work was making food for forty workers. She ground maize, made *tortillas*, put the *nixtamal* on the fire and cooked beans for the workers' food. That's a difficult job in the *finca*. All the dough made in the morning has to be finished the same morning because it goes bad. My mother had to make the number of *tortillas* the workers would eat. She was very appreciated by the workers because the food she gave them was fresh. The food we ate was cooked by another woman who sometimes gave us things that had gone bad, or *tortillas* that were tough and beans which jumped when you tried to pick them up. In the *finca* the women who do the cooking don't know which people they will cook for. The overseer comes and says: 'This is your group . . . this is what you give them to eat, these are the people you feed, you feed them at such and such a time . . . so get to work.' So different women fed us. My mother liked to give the workers the food they deserved, even if it meant she didn't sleep all night. They came back tired from the fields and she wanted to see that they ate well, even though her own family were eating badly somewhere else.

I was five when she was doing this work and I looked after my little brother. I wasn't earning yet. I used to watch my mother, who often had the food ready at three o'clock in the morning for the workers who started work early, and at eleven she had the food for the midday meal ready. At seven in the evening she had to run around again making food for her group. In between times, she worked picking coffee to supplement what she earned. Watching her made me feel useless and weak because I couldn't do anything to help her except look after my brother. That's when my consciousness was born. It's true. My mother didn't like the idea of me working, of earning my own money, but I did. I wanted to work, more than anything to help her, both economically and physically. The thing was that my mother was very brave and stood up to everything well, but there were times when one of my brothers or sisters was ill – if it wasn't one of them it was another – and everything she earned went on medicine for them. This made me very sad as well. It was that time, I remember, that when we went back to the *Altiplano* after five months in the *finca*, I was ill and it looked as if I'd die. I was six and my mother was distressed because I nearly died. The change of climate was too abrupt for me. After that, though, I made a big effort not to get ill again and, although my head ached a lot, I didn't say so.

When I turned eight, I started to earn money on the *finca*. I set myself the task of picking thirty-five pounds of coffee a day. In those days, I was paid twenty *centavos* for that amount. If I picked the thirty-five pounds, I earned twenty *centavos* a day, but if I didn't, I had to go on earning those same twenty *centavos* the next day. So I set myself this task and I remember that my brothers and sisters finished work at about seven or eight in the evening and sometimes offered to help me, but I said; 'No, I have to learn because if I don't learn myself, who's going to teach me?' I had to finish my workload myself. Sometimes I picked barely twenty-eight pounds because I got tired, especially when it was very hot. It gave me a headache. I'd fall asleep under a coffee bush, when suddenly I'd hear my brothers and sisters coming to look for me.

In the mornings we'd take turns to go off into the scrub and do our business. There are no toilets in the *finca*. There was only this place up in the hills where everybody went. There were about four hundred of us living there and everyone went to this same place. It was the toilet for all those people. We had to take it in turns. When one lot of people came back, another lot would go. There were lots of flies on all that filth up there. There was only one tap in the shed where we lived, not even enough for us to wash our hands. A little way away, there were water holes which the landowners used for irrigating the coffee or any other crops. So we had to go over to those water holes to get a drink and fill the water bottles we took with us to the fields.

Coffee is picked from the branch, but sometimes when it was ripe and fell off the branch, we'd have to collect it up off the ground. It's more difficult to pick up than pick from the branch. Sometimes we have to move the bushes to get at the coffee. We have to pick the nearest beans very carefully – bean by bean – because if we break a branch we have to pay for it out of our wages. It's worse when the coffee bushes are young. The branches are more valuable than on the old bushes. That's the job of the overseer, watching how the workers pick the coffee and seeing if they damage the leaves. We had to work very carefully. We learned that very early in our lives. I remember that it's one of the things that taught me to treat things very gently. Picking coffee is like caring for a wounded person. I worked more and more as I set myself bigger quotas. For instance, I made myself collect up off the ground a pound over what I picked every day. So I kept working harder but they didn't pay me more, they didn't pay me the extra work I did. They paid me very little.

I went on working and, as I said, for two years they paid me only twenty *centavos*. I picked more and more coffee. It increased by one pound, two pounds, three pounds. I worked like an adult. Then, finally, they started paying me more. By the time I was picking seventy pounds of coffee, they payed me thirty-five *centavos*. When I began earning, I felt as if I were an adult, as if I was making a direct contribution to our subsistence, together with my parents; because when I got my first pay, the little I got was added to what my parents earned. So I now felt I was part of the life my parents lived. It was very hard on me. I remember very well never wasting a single moment, mainly out of love for my parents and so that they could save a little of their money, although they couldn't really save any because they had to tighten their belts so much anyway.

It was during this period, when I was eight, that I fell ill. I'd been in the *finca* barely three months when I became ill and we had to go back home. It was in March, the time when we had to go back to the *Altiplano* anyway to sow our maize. So we went back and that's when I began working with my parents in the fields as well. It was another life, life in the fields – we were much happier. Although things were hard there too, because it rains a lot in the mountains and we were always wet. Our house was very draughty, we were never out of the wind, and the animals came into the house whenever they wanted. It meant we were never comfortable, and we were never warm because we didn't have clothes.

We went down to the *finca* again. It was round about May. My father went to cut cane on another plantation, one of my brothers went to pick cotton, and the rest of us stayed on the coffee plantation. When my father worked nearby he used to come back and stay, but when we worked on another *finca* we wouldn't see him until the end of the month. It was like that most of the time, with my father cutting, sowing or cleaning cane somewhere else. My father usually worked in sugar and the rest of us in coffee. So we were in different *fincas*. Sometimes we saw each other every month and sometimes every three months.

When my parents came back from work, they were very tired. My father, for instance, used to get very, very tired and he often didn't feel like talking or telling us anything. My mother didn't either. They were never cross but very often we had to keep quiet and do everything right so that mother and father could rest for a while. Even more so with the noise of all those people living together, thousands of people we don't know all living together. Among them are people who've gone through a great deal, a lot of upheavals in their lives. Prostitutes and people like that. So it's a very difficult atmosphere to live in and children are often not looked after very well. Mothers are very tired and just can't do it. This is where you see the situation of women in Guatemala very clearly. Most of the women who work picking cotton and coffee, or sometimes cane, have nine or ten children with them. Of these, three or four will be more or less healthy, and can survive, but most of them have bellies swollen from malnutrition and the mother knows that four or five of her children could die. This is a terrible situation and makes the men want to rebel, but they just try and forget because there is no other way out. So it's the mother who has to be with her children during their final moments. Suffering is everywhere. Women show a great deal of courage faced with this whole situation. Another thing that happens is that men who've been in the army, for example, often abuse young girls. Many girls have no families and earn only the little they get in the *finca*, so you start getting prostitution. This is something that doesn't exist among Indians, because of our culture and the traditions we preserve and respect.

In the eyes of our community, the fact that anyone should even change the way they dress shows a lack of dignity. Anyone who doesn't dress as our grandfathers, our ancestors, dressed, is on the road to ruin.

VII

DEATH OF HER LITTLE BROTHER IN THE FINCA. DIFFICULTY OF COMMUNICATING WITH OTHER INDIANS

'... those who sow maize for profit leave the earth empty of bones, because it is the bones of the forefathers that give the maize, and then the earth demands bones, and the softest ones, those of children, pile up on top of her and beneath her black crust, to feed her.'
—Miguel Angel Asturias, *Men of Maize*

We'd been in the *finca* for fifteen days, when one of my brothers died from malnutrition. My mother had to miss some days' work to bury him. Two of my brothers died in the *finca*. The first, he was the eldest, was called Felipe. I never knew him. He died when my mother started working. They'd sprayed the coffee with pesticide by plane while we were working, as they usually did, and my brother couldn't stand the fumes and died of intoxication. The second one, I did see die. His name was Nicolás. He died when I was eight. He was the youngest of all of us, the one my mother used to carry about. He was two then. When my little brother started crying, crying, crying, my mother didn't know what to do with him because his belly was swollen by malnutrition too. His belly was enormous and my mother didn't know what to do about it. The time came when my mother couldn't spend any more time with him or they'd take her job away from her. My brother had been ill from the day we arrived in the *finca*, very ill. My mother kept on working and so did we. He lasted fifteen days and then went into his death throes, and we didn't know what to do. Our neighbours from our village had gone to different *fincas*, there were only two with us. We weren't all together. We didn't know what to do because in our group we were with people from other communities who spoke different languages. We couldn't talk to them. We couldn't speak Spanish either. We couldn't understand each other and we needed help. Who was there to turn to? There was no-one we could count on, least of all the overseer, he might even throw us out of the *finca*. We couldn't count on the owner, we didn't even know who he was since he always did everything through intermediaries: the overseers, the contracting agents, etc. So that's how it was. When my mother needed help to bury my brother, we couldn't talk to anyone, we couldn't communicate, and she was desolate at the sight of my brother's body. I remember only being able to communicate with the others through signs. Most of them have had the same experiences; every day they're stuck in situations in which they can't call on help from outside and have to help each other. But it was very difficult. I remember also wanting to make friends with the children who lived in our shed with us – we were three hundred . . . four hundred people working in the *finca* – but we couldn't get to know each other.

A *galera* is a house, a large shack, where all the workers live. It's called a *galera* because it has only palm leaves or banana leaves for a roof, and the sides are open, it has no walls. All the workers live there together, with their dogs and cats, everything they bring with them from the *Altiplano*. There are no divisions, they put us in any old how, and with anybody. That's what life is like on the coast. Just one house to hold four, five hundred people.

It was difficult to get to know each other anyway, but our work made it even more difficult because we had to get up at three in the morning and start work straight away. It's worst when we're picking cotton because it isn't the weight that counts, it's the quantity. In the early morning it's nice and cool but by midday it's like being in an oven; it's very, very hot. That's why they make us start work so early. We stop work at midday to eat but go on working straight away afterwards until night-time. So, we didn't have much time to get to know any of the others, in spite of our all being one people. That's what is really distressing for us Indians, because when we're together, well, we're a community, we're all from the same place, but down in the *finca* we're together with other Indians we don't know. All the workers on the coastal estates, in coffee or in other things, are Indians who either live there at the *fincas* or emigrate there to work. They're all Indians but from different ethnic groups who speak different languages. This makes it very difficult for us because the linguistic barriers prevent any dialogue between us Indians, between ourselves. We can only understand the people from our own ethnic group, because we can't speak Spanish and we can't speak the other languages. So although we want to get closer to other groups, we can't. And so what we used to do in the *finca* was to go on celebrating our customs and everything, but without understanding each other. It was as if we'd been talking to foreigners.

The little boy died early in the morning. We didn't know what to do. Our two neighbours were anxious to help my mother but they didn't know what to do either – how to bury him or anything. Then the *caporal* told my mother she could bury my brother in the *finca* but she had to pay a tax to keep him buried there. My mother said: 'I have no money at all.' He told her: 'Yes, and you already owe a lot of money for medicine and other things, so take his body and leave.' We didn't know what to do. It was impossible to take his body back to the *Altiplano*. It was already starting to smell because of the humidity, the heat, on the coast. None of the people living in our *galera* wanted my brother's body to stay there, of course, because it was upsetting. So my mother decided that, even if she had to work for a month without earning, she would pay the tax to the landowner, or the overseer, to bury my brother in the *finca*. Out of real kindness and a desire to help one of the men brought a little box, a bit like a suitcase. We put my brother in it and took him to be buried. We lost practically a whole day's work over mourning my brother. We were all so very sad for him. That night the overseer told us: 'Leave here tomorrow.' 'Why?' asked my mother. 'Because you missed a day's work. You're to leave at once and you won't get any pay. So tomorrow I don't want to see you round here.' It was terrible for my mother, she didn't know what to do. She didn't know how to find my father because he was working somewhere else. When they throw people out of the *finca*, they don't take them back home as they usually do. Usually when the time comes to go back to the *Altiplano*, the same contracting agents take us back to our village, so we don't have to worry about how we're getting back, or about any transport, or even where we are. We didn't know our whereabouts, we didn't know where we were or anything. My mother didn't even know the name of the town we were in. But we knew we had to leave so my mother began getting our things together. So our neighbours said: 'We'll go with you even though it means losing everything we worked for too.' One of them lent my mother some money to pay for the burial since she'd been in the *finca* for about four months and had saved a little money. The fifteen days we had worked we weren't paid. Not only my mother and I, but my brother had worked fifteen days and wasn't paid either. The overseer said: 'No, it's because you owe a lot to the pharmacy. So, go on, out of here. I don't want to see you around here again.' But my mother knew that she hadn't been able to buy medicine for her son and that's why he'd died. The trouble is that we couldn't speak Spanish and the overseer spoke our language because he came from our region. He threw us out and said he didn't want to see us round there again. The boss's orders. So we had to leave.

We arrived back at our house in the *Altiplano*. My mother was very sad, so was my brother who was with us. My father didn't know his son had died, nor did my other brothers and sisters because they were working on other *fincas*. Fifteen days later, they all arrived home to be greeted by the news that the little boy had died and that we owed a lot of money. My father and my brothers and sisters had been earning in the other *fincas* and had enough money to settle up with our neighbour. The neighbour also gave what he felt he should to the dead child. That's how they helped us – the community, everyone – once we'd got home.

From that moment, I was both angry with life and afraid of it, because I told myself: 'This is the life I will lead too; having many children, and having them die.' It's not easy for a mother to watch her child die, and have nothing to cure him with or help him live. Those fifteen days working in the *finca* was one of my earliest experiences and I remember it with enormous hatred. That hatred has stayed with me until today.

We went down to the *finca* again. Christmas is the last month we spend in the *finca*. In January we start working our land in the *Altiplano*. January and February are the months we sow our crops. In March we go back down to the coast to earn money to spend on the maize fields, and when the first work on the maize is over, we return to the *finca* to carry on earning for food.

When I was ten, they raised my pay because by then I was picking forty pounds of coffee. For picking cotton I still got very little because it was a lot in quantity but not in weight. There's an office in every *finca* where all the work you deliver is taken. It's weighed and noted down for their accounts. Towards the end, my brothers (who are not stupid) managed to figure out the ways in which they fiddled the amounts weighed. They have tricks to make it weigh less, when the real amount is much more. That happens everywhere. It's a special trick of the men in charge of weighing the workers' loads; that's when they steal many pounds of coffee. They put large amounts on one side so that they can deliver more and get paid more. It's part of a long process which starts the moment the agents contract the workers in their villages and load them into the lorries like animals. It's one long process of robbing them of their pay. They're charged for absolutely everything, even for the loading of the lorry. Then, in the *finca*, the overseers steal from the workers from the very first day. The *cantina* steals from them too. It continues until the last day. It's so bad that we have had the bad experience of getting home again without a *centavo*. Coffee is measured by the workload set but cotton is measured by a different method. If you pick sixty-five pounds of cotton per day, you're paid according to the weight. But with coffee, you have to pick a *quintal* per day and if you don't it's added on and the next day you have to finish that *quintal* before starting another one. In my case, when I started work I had to do a third of what an adult's task would be. That was thirty-five pounds. But some days I could only do twenty-eight pounds so the next day I had to carry on with the same one. This way you fall further and further behind until you have to spend two days just making up the amount you're missing. With cotton, the situation is different but it's very difficult too. The worst work is when it's second 'hand'. First 'hand' is when the flowers are nicely grouped together, but second hand is when you have to pick between the branches the cotton which has been left behind the first time. That's much harder work but the pay is the same.

VIII

LIFE IN THE ALTIPLANO. RIGOBERTA'S TENTH BIRTHDAY

'We Indians never do anything which goes against the laws of our ancestors.'
—Rigoberta Menchú

Back in the *Altiplano*, we all set to work with our hoes. I remember from the age of nine going off to the fields with my hoe to help my father. I was like a boy, chopping wood with an axe, or with a machete. There was very little water near our village. We had to walk about four kilometres to fetch our water, and that added to our work a lot. But we were happy because that was the time of year we sowed our bit of maize and it was sometimes enough for us to live on. At times, we managed to scrape a living in the *Altiplano* and didn't go down to the *fincas*. When the fields were full of plants and we had a bit of maize and a few *tortillas*, we were very happy up there. The land was fertile and I remember my mother giving us different types of beans like *ayote*, *chilacayote* and others that grew up there. But we didn't eat a lot of beans because most of what my mother grew was taken to market to buy soap, or some chile. That's what we ate – chile. And if we wanted to, we could pick plants in the fields. So, with chile, plants and *tortillas*, we ate very well. That was our menu most of the time.

It's not the custom among our people to use a mill to grind the maize to make dough. We use a grinding stone; that is, an ancient stone passed down from our ancestors. We don't use ovens either. We only use wood fires to cook our *tortillas*. First we get up at three in the morning and start grinding and washing the *nixtamal*, turning it into dough by using the grinding stone. We all have different chores in the morning. Some of us wash the *nixtamal*, others make the fire to heat water for the coffee or whatever. In our house there were a lot of us – my elder sister, my mother, myself, and my sister-in-law, my elder brother's wife. So there were four women working in the house. Each of us had her job to do and we all had to get up at a certain time, our time was three in the morning. The men get up at that time too because they have to sharpen their hoes, machetes and axes before going off to work. So they get up at the same time. There are no lights in our village so at night we see by the light of *ocotes*. An *ocote* is a piece cut from a pine tree. It lights up immediately as if petrol had been poured on it. It burns easily. You can light it with matches and it flames up. That's what we use for light to move about the house. It burns slowly and if you put a bunch of *ocote* somewhere, it lights everything up.

Whoever gets up first, lights the fire. She makes the fire, gets the wood hot and prepares everything for making *tortillas*. She heats the water. The one who gets up next washes the *nixtamal* outside, and the third one up washes the grinding stone, gets the water ready and prepares everything needed for grinding the maize. In our house, I made the food for the dogs. My father had a lot of dogs because of the animals which came down from the mountain. These dogs guarded our animals. It was my job to make food for them. Their food was the hard core of the maize, the cob. We had a little place just outside the house, a sort of little hollow, where we'd throw the cob when we'd taken the grains of corn off. With time, the cobs rot and go soft, and are cooked with lime. Then it's all ground up for the dogs' food. Lime makes our dogs strong, otherwise they'd all die. They don't eat our food, which is maize, but sometimes, when there's no maize, we eat the dogs' food.* We make it into *tortillas*, just as we do with the maize dough. Anyway, it was my job to make the dogs' food. I'd get up, wash the stone and things I needed and start grinding the dogs' food. I started doing this when I was seven. When the fire is made and the *nixtamal* washed, everyone starts grinding. One person grinds the maize, another grinds it a second time with a stone to make it finer, and another makes it into little balls for the *tortilla*. When that's all ready, we all start making *tortillas*. We have a flat earthenware pan big enough to hold all the *tortillas*. Then the men – my brothers and my father – all come and get their *tortillas* from the pan and start eating. In the mornings, we sometimes drink coffee or sometimes only water. We usually make *pinol*; that is, maize toasted and ground. This is drunk instead of coffee because coffee is too expensive for my parents to buy. Sometimes my parents haven't enough money for *panela* either; we don't use sugar but *panela* which comes straight from the sugar cane. When there's no *panela* in the house, we can't drink *pinol* or coffee. So we drink water. In the mornings, we usually have a big plate of chile, and all of us have a good meal of *tortilla* and chile before going off to work. Our dogs are used to being with people, they enjoy the natural world as well and like going off to work with the men. So we have to feed the dogs before the workers leave, as the dogs always go with them. If the men are going to work a long way off, we have to make *tortillas* for them to take with them, but if they're working nearby, one of the women stays at home and makes the midday meal for them.

Our men usually leave around five or half past every morning. They go and tend the maize or cultivate the ground. Some of the women go with them because we sow the beans and, when the plant starts sprouting, we stick in little branches for it to wind itself around, so that it doesn't damage the maize.

---

* It often happened that we had no maize and my brothers and sisters and I, even when we were ill, had to eat the dogs' food.

So, yes, at times we're working alongside the men all day. What we used to do, was that my sister-in-law stayed at home because she had a baby. She stayed at home, looked after the animals, made the food and brought it to us at midday. She'd bring *atol, tortillas,* and if she saw anything she could use in the fields, she'd prepare that too and bring it along for us to eat. *Atol* is the maize dough. We use it for a drink, as refreshment. It's dissolved in water, boiled, and it thickens, according to how you want to drink it. Of course, sometimes we take it in turns to stay home because my sister-in-law grew up on the *fincas* and in the *Altiplano* too, so she gets bored in the house because the food only takes a minute to make and the rest of the time she has to herself. She uses the time to do a lot of weaving. She makes mats, cloth, *huipiles*, blouses, or other things like that. But she often gets bored and wants to work in the fields, even though she's carrying her baby on her back. So we take it in turns, my sister, my mother and I.

In our village we have the habit of talking very loudly because we haven't really any close neighbours. When the workers leave in the morning, they call out to all their neighbours because the neighbours' maize fields are all near each other, so they all go together. We all get together like one family. Our maize fields aren't in the village itself. They're a short distance away, towards the mountain, so we call all our neighbours and we all go together – twenty or thirty people going off to work together with our dogs. We eat at midday or whenever we feel hungry. We usually go home again at six in the evening. Six o'clock is when our men come home, hungry and thirsty, and the woman who stays at home has to make food again. That's when we do all the extra chores in the house. The men tie up the dogs in the *corrales* where the animals are and the women fetch water to wash the *nixtamal* and washing pots, chop wood and prepare the torches for the night. We prepare all our things for the next day to save time in the morning. When nights falls, we're still working. Afterwards, we sing a bit; songs we Indians have in our own language. I don't know how, but my brothers got hold of an accordion, and we'd sing until our parents told us off because we were very tired and they sent us to bed. We usually go to bed at ten or half past because we have to get up so early and since our house is very small, when one person gets up, we all have to get up.

Our house measures about eight *varas*. It's not made of wood but of cane; straight sticks of it we find in the fields and fasten together with *agave* fibres. Any tree will do to make a house, but (I think this is part of our culture) only if it's cut at full moon. We say the wood lasts longer if it's cut when the moon is young. When we build a house, we make the roof from a sort of palm tree found near the foot of the mountains. We call it *pamac*. For us, the most elegant houses are made with cane leaves, because you have to go a long way to get them. You have to have men to go and get them to make the house. We were poor and had neither money to buy cane leaves nor anyone to go and get them. They're only found down in the *fincas* on the coast and they're very expensive. The landowners charge by the bunch – seventy-five *centavos* the bunch – and it takes fifty bunches for a house. We didn't have the means to buy cane leaves, so what we did was go to the mountains and collect this leaf called *pamac*. The mature leaves last about two years and after that you have to start again. So we all went to cut the mature leaves. Between us – men, women and children – we could build a house in fifteen days. We had a very big family, and we were able to use sticks, although many people used maize stalks. After the maize is harvested, people cut the stalks and use them for walls. But our house was made of sticks of cane: that lasts longer. The houses are not very high because, if there's a lot of wind, it can lift the house and carry it all away. That's why we make them small and put sticks all round. The sticks are stuck in the ground and tied together with *agave* fibres. There are no nails in our houses – you won't find a single nail. Even the roof props, the corners, or anything supporting the house, comes from trees.

We all sleep in there together. The house has two floors; one above, where the corn cobs are stored (we call it the *tapanco*) and another below where we all live. But at the times of the year when there's no maize, many of us go up and sleep in the *tapanco*. When the cobs are stored there, we have to sleep on the ground floor. We don't usually have beds with mattresses or anything like that. We just have our own few clothes and we're used to being cold, because the roof doesn't give much protection. The wind comes in as if we were out on the mountain. As for sex, that's something we Indians know about because most of the family sees everything that goes on. Couples sleep together but don't have a separate place for themselves. Even the children realize most of the time, but sometimes they don't, because I think married couples don't have enough time to enjoy their life together and, anyway, we're all in there together. Of course, when we sleep, we sleep like logs, we're so tired. We often get home so tired we don't want to eat anything, or do anything. We just want to sleep. So we sleep. Perhaps that's when the others take the opportunity to have sexual relations, but there's hardly any room. Often just the children go down to the *finca* and the parents stay at home and look after the animals. That's when they have a bit more time to themselves. But most of the time my father goes to one *finca* and my mother takes the children to another *finca* so they're apart for three months. Or we all go together to one *finca* but there it's even worse for sleeping than at home, because we're with people we don't even know and there are hundreds of people and animals sleeping together. It is really difficult there. We're piled up in one place, almost on top of one another. I'm sure the children notice a lot of things. In our case, all the brothers and sisters in our family slept together in one row. My older brother, who'd been married for some time, slept with his *compañera*, but the ones who weren't married (my other two older brothers, my sister, myself, and my three younger brothers who were alive then), we all slept together in a row. We put all the women's *cortes* together and used them for blankets. My parents slept in another corner quite near us. We each had a mat to sleep on and a little cover over us. We slept in the same clothes we worked in. That's why society rejects us. Me, I felt this rejection very personally, deep inside me. They say we Indians are dirty, but it's our circumstances which force us to be like that. For example, if we have time, we go to the river every week, every Sunday, and wash our clothes. These clothes have to last us all week because we haven't any other time for washing and we haven't any soap either. That's how it is. We sleep in our clothes, we get up next day, we tidy ourselves up a bit and off to work, just like that.

My tenth birthday was celebrated in the same way as all our people. I was up in the *Altiplano*. It might not have been the exact date of my birth because I was in the *finca* at the time, but when we went back up to the *Altiplano*, that was when we celebrated my birthday. My parents called me to them and explained what an adult's life is like. I didn't really need them to explain because it was the life I'd seen and lived with my mother; so it was really only a show of accepting what parents tell us.

My elder brothers were present and my sister who's now married. But my younger brothers were not. I'm the sixth in the family, with three brothers after me, but they weren't present because it's a ceremony in which my parents tell me about the new life I'm about to start. They told me I would have many ambitions but I wouldn't have the opportunity to realize them. They said my life wouldn't change, it would go on the same – work, poverty, suffering. At the same time, my parents thanked me for the contribution I'd made through my work, for having earned for all of us. Then they told me a bit about being a woman; that I would soon have my period and that was when a woman could start having children. They said that would happen one day, and for that they asked me to become closer to my mother so I could ask her everything. My mother would be by my side all this time in case I had any doubts or felt alone. They talked about the experiences with my elder brothers and sisters. My elder sister, who was already grown-up (she'd be about twenty-four, I think) told me about when she was young: when she was ten, twelve, thirteen, fifteen. My father said that sometimes she didn't do things as she should but that that wasn't right: we should not stop doing good things but accept life as it is. We shouldn't become bitter or look for diversions or escape outside the laws of our parents. All this helps you to be a girl who is respected by the community. My father explained the importance of our example and the example of every one of our neighbours' children. We know that not just one pair of eyes is watching us, but the eyes of the whole community are on us. It's not a case of giving things up. We have a lot of freedom, but at the same time, within that freedom we must respect ourselves.

Well, my mother, father, and all my brothers and sisters, gave me their experiences. Suddenly they treated me like an adult. My father said: 'You have a lot of responsibility; you have many duties to fulfil in our community as an adult. From now on you must contribute to the common good.' Then they made me repeat the promises my parents had made for me when I was born; when I was accepted into the community; when they said I belonged to the community and would have to serve it when I grew up. They said they'd made these promises and now it was up to me to keep them, because now I had to participate in the community as one more member of it. In those days, there was already the mixture of our culture with the Catholic religion, let's say Catholic customs. So my duty was to promise to serve the community and I looked for ways in which I could work for the community. When you reach the age of ten, your family and the whole community holds a meeting. It's very important. There's a ceremony as if we were praying to God. The discussion is very important because, as I said, it initiated me into adult life. Not the life of a young girl but adult life with all its responsibilities. I'm no longer a child, I become a woman. So in front of my parents, in front of my brothers and sisters, I promised to do many things for the community. That's when I started to take over some of my father's duties: that is, praying in our neighbours' houses like my father does. Whenever there's a meeting, it's always my father who speaks, and he coordinates a lot of things in the community. I felt responsible for many things and my mother let us into many secrets, telling us to try and do things the way she had. It was then, I remember, I became a catechist, and began working with the children both in the community and down in the *finca*, since, when some of the community go to the *finca*, others stay in the *Altiplano* looking after our animals, or whatever, so we don't have to take them with us to the coast.

IX

CEREMONIES FOR SOWING TIME AND HARVEST. RELATIONSHIPS WITH THE EARTH

'Sown to be eaten, it is the sacred sustenance of the men who were made of maize. Sown to make money, it means famine for the men who were made of maize.'

—Miguel Angel Asturias, *Men of Maize*

'The seed is something pure, something sacred. For our people the seed is very significant.'

—Rigoberta Menchú

There's another custom for our twelfth birthday. We're given a little pig, or a lamb, or one or two chickens. These little animals have to reproduce and that depends on each person, on the love we give our parents' present. I remember when I was twelve, my father gave me a little pig. I was also given two little chickens and a lamb. I love sheep very much. These animals are not to be touched or sold without my permission. The idea is for a child to start looking after his own needs. I intended my animals to reproduce but I also intended to love the animals belonging to my brothers and sisters and my parents. I felt really happy. It's one of the most wonderful things that can happen. I was very pleased with my little animals. They had a fiesta for me. We eat chicken whenever there is a fiesta. Years and years can go past without us eating beef. With us, eating a chicken is a big event.

It wasn't long before my little pig grew and had five little piglets. I had to feed them without neglecting my work for my parents. I had to find food for them myself. So what I used to do was, after work in the fields, I'd come back home at six or seven in the evening, do all my jobs in the house for the next morning, and then at about nine o'clock I'd start weaving. Sometimes I'd weave until ten. When we'd stop for our food out in the fields, I'd hang my weaving up on a branch and carry on weaving there. After about fifteen days, I'd have three or four pieces of cloth to sell, and I'd buy maize or other little things for my pigs to eat. That's how I looked after my little pigs. I also started preparing some ground with a hoe to sow a bit of maize for them. When my pigs were seven months old, I sold them and was able to sow a bit of maize for the mother pig so she could go on having piglets. I could also buy myself a *corte* and other things to put on, and enough thread to make or weave a blouse, a *huipil*. That's how you provide for your needs and, in the end, I had three grown-up pigs, ready for me to sell. At the beginning it's difficult, I didn't know what to give them to eat. I'd collect plants in the fields to give my piglets and when I made the dogs' food, I used to take a bit for them too. By the time the first little animals are born, our parents can tell if our *nahual* gives us the qualities for getting on well with animals. I was one of those who loved animals, and they always turned out very well for me. Animals loved me too. Cows, for instance, were never awkward with me. My parents were very pleased with me.

For us women, Sunday was the day we went to the river to wash clothes. Mother or father would go to market to buy things, but some Sundays they didn't have to go because we don't eat very much that comes from the market. We mostly eat maize and plants. We go there to sell, when we harvest our beans. We grow little beans but we don't eat them. They all go to market so we can buy the few provisions we use from the market, like soap, salt, and some chile. Sometimes we can't sell our beans because nobody buys them. Everyone is selling the beans they've grown, so the traders come and pay what they choose. If we ask a little more, they don't buy. But for us it's almost a day's walk to the town and it's difficult to get horses because only two or three people have horses. When we need one we ask a neighbour to lend us one, but many people want to borrow and some are left without horses. So we have to carry our beans on our backs. I used to carry forty or fifty pounds of beans or maize from our house to the town. We'd sell maize too when there was something we needed to buy.

Most villagers hardly ever go down to the town. We only go when we're needed to carry all our goods to town, and then two or three of my brothers and sisters would go. Otherwise, just my father, or my mother, or a neighbour would go. It's the custom with us on Saturday nights to go from house to house asking if any neighbour is going to town next day and if they say, 'Yes,' we say: 'Will you bring us this thing or that thing?' And that neighbour buys what the whole community needs. So when my mother goes to town, she shouts very loud to all the neighbours: 'I'm going to market,' and they say: 'Buy us soap, buy us salt, buy us chile,' and tell her how much she should buy. Then another neighbour will come and offer a horse, if a horse is needed. So we all help one another. This is how we sell things as well. Most people in our village make straw plaits for hats, or they make mats, or weave cloth, so at the weekend they get it all together for one person to sell. This way we don't all have to go to market.

The times we spend up in our village are happy times because we're there to harvest the maize, and before we harvest the maize, we have a fiesta. The fiesta really starts months before when we asked the earth's permission to cultivate her. In that ceremony we burn incense, the elected leaders say prayers, and then the whole community prays. We burn candles in our own houses and other candles for the whole community. Then we bring out the seeds we will be sowing. With maize, for instance, the seeds for the coming year are picked out as soon as the cobs start to grow. We choose them and put a mark on them. The cob is peeled or left in its leaves but those grains are taken off, and the big ones are wrapped in the leaves and made into a little ball. The small ones are cooked straight away and made into a *tortilla* the next day and eaten, so we don't waste even the smallest part of these cobs. The big seeds, wrapped in the leaves in little balls, are left in the branches of a tree to wait, to be dried as carefully as possible. It has to be a place where none of the women pass over them, or jump on them or anything, nor where the hens and chickens or any other animal can walk on them – where dogs, for example, can't get them. In front of our house there is a big tree where we put everything like that. A child stands watch to see that nothing gets at them.

Before the seeds are sown in the ground, we perform a ceremony. We choose two or three of the biggest seeds and place them in a ring, candles representing earth, water, animals and the universe (that is, man). In our culture, the universe is man. Th seed is honoured because it will be buried in something sacred – the earth – and because it will multiply and bear fruit the next year. We do it mainly because the seed is something pure, something sacred. For us the word 'seed' is very significant. The candles are lit in every house. We put in some *ayote* too, because that will be sown together with the maize. And we do the same with beans. It is like an offering to the one God. This will be our food for the coming year. During the fiesta, prayers are given up to the earth, the moon, the sun, the animals and the water, all of which join with the seed to provide our food. Each member of the family makes a vow and promises not to waste the food.

The next day everyone calls to each other to go and start sowing. The whole community rejoices when we begin to sow our maize. When we reach the fields, the men sow the maize and the beans. The seeds go in the same hole. The women follow, planting the *ayotes* in between the furrows to make the most of every bit of land. Others, children usually, follow sowing gourds, *chilacayote*, or potatoes. Children like sowing potatoes. We plant everything at the same time. Then we have to look after the maize because there are many kinds of animals in the mountains and, at sowing time, they come and dig up the seeds. So we take it in turns to keep watch in the fields, taking a turn around the fields now and again during the night. Racoons, squirrels, *taltuzas* and other rodents are the ones that come at night. During the day, it's the birds. We're happy to take turns keeping watch because we fall asleep by the tree trunks. We like setting traps everywhere we think an animal is likely to come. We set traps but when the poor animals cry out, we go and see. Since they are animals and our parents have forbidden us to kill them, we let them go after we've given them a telling off so that they won't come back. If the dogs kill them, we eat them, but, generally, we don't kill animals. We only kill them accidentally. When the leaves start sprouting, they stop digging up the seeds.

When the maize starts growing, we all go back down to the *fincas* on the coast to work. When we come back, the maize has grown and needs attention. It needs weeding out. When that's done, we go back to the *finca*. When the maize is high, it needs attending to again. These are the two most difficult parts of growing maize; after that it can be left to itself. We have to put little pieces of earth round the roots so that the stalks don't get knocked over by the wind. While it is growing, the women often don't go to the *fincas* but stay and look after the beans, putting in little sticks for them to wind round so they don't interfere with the maize. They look after the *ayotes* too, and all the varieties of gourds.

Maize is the centre of everything for us. It is our culture. The *milpa* is the maize field. *Maíz* is the grain. The *mazorca* is the body of the maize, the cob. The *tuza* is the leaf which envelopes the cob, especially when it's dry. The *xilote* is the core. That's why we called it *xilotear* when the fruit begins to grow. Maize is used for food and for drink, and we also use the *xilote* for bottle stoppers and food for the dogs and pigs.

The animals start coming into the maize fields again when the cobs appear. The birds eat them and the animals come from the mountains for them. So we have to keep guard again. It's usually the children who look after the fields; shouting and throwing earth all day to keep the birds away. All the neighbours are in their fields shouting. When the cob starts to grow, we have other customs. One custom is when we start using the leaves of the maize plant to make *tamales*. We don't cut them or use them straight away, but have a special ceremony before we cut the first leaf. All our village sows their maize in the same way but it doesn't always grow the same. Some turn out small, some big, and some even bigger. So the neighbours with the most maize must share their big leaves with the others. For us, using a maize leaf for our *tamales* makes them very tasty and we want to give some meaning to it, so that's why we celebrate the first leaves. Then comes the fiesta. After we've used the first leaves, when we've eaten the *tamales* inside, we don't throw the leaves away but make a pile of them. We roll them up and hang them in a corner of the house in remembrance of the first harvest the earth gave up. Then comes the ripe maize cob. Sometimes we eat it when it's still very young but only if we really need to because it's bigger when the cob has matured. But it's mountainous there and the cobs fall off with the winds. We have to pick up the maize which falls and eat that too.

At harvest time, we also celebrate the first day we pick the maize cobs, and the rest of what our small plots of land yield. The women pick the beans and the men pick the maize; we all harvest the fruits of our labour together. But before we pick them, we have a ceremony in which the whole community thanks the earth and the God who feeds us. Everyone is very happy because they don't have to go down to the *finca* and work now that they have food. The ceremony to celebrate the harvest is nearly the same as the one where we ask the earth's permission to cultivate her. We thank her for the harvest she's given us. Our people show their happiness, their gratitude for this food, this maize, which took so long to grow. It's a victory for the whole community when they harvest their crops and they all get together for a feast. So we have a celebration at the beginning of the *tapizca*, and at the end of the *tapizca* we have another.

Every village has a community house which is used for meetings, for prayers, for fiestas, or anything else. It's a big house which can hold a lot of people. It has a kitchen and a *tapanco* to store the communal maize. The whole community assembles there to celebrate our faith, to pray. If we don't do it every Friday, then it's every Monday. So the whole village gets together, even when there are no special ceremonies or fiestas to celebrate. We get together to pray or just to talk to each other. We tell each other our experiences. We don't need an agenda, it's a dialogue between us. We also play with the children for a while. This happens once a week. Either on a Friday or a Monday.

At the beginning everybody works communally, clearing the bush in the mountains. How many years would that take one family? We work together: the women pulling out the small plants below and the men cutting down trees on the mountainside. When sowing time comes, the community meets to discuss how to share out the land – whether each one will have his own plot or if they will work collectively. Everyone joins in the discussion. In my village, for example, we said it was up to all of us if we wanted our own plot or not. But we also decided to keep a common piece of land, shared by the whole community, so that if anyone was ill or injured, they would have food to eat. We worked in that way: each family with their own plot and a large piece of common land for emergencies in the community or in the family. It was mostly to help widows. Each day of the week, someone would go and work that common land.

X

THE NATURAL WORLD.
THE EARTH, MOTHER OF MAN

'We must respect the one God at the heart of the sky, which is the Sun.'

—Rigoberta Menchú

'Tojil, in his own natural darkness, struck the leather of his sandal with a stone, and from it, at that very moment, came a spark, then a flash, followed by a flame, and the new fire burned in all its splendour.'

—Popul Vuh

From very small children we receive an education which is very different from white children, *ladinos*. We Indians have more contact with nature. That's why they call us polytheistic. But we're not polytheistic ... or if we are, it's good, because it's our culture, our customs. We worship – or rather not worship but respect – a lot of things to do with the natural world, the most important things for us. For instance, to us, water is sacred. Our parents tell us when we're very small not to waste water, even when we have it. Water is pure, clean, and gives life to man. Without water we cannot survive, nor could our ancestors have survived. The idea that water is sacred is in us children, and we never stop thinking of it as something pure. The same goes for the earth. Our parents tell us: 'Children, the earth is the mother of man, because she gives him food.' This is especially true for us whose life is based on the crops we grow. Our people eat maize, beans and plants. We can't eat ham, or cheese, or things made with equipment, with machines. So we think of the earth as the mother of man, and our parents teach us to respect the earth. We must only harm the earth when we are in need. This is why, before we sow our maize, we have to ask the earth's permission. *Pom, copal*, is a sacred ingredient for our people. We use it to express our feelings for the earth, so that she will allow us to cultivate her. *Copal* is the resin of a tree. It has a smell like incense. We burn it and it gives off a very strong smell: a smoke with a very rich, delicious, aroma. We use the candle, water and lime a great deal in our ceremonies. We use candles to represent the earth, water and maize, which is the food of man. We believe (and this has been passed down to us by our ancestors) that our people are made of maize. We're made of white maize and yellow maize. We must remember this. We put a candle out for man, as the son of the natural world, the universe, and the members of the family join together in prayer. The prayers usually ask the earth for permission to plant our crops at sowing time, to give us a good harvest, and then to give thanks with all our might, with all our being, for a good harvest.

The prayers and ceremonies are for the whole community. We pray to our ancestors, reciting their prayers which have been known to us for a long time – a very, very long time. We evoke the representatives of the animal world; we say the names of dogs. We say the names of the earth, the god of the earth, and the god of water. Then we say the name of the heart of the sky – the sun. Our grandfathers say we must ask the sun to shine on all its children: the trees, animals, water, man. We ask it to shine on our enemies. To us an enemy is someone who steals or goes into prostitution. So, you see, it's a different world. This is how we make our pleas and our promises. It doesn't refer so much to the real world, but it includes part of our reality. A prayer is made up of all this. We make a definite plea to the earth. We say: 'Mother Earth, you who give us food, whose children we are and on whom we depend, please make this produce you give us flourish and make our children and our animals grow . . .', and other things as well. Or we say: 'We make our vows for ten days so that you concede us permission, your permission, Mother Earth, who are sacred, to feed us and give our children what they need. We do not abuse you, we only beg your permission, you who are part of the natural world and part of the family of our parents and our grandparents.' This means we believe, for instance, that the sun is our grandfather, that he is a member of our family. 'We respect you and love you and ask that you love us as we love you' – those prayers are specially for the earth. For the sun, we say: 'Heart of the sky, you are our father, we ask you to give your warmth and light to our animals, our maize, our beans, our plants, so that they may grow and our children may eat.' We evoke the colour of the sun, and this has a special importance for us because this is how we want our children to live – like a light which shines, which shines with generosity. It means a warm heart and it means strength, life-giving strength. It's something you never lose and you find it everywhere. So when we evoke the colour of the sun, it's like evoking all the elements which go to make up our life. The sun, as the channel to the one God, receives the plea from his children that they should never violate the rights of all the other beings which surround them. This is how we renew our prayer which says that men, the children of the one God, must respect the life of the trees, the birds, the animals around us. We say the names of birds and animals – cows, horses, dogs, cats. All these. We mention them all. We must respect the life of every single one of them. We must respect the life, the purity, the sacredness, which is water. We must respect the one God, the heart of the sky, which is the sun. We must not do evil while the sun shines upon his children. This is a promise. Then we promise to respect the life of the one creature, which is man. This is very important. We say: 'We cannot harm the life of one of your children, we are your children. We cannot kill any of your creatures, neither trees nor animals.' Then we offer up a sheep or chickens, because we believe sheep to be sacred animals, quiet animals, saintly animals, animals which don't harm other animals. They are the most tranquil animals that exist, like birds. So the community chooses certain small animals for the feast after the ceremonies.

XI

MARRIAGE CEREMONIES

'Children, wherever you may be, do not abandon the crafts taught to you by Ixpiyacoc, because they are crafts passed down to you from your forefathers. If you forget them, you will be betraying your lineage.'

—Popol Vuh

'The magic secrets of your forefathers were revealed to them by voices which came by the path of silence and the night.'

—Popol Vuh

I remember that, when we grew up our parents talked to us about having children. That's the time parents dedicate themselves to the child. In my case, because I was a girl, my parents told me: 'You're a young woman and a woman has to be a mother.' They said I was beginning my life as a woman and I would want many things that I couldn't have. They tried to tell me that, whatever my ambitions, I'd no way of achieving them. That's how life is. They explained what life is like among our people for a young person, and then they said I shouldn't wait too long before getting married. I had to think for myself, learn to be independent, not rely on my parents, and learn many things which would be useful to me in my life. They gave me the freedom to do what I wanted with my life as long as, first and foremost, I obeyed the laws of our ancestors. That's when they taught me not to abuse my own dignity – both as a woman and a member of our race. They always give the *ladinos* as an example. Most of them paint their faces and kiss in the street. To our parents this was scandalous. It was a show of disrespect to our ancestors and I was not to do it. If you have a home, your betrothed can come there, if he abides by various customs and the laws of our ancestors. These are all the things our parents tell us. A girl must listen to what her mother tells her; she'll teach her things she will need one day. They explained all this to me so that I might open the doors of life; so I might learn many things. This is when I began spending more time with my mother and developing as a woman. My mother explained that when I started menstruating, I had begun developing as a woman and could have children. She told me how young women should behave, according to what is laid down in our traditions. For example, if a young man talks to us in the street, we have the right to insult him or ignore him, because our ancestors say it is scandalous for a woman to start courting in the street or do anything behind her parents' back.

Most children know when their parents are having relations but this doesn't mean they have a clear idea of what that is. Our parents tell us that we should develop and know all about this aspect, but that's as far as they go. We don't even know about the parts of our own bodies, and we don't know what having babies means. Now I'm critical of that in many ways because I don't think it is a good thing, and it can be a problem being ignorant of so many things about life.

It's very rare for a couple not to have children. A lot depends on the medicines the midwife uses. They cure many people with their herbs. I have a cousin who is married and hasn't any children. The community gives her a lot of affection because they do need a child. Under these circumstances the man can often give in to vices and start drinking. If he hasn't any children, he only thinks about himself. The woman can become quarrelsome too. If this happens the community slowly loses their sympathy for the couple. They provoke most of the quarrels themselves but sometimes there are women who just don't like to see a woman without children and some men just don't like men who've no children. This is not the same as rejecting the *huecos*, as we call homosexuals. Our people don't differentiate between people who are homosexual and people who aren't; that only happens when we go out of our community. We don't have the rejection of homosexuality the *ladinos* do; they really cannot stand it. What's good about our way of life is that everything is considered part of nature. So an animal which didn't turn out right is part of nature, so is a harvest that didn't give a good yield. We say you shouldn't ask for more than you can receive. That's what the *ladinos* brought with them. It's a phenomenon that arrived with the foreigners.

Having said that, when our women migrate (leave the village and then come back), they bring with them all the nastiness of the world outside. And they use those plants – medicinal plants found in the fields – to stop themselves having children. In our fields there are remedies which can make you have children at certain times, and at others stop you having children. The outside world – which we know is disgusting – has set a bad example and has started giving us pills and gadgets. There was a big scandal in Guatemala when the Guatemalan Social Security Institute began sterilizing women without telling them, in order to reduce the population. The thing is, to us, using medicine to stop having children is like killing your own children. It's negating the laws of our ancestors which say we should love everything that exists. So what happens is, our children either die before they are born, or two or so years afterwards, from no fault of our own. It's the fault of others. The real culprits are those who sow bad seeds on our land. It's not the Indian's fault if he gives life to a child and then sees it die of hunger anyway.

The community is very suspicious of a woman like me who is twenty-three but they don't know where I've been or where I've lived. She loses the confidence of the community and contact with her neighbours, who are supposed to be looking after her all the time. In this sense, it's not such a problem when her parents are sure she's a virgin.

We have four marriage customs to respect. The first is the 'open door'. It is flexible and there's no commitment. The second is a commitment to the parents when the girl has accepted the boy. This is a very important custom. The third is the ceremony when the girl and boy make their vows to one another. The fourth is the wedding itself, the *despedida*. The formalities for getting married are usually carried out in the following way.

The boy first tells his own parents that he likes a certain girl and they tell him what sort of commitment marriage is: 'You must have children, you have to feed them, and you must never regret what you've done for a single day.' They tell him about the responsibilities a father has. Then, when the young man has made up his mind and so have his parents, they go to the village representative and tell him the boy wants to get married and is going to ask the girl. Then comes the first custom, the 'open door', as we say. A door is opened by the village representative, the young man's parents and then the young man. These requests for marriage usually take place at four in the morning because most Indians leave home before five, and when they come home from work at six in the evening they're usually busy with other things. It's done at four in the morning so as not to cause too much inconvenience and they leave when the dogs start barking.

Fathers don't usually agree to start with, because it's the custom here to get married very early. Girls often get married at fourteen and are expecting babies by the age of fifteen. The parents object. They say: 'No, our daughter is too young. She's too little; she's a very obedient daughter and we have faith in her.' So the village representatives go and plead with them, and go back and plead again. The father resists and won't open the door to ask them in. So they go away. If the young man and his parents are really interested, they have to go back at least three times. After the first time they've been, the father begins to talk to his daughter. He explains that a young man is interested in her and tells her all the formalities she will have to go through. The second time the representatives and parents come, they usually bring a little *guaro* or cigarettes. If the girl's parents accept a cigarette, that means there is already some small commitment. The door starts to open for the young man. In my sister's case, when the representatives came the first time, they were refused. My father wouldn't receive them the second time either because he said; 'My daughter is too young to be a mother, isn't she?' This is because when our people think of marriage, they think of becoming a mother or fulfilling their duty as the father of a family. They also think of gaining the respect of the community, because when a couple gets married in our community, they have to preserve our traditions, and act as an example for their brothers and sisters and for their neighbours' children. It's a very important commitment for us.

Well, the young girl starts talking to her parents and she says she would like to know the young man. My father opened the door for my sister when they came for the third time. He was the elected leader of our village, so they had to come with another of the community's representatives, and my parents finally received them. My father accepted a glass of *guaro* and some cigarettes. From then on the door was open.

At this stage the parents tell the young man that their daughter is honest and hardworking. This is his parents' main concern; that the girl is sturdy and works hard and has the energy to stand up to life's challenges. My parents said my sister had worked like an adult since she was three, that she was an early riser and very diligent. She liked finishing her work quickly; when she worked tilling the land, she'd already finished her task by three in the afternoon. My parents said they never wanted to hear any complaints about her or her behaviour, because she was hardworking and knew how to observe all the traditions of our ancestors.

The young man's parents also tell them about their son's bad and good points. They say: 'Our son is not very good at such and such a thing, but, on the other hand, he knows how to do this and the other.' It's a dialogue. Then the representatives leave because the father has to go off to work. But if he's going to open his door, he must show them hospitality even if he has to stay and chat with them for half a day or a day. The young man is then given permission to call on the daughter another day. But he knows he can't go just any day because the father, the mother, everybody, are out working in the fields. So he only goes on Sundays. On Sundays, the mother is usually at home doing the washing, or the father is at home while the mother goes to market. One or other of the parents must be at home when the young man arrives. . . . He doesn't come empty handed, but brings a little present for the parents – a few rolls of bread, a few cigarettes, or something to drink. He arrives and starts talking to the girl for the first time, since he'd never, never, get to know her in the street. This way the community will respect the girl: they will love her because they know she has begun her marriage with her hands clean. That's what they say: 'She's not one of those girls who hang around the streets. She's never been seen with a boy in the street.' In our community, if a girl is seen in the street with a boy, she both loses her dignity and breaks the customs of our forefathers.

Of course, if the girl doesn't like the boy, she can say so. If she doesn't like him, she carries on working even if her parents open the door. She finds things to do and has no time for him. She doesn't talk to him. That's a signal she doesn't like him. Everyone waits for fifteen days to see if she's going to talk to him. If she doesn't, they tell him it isn't the family, but the girl who isn't interested. This often happens. But if she accepts him, there will always be someone in the house when he calls; they'll never be alone. This is to preserve the woman's purity, which is something sacred, something special, something which will engender many lives. The woman has to be respected, so the parents are always around. In my sister's case, she decided about seven months after she and the young man first talked together. He came to see her all the time without any commitment either on her part or his.

Just the 'open door'. Then my sister decided. The day the girl agrees, the young man gets down on his knees in front of her parents and says that on such and such a day he will come with his parents.

Certain traditions are respected. For example, when the people come to ask for the door to be opened for the first time, they don't stand up but go down on their knees in front of the door. My father didn't open the door the first time, and the second time they kneeled at the door, he still didn't open. On the third occasion the door was opened and they offered my father a drink; the young man remaining on his knees. It's a form of great respect. As my parents say, a person who knows how to kneel is a humble person, so from the way the young man kneels the parents can tell whether he knows how to respect our ancestors.

It is decided straight away who will take part in the ceremonies. There will be the couples' eldest uncle and his wife, their brothers and sisters, or rather their elder brothers and sisters, the village representatives, and the grandparents of both the young man and the girl. So the second stage of the marriage ritual begins. There is a fiesta at home with all the family; grandmother, grandfather, uncles and aunts, elder brothers and sisters are all there. It's like the fiesta for the birth of a baby, when a lamb is killed. Now the parents kill the biggest lamb in their flock and bring it to the house. The uncles arrive with dough for the *tortillas*. The whole family makes a contribution. The grandmother must bring her granddaughter a present. Grandmothers keep the silver jewellery passed down from our forefathers, and now the grandmother gives the young girl a necklace or something as a keepsake and to encourage her. In return, she makes a promise to be just like her grandmother and to keep our ancestors' traditions in the same ways she did.

Then the house is prepared and the food is made for the fiesta. For their part, the young man's parents make preparations too. They bring something for the girl as an engagement present: usually something given to the young man when he was born. They also bring a live lamb and another already prepared to eat. The dough for the feast is made into larger *tamales* than usual and they usually make about seventy-five of them. These *tamales* last a long time: they will last the girl's parents about a week because they're big and don't go bad, or at least the outside does but not the inside. These big *tamales* give a party feeling to the meal.

These seventy-five big *tamales* brought by the boy's parents weigh about two or three *quintals* altogether, because each *tamal* is about eight pounds in weight. For us Indians, each *tamal* represents a sacred day. We count the days that we ask the earth's permission to sow our crops, the eight sacred days a baby is with his mother, the sacred days of our fiestas and the ceremonies throughout a child's life from birth to marriage: when he was born, when he became a member of the community, when he was baptized, his tenth birthday, and so on. Each child has his own sacred day. Even if he's working, it's still his sacred day. These days are always sacred for him. In addition, we count other sacred days, like the day we ask the trees' permission to cut them down because we need to clear the land for cultivation. For us, all things have their sacred days even if, because of our circumstances, we don't have the time to observe their rituals very faithfully. Then there are all the saints' days, from the Catholic Action. But ours are not the saints of the pictures. We celebrate special days talking about our ancestors; for us in the month of October, a whole part of the month is sacred because this is the time they used to worship and keep their silence. We preserve this tradition too. All the sacred days of the year add up to seventy-two or seventy-five days, and each *tamal* represents one day.

So the young man's family brings seventy-five *tamales*, a live lamb and one ready prepared for eating. They also usually bring a large earthenware jar of soup made from the lamb when it's killed. Altogether this is a pretty big load. They take the cooked meat to a place set aside for it and one person is put in charge of it. The *tamales* need at least four boys in charge of them, so a whole lot of them line up for the job. But not just any boys are chosen, they have to be ones who are respected by the community. They will serve the drinks and give out the cigarettes at the fiesta after the ceremony. They are usually the young man's brothers or cousins, except if any of them are naughty, or not very sociable, he won't be chosen to help at the fiesta.

When the guests arrive, they come in in a line. First comes the representative of the young man's village with his wife, and greet the girl's parents. Then the father kneels in a corner that has been specially prepared. If they still live in the same house where the girl was born, this will be the place where they put the candles when she was received into the natural world. If it is the same place, the parents will still have the remains of those candles and will use them now. This is still not the marriage rites, however, as there are still certain customs to perform. They come and kneel down in the corner where the candles are, without saying a word or acknowledging each other. The doors are opened and the rest of the people come in and kneel down. Then the girl's mother and father come in. The mother's role is very important here, because she is someone special, the person who has given life to her daughter and in whose image her daughter must live. She is the one who goes to each person and asks them to get up off their knees. She goes first to the young man's mother and asks her to stand and then goes to each person who is kneeling, individually. The father shows them where to sit. They can't sit just anywhere all mixed up, because the order in which the cups of *guaro* are drunk is very important and the elderly people have to be served first and then the rest. We drink a lot of *guaro*, more than anything else. Some *guaro* is clandestine: forbidden by the Guatemalan government. We Indians make it and use it for all our ceremonies. This *guaro* is very strong, and it's very cheap. They don't like us making it because it lowers the price in the *cantinas*. It's made in the mountains, in tree trunks and in earthenware jars. It's made from fermented maize and the bran we use to feed our horses, or from wheat – the chaff of the wheat. It can also be made from rice or sugar cane. It's always very strong. The parents provide enough *guaro* for everybody.

The mother asks the boy's mother to stand first, then his grandmother and then all the other people. The girl's father is busy showing everyone where to sit. There is a special seat for each one. The ceremony begins. The girl goes out. The young man remains on his knees. She comes in again and kneels some way away from him. They remain kneeling for about fifteen or twenty minutes. The ceremony begins with the grandparents' account of their suffering, the sadness and the joy in their life. They give a sort of general account of their life – that at this moment or that moment they were ill but they never lost hope, that their ancestors had also suffered in the same way, and many, many other things. Then the couple who are getting married say a prayer: 'Mother Earth, may you feed us. We are made of maize, of yellow maize and white maize.' And then the couple says other prayers to our one God, the heart of the sky who embraces the whole natural world. They talk to the heart of the sky, saying: 'Father and Mother, Heart of the Sky, may you give us light, may you give us heat, may you give us hope and punish our enemies – all those who wish to destroy our ancestors. We, poor and humble as we are, will never abandon you.'

They make a new pledge to honour the Indian race. They affirm our importance. They say it is the duty of each one of us to reproduce the earth and the traditions of our ancestors, who were humble. They refer back to the time of Columbus and say: 'Our forefathers were dishonoured by the white man – sinners and murderers'; and: 'It is not the fault of our ancestors. They died from hunger because they weren't paid. We want to destroy the wicked lessons we were taught by them. If they hadn't come, we would all be united, equal, and our children would not suffer. We would not have boundaries to our land.' This is, in part, recalling history and, in part, a call to awareness. Then they make their vows and say: 'We will be father and mother. We will try to defend the rights of our ancestors to the last.' 'We promise that our ancestors will live on through our children and no rich man nor landowner can destroy our children.' When they've made their vows, the young people get up. It's the turn of the girl's grandmother and the boy's grandfather to help them up and lead them to their seats. Then the ones giving out the drink serve the first cups to the grandfathers, grandmothers, the village elders, the village representatives, and the parents. When they are on their third drink, the couple kneels down again and begins kissing the hands of all those present at the ceremony. They ask forgiveness for any occasion on which they may have abused traditions, and admit they might not have paid enough attention to many of the lessons and advice of their parents. They say: 'We did not apologize to such and such a person . . .'; or: 'We offended the laws of the natural kingdom.' After that they ask forgiveness from their parents and for help with bringing their children up in Indian ways, remembering their traditions, and always remaining true to their race no matter how much trouble, sadness and hunger they endure. And the parents answer: 'Generations and generations will pass but we will always be Indians. It is our duty as parents to keep our secrets safe generation after generation, to prevent the *ladinos* learning anything of our ancestors' ways.'

Then the grandparents tell us many things that they've been witness to, things which must be passed on by their children. They are witnesses that our ancestors were not sinners, they did not kill. They apply past experience to the present. They say: 'Today human life is not respected, now people are killed, our children die – our younger brothers and sisters. Children haven't always died young. Our forefathers told us that our old people used to live until they were a hundred and twenty-five, and now we die at forty or thirty. You younger people must ask yourselves why this is so.' The elders examine our lives now. They are given the floor because of their experience, their example, what they know of life. They say: 'Our ancestors always asked the permission of every living thing before using it to help us feed ourselves.' This is no longer so and our ancestors are saddened and troubled by it. Many of our race now know how to kill. The white man is responsible for this. They blame the white man for coming and teaching us to kill. Even now we must prevent him from teaching us how to kill. It is wonderful listening to this, because it is the elders' opportunity to unburden themselves about what they have lived through. When the parents receive the guests of honour, only adults are present, but when the elders start speaking, everyone comes in to listen. The children wait outside during the first part and then are all called in. Our little house is full to bursting. All this takes about half a day.

There is a lot of smoking; and the drinking is very significant. With each drink goes a sort of prayer. First they say: 'This is the sacred wine of our ancestors, they were not forbidden to grow their own wine, to make their own drink. Today everything is different. Now we are not allowed to make our drink.' So they say this drink is sacred and it makes us think a lot. The prayer for the second drink is different. It says: 'We promise to defend this drink. We will go on making it even if we have to do it secretly, and our children will continue to make it throughout the generations.' With the third drink, the engaged couple take their vows. At the fourth drink, the grandparents are given the floor to say what they wish. Then it's the turn of the village representatives and they too make various recommendations to the couple: 'You must have children for our ancestors' sake, so that our seed does not die or be effaced. The first child must bear the name of the boy's parents and the second the name of the girl's parents.' After them come more rounds of speeches – the parents, the uncles, and the members of the families who serve the drinks. We younger ones are also given a turn to speak but we don't usually say anything because we're used to respecting our elders, and our words might show a lack of respect. So we don't join in very much.

The bride and bridegroom get up. Remaining on their knees until the elders have finished speaking has been a sort of penance for them. Now they get up, take their seats and the ceremony becomes a general talking session – a whole day of sitting and talking. They say: 'This is what our ancestors were like; this is what the white man did; it's the fault of the white man. Our ancestors used to sow enough maize, there was enough for each tribe, each community. They all lived together. We had a king and he used to share everything out among everybody. Now we no longer grow cocoa, it belongs to the white man, to the rich. We can no longer sow tobacco. Before there was enough tobacco for all our people. Before we weren't divided into communities and languages. We understood each other. Who is to blame for all this? The white man who came to our country. We must not trust them, white men are all thieves. We mut keep our secrets from them. We had no artificial medicines or pills before, our medicines were the plants. Our king sowed many plants and our children need to know about them too. Animals used not to bite us before, but now even that is something which happens.' The last part of the ceremony is rather sad because our grandparents remember all this with great feeling and begin to tell what things will be like from now on. It worries them a great deal. Now our children don't live very long. Will it be like that from now on? Now a lot of people go around in cars. Our old Guatemala wasn't like this. We all went around on foot but we all lived very well. They killed our most important, most revered ancestors. Because of this, we must learn to have respect for the natural world – trees, the earth, water, the sun, and our brother human beings too. We must respect our elders. The discussion is for everyone. We all join in, and give our opinions. We stop drinking. We don't drink all the *guaro* brought. It is a sacred fiesta so nobody gets drunk. When all our close friends and neighbours (i.e. most of the community) have finished discussing, we start eating. The brothers and sisters and secondary uncles and aunts get up and bring in the food. We eat the food offered by the bride, not the food brought by the bridegroom's family. It's all prepared, we pass it round and eat with great pleasure. After the meal, the parents and neighbours go on talking, with a lot of feeling. It's a common dialogue. At four in the afternoon, everyone goes home.

In my sister's case, after the second ritual we all had to go down to the *finca*. We spent four months on the coast, so it was five months later that we celebrated the third ritual. The same people were present as for the second and we had a lot of food and drink. They bring a lot to drink, but not many *tamales*. It was the time for starting to sow our land and everyone came again. The engaged couple saw each other again after four months. My sister was very mature. A child becomes an adult very early among our people. We have no adolescence. We have a lot of responsibility from an early age. My sister was very mature and she knew that if she didn't see her betrothed, it was because of our circumstances, so it was quite all right. When he got back, the young man came to visit us again. It was quite normal, nothing strange at all. The young man said his parents were ready for the third ritual and everyone agreed on a day. We had to get our maize in very quickly because it was raining hard and the maize rots. The boy has to work for the girl's parents for a few months as a member of the family, so as the second ritual was over, he said: 'I'll come and live with you now.' After three months he went back to his family. It was just as if he'd gone to the *finca*.

The third ceremony is when the boy and girl make their vows to one another. It's rather like the Catholic Action wedding ceremony when the couple make their promises in church. Our vows aren't made before God, though, but before our elders. The girl says: 'I will be a mother, I will suffer, my children will suffer, many of my children will die young because of the circumstances created for us by white men. It will be hard for me to accept my children's death but I will bear it because our ancestors bore it without giving up. We will not give up either.' This is the girl's promise. The young man promises: 'I will be responsible. We will see our children die before they have grown, but we must still go on following

Indian ways.' Then they both promise: 'We will try to leave two or three seeds to reproduce the lineage of our ancestors. Although some of our children will die young, others will live on. From now on we will be mother and father.' This is their joint vow, taken before our elders. It demonstrates the mixture in the life the couple will lead, the life their children will lead, whereas the previous ceremony was trying to enact our ancestors' traditions from the very beginning, all the things they used, all the things they conserved. To represent this mixture, they bring crates of lemonade, a bit of bread, some bought *guaro*, bought candles – all those things we Indians find so outrageous – and explain the meaning of each of those things. First they show these candles made of artificial wax. They are not like the beeswax candles used in the birth ceremony and the engagement ceremony. Ours have to be of natural wax, not those you buy in the market. Everything we use is natural, everything is our own. Our cooking pots are earthenware, made by grandmothers, mothers or aunts. We make our own *guaro* and light our cigarettes with little stones. *Tortillas* are shown to symbolize the maize, sacred to man, his food, his life. The modern things that are shown are the fizzy drinks, the bought *guaro*, eggs, chocolate, bread, coffee. According to them, coffee didn't exist before. Everyone gets together and gives their opinion on these things. For example, our grandparents say of Coca-Cola: 'Never let your children drink this dreadful stuff because it is something which threatens our culture.' They say: 'These things are made by machines; our forefathers never used machines. The *fincas* mean an early death for our people. They provide food for white people, and white people get rich from them.' We never let our children eat or drink these horrible things. This is what the ceremony is about. When they talk about the bread, they say: 'Bread is very meaningful for the Indian, because of the fact that it was mixed with egg, flour with egg. In the past, our ancestors grew wheat. Then the Spaniards came and mixed it with egg. It was a mixture, no longer what our ancestors ate. It was white man's food, and white men are like their bread, they are not wholesome. The blood of our most noble ancestors was mixed with the blood of white men. They are a mixture, just like their food.' This is the grandparents' lesson to us about the bread. Then they say: 'They put the juice of our crop, our natural sugar cane, through a machine and made sugar. They put sugar in the cane and it became mixed. We must not mix our customs with those of the whites. So we don't eat bread. It is not our *tortilla*.' They say: 'Don't let our children get used to eating bread; our ancestors had no bread.' All this comes first from the grandparents. Then comes the turn of the parents. They say: 'We never taught them to eat bread. We didn't give them any, we didn't have any. Why not? Because it is not ours. It is the white man's.' All these recommendations are made to the couple about how to bring up children. The uncles bring in a bit more about Catholic customs. They show a small picture, the likeness of a saint. They say: 'This is such and such a saint – Saint Judas, saint Augustine or Saint Anthony, for example; this one does the most miraculous things, this one does the most good works,' depending on what ideas prevail about them among the people. They say: 'These are some of the saints, but they're not the only ones. There's the god of the sky, and the god of the earth.' They explain everything – that they all lead to the one God, the only God, and that the saints are channels through which we communicate with the one God. Then the couple make its vows to one another. Now there's only the marriage itself to come.

The guests of honour congratulate the couple and exhort them to be good parents. They hope they'll have good children, that they'll bear life with fortitude and live as human beings, and won't abuse the natural world. Then the couple is given the floor. When they have finished speaking, there's a discussion about all the things that happen in the country. They talk about cars, about the *ladinos'* bathrooms, and about the rich. They do it to shake themselves free of it. They say that the bathrooms of the rich shine like new dresses whereas we, the poor, have nothing but a hole to go to. And our cooking pots are different from theirs too. But they also insist that we don't desire what the rich have. We have hands to make our pottery with and we don't want to lose the skill. They say: 'These things may be modern but we mustn't buy the rubbish they have, even if we have the money. We must keep our ways of making our own.' Our village does not have a grinder for our maize. This is not because we could not get one. Many landowners would gladly install one to grind the maize for the whole village. But our people say no. The *ladinos* bring their machines in little by little and very soon they own everything.

Between the third and fourth ceremonies, there is a separate little fiesta just for the family. It's when the father tells his daughter that his responsibility towards her is over. From now on her life will be different, although she must still live within a community the way all Indians should, and keep in close communion with nature. Her mother buys something or has something woven for her daughter as a surprise, and she's shown all the presents she will be taking with her, although she won't be given them until the fourth ceremony when the husband-to-be's parents are present. These days this small fiesta is held any day, whenever there's time. But my grandfather says that before they always had it on a special day – forty days before the girl left home. We didn't do that for my sister because there wasn't time. At the family fiesta, the girl's brothers and sisters all speak, the younger ones as well as the older ones. The little ones say things like: 'Thank you for all you've done for us, for looking after us, for carrying us around, and for changing our nappies.' We look on a sister rather like a mother, because she's part of what our mother has done for us. So they thank their sister for all her work, and for the difficult experiences of their parents. They tell her whatever nice feeling they want to express. The older ones tell her to remain pure and wholesome because they looked after her since she was small. They also promise to gather the flowers to arrange for her farewell fiesta. One of them says: 'I promise on behalf of all your brothers and sisters to arrange the flowers.' The bride-to-be then thanks them for all they have done for her. She also kneels before her parents and thanks them too. They know it will be very painful and sad for her to leave the community she has known for so long and they give her a lot of good family advice. They tell her never to forget them. There's no special time for this fiesta to finish. They can go on talking as long as they like. The parents tell the girl what most of the presents she'll be getting when she leaves are – hens, a dog, a sheep, cooking pots. Her mother has been making the earthenware cooking pots Indians use for her. We never buy anything like that from the market. Mothers always make them. Her mother also makes some small mats for her. Indians think it is dreadful to sit on chairs, women especially, because the woman is the mother of the home and the earth is the mother of the whole world – the mother of all our indigenous people. The importance of the mother is related to the importance of the earth. So we usually sit on the ground, on the mats our women weave. The girl takes with her half a dozen small and some large mats, and some little presents from her mother, but the rest she will receive at her farewell fiesta. As a symbol of all the happiness and sadness the parents and brothers and sisters feel for their sister, we always, always, burn some incense. We always burn incense, our sacred smoke, in all our ceremonies. It's as if we are making a sacrifice to our one Lord. The family burns incense for the young girl because she's bound to be very sad at leaving her family, her work and everything. She'll have to do the other family's work now, but it will be the same sort of work because most communities have the same customs. My sister's problem was that she went to live in another community with a different language and different customs.

The fourth and last ritual is the *despedida*, the farewell ceremony, when the young girl is given her presents and says goodbye to the community. This is the saddest part. Both sets of parents must be present. There are two locations because there are two forms of marriage now. There is our traditional ceremony according to our customs. Then there's the civil ceremony or the Catholic church ceremony. Some people go to the civil registry or the church, then back to the girl's house for the traditional *despedida*, and then the girl leaves from there for the young man's home. But others have the *despedida* first, then go to the registry or the church, and the girl is delivered to the boy's home after that.

The actual *despedida* is like this. First, the house is decorated by the brothers and sisters who promised to collect flowers and arrange them. Indians think of flowers as part of nature and you never see flowers in an Indian house. There are some flowers, though, like this white flower, the *cartucho*, which you get more in cold countries and we sow that, not in the house but in our neighbours' fields or in a corner away from the house. We pick them on special occasions, like a fiesta or an important ceremony. My father explained that we don't need flowers in the house any other time because we live amongst plants and trees, which are all part of nature. The brothers and sisters have to pick them and decorate the house. Some of the cost of the *despedida* is born by the parents but the community provides most of the things. All the neighbours know when the young girl is going away, and they all come around and bring things (just like when a baby is born). They bring wood, dough, meat, and the parents only have to provide the *guaro*. We make two types of *guaro*. One is a strong alcohol like rum or tequila, and the other is a sort of smooth, rather sweet, wine. So the parents make the drink and the neighbours bring everything else. They all arrive and act as if they were in their own homes. They take out the pots and utensils, make the food, and prepare the house. The community does everything. The same happens when the girl is received into the young man's home – it is the community that receives her. The girl is there ready with all her new things (except for the ones she'll be given when her young man is there), and all the things that belonged to her before. The neighbours all bring her little presents too, a cooking pot or a *sobainita*. One of the neighbours is chosen on behalf of the community to present the young girl with all the little things they have brought. If the guests are expected at ten in the morning, the neighbours will be there from five o'clock onwards preparing the house and the food. At ten everything is ready. The neighbours have another important way of showing their affection. All the wood the girl will be given has to be cut on the very day of the *despedida*, so the men are out from five in the morning cutting the wood and chopping it up ready for the party.

It is a big party. First, they receive the parents of the young girl and all the neighbours eat together. Then the parents of the young man arrive accompanied by another couple, all the uncles and aunts, the elder brothers and sisters, the grandparents and the village representatives. The girl meets the young man's godparents for the first time and her father introduces her godparents to him. Godparents are chosen when a child is born and they must be present at this ceremony. After the first greeting, the mother brings out all the presents for the girl and says: 'This is all we can give you, may it give you encouragement.' The parents-in-law accept the girl's things. Then the grandmother begins talking about everything that is happening at that time. She gives the girl a large bunch of flowers prepared for her by her own grandchildren. As she offers the bunch she explains that this flower is sacred, pure and that the young girl must live as all our women live. She must be a mother. She explains about all the things that happen to our women – about prostitution, about working as maids in the towns, the women who work on the coast. She tells her of the bad examples to avoid and gives her advice for her to think about. She tells her she mustn't have more than one husband because our ancestors disapproved of that vanity. She talks about this important thing like this: 'My children, these days to get married you have to sign a silly piece of paper. They say there is a mayor, files, and papers even for our people. We didn't have any of this before. We got married the way our customs, our ceremonies laid down for us. We didn't have to sign any bits of paper. Under our ancestors' laws, men and women didn't separate, but if a woman was suffering, she could leave her husband. Now, she can't leave her husband because she's signed a paper. The Church's laws and the *ladinos*' laws are the same in this – you cannot separate. But the Indian feels responsible for every member of his community, and it's hard for him to accept that, if a woman is suffering, the community can do nothing for her because the law says she cannot leave her husband.' The grandmother tries to give her granddaughter a general idea of what she feels about what is happening in the world, in Guatemala. She finishes with her voice full of feeling. It hurts her very much to see many of the things that happen. She would never want any granddaughter of hers to be a prostitute. It is the grandfather who talks to the young man. He goes through certain customs in his house with his own family. This is the real *despedida* when the grandmother offers these flowers.

The fiesta goes on with other people, especially the women, talking to the girl. They ask her not to forget all her memories of the community. She must make sure she is respected as a woman, as our ancestors would wish. She must have the courage to face our hard life but be tender as a mother and teach her children to respect nature. We don't kiss each other on the cheek. One way of showing respect is to kneel and kiss our parents' hands. The girl kneels to everyone present and kisses the hands of her parents, grandparents, aunts and uncles and elder brother. Then she kneels and kisses the hands of all the young man's family. They take her hand and tell her to get up. The young man does the same with his family and with the girl's family. This is the promise sworn. This is the marriage.

The parents of the girl then say, 'In fifteen days we want to see our daughter again here.' When the girl goes out of the door of her house, she may not look back, and can't go back to that house until fifteen days have passed. The explanation my parents gave was that my sister was now a grown-up person and that she must not look back when she's faced with all the problems she will meet. She must always go forward.

Her nest, the house where she was born, will no longer be her house. She will never be a child again. It has now been decided where the girl will live, whether she'll have a hut of her own or if she'll live with the boy's parents. In our community, we are all used to living as brothers and sisters, so a girl will be sad if she is going to live alone. These days, we don't have time for many of the customs our ancestors honoured, but if there is time, the girl's parents or grandparents will go with her. There wasn't really any time when my sister was married but since my father was the elected leader of our village, he was able to send my sister's godparents and my elder brother with her to her new home. The whole community was waiting to receive her in the young man's house. They had a bunch of flowers too. There she is given her grinding stone and her cooking pot. She must always keep her pot for washing the *nixtamal*, her kitchen utensils and the maize. They also give her her big mat and her smaller mats and show her where her place in the house will be. Most houses don't have separate rooms for each couple. But first they cut a little bit from each of the four corners of the house for her. The houses are made from palm leaves or cane so they can cut a bit off. In each of the corners they light the young man's candle. They burn some incense and the bits from the four corners to welcome the young bride. This is how they ask the house's permission to allow another person to live there.

There may come a time when the couple don't get on together and do not have a happy life. Then there are problems. But it is important that we all try to solve these matrimonial problems by explaining to the couple that they must make their life together and that it will be a different life. The elected leaders will come and try and talk to them as if they were their own children, and it is the responsibility of both sets of godparents to help the couple. If the problem can't be solved, however, the girl is protected by her parents. She can go back to them as long as she hasn't broken with any of their traditions. There have been cases where the girl gets tired of waiting for the different rituals to take place and her young man takes her away. But then they run the risk of her father refusing to have her back if the marriage doesn't work. The young man's parents also reject him because he did not obey the laws – what our forefathers taught us. In the past, there was no law to bind a couple forever, as the Church and the State have now. There were laws which had to be obeyed but there was nothing which tied people together forever. The community gives as much support as they can to the young girl who goes away. The whole village is present when she leaves and expresses its feelings. They say: 'Whatever happens, we are always here. You must lead your own life but if things go wrong, we will help you.' All Indian women have this – the support of their community – as long as they don't break our laws. If a girl does break them, the community does have a heart, but it will look at her with different eyes. It all depends on the girl. Among our people, there are men who come home drunk and beat their wives. But a wife who is very fond of her husband, and thinks of him as the father of her children, doesn't complain as much as her community allows her to.

In my sister's marriage, things went rather wrong. She couldn't get used to the new community, because of the different language and customs of her husband's parents and her husband himself. We live very much within a community, so how could she be happy there if she didn't understand them? So my parents discussed the problem with the husband's parents and the village leader. My father said: 'Our community is willing to help you as a family. I think my daughter should come back and live near here so we can help you better.' They agreed my sister should come back to our village. She didn't come back to our house, of course. The whole village helped and two weeks later she was fixing up her own little house. She couldn't come back to our house because we have a very large family and my cousins were living with us then. My sister had a little boy and my father said they should lead their own life. The community gave them part of our collective land, and a few beans and maize so that they could work and live. A woman has no problem, whether she works on her own or collectively, whether she's married or single, as long as she obeys the laws of the community. If anything goes wrong, her neighbours will always help her and she can count on the community. This is exactly what our parents tell us on our tenth birthday.

XII

LIFE IN THE COMMUNITY

'Don't you understand that the game is a sign of freedom, of death, and of fate, which governs the sentences of the judges. The only ones daring enough to play are dead.'

—Popol Vuh

'I'm a catechist who walks upon this earth, not one who thinks only of the kingdom of God.'

—Rigoberta Menchú

I remember things very, very well from the time I was twelve. It's then that I thought like a responsible woman. When we do collective work, to have something extra in case someone in the community dies, or is ill, only the adults work. Of course, we have this relationship with our community from the very beginning but, even so, it becomes much stronger when we start having a real obligation to the community. Each member of the family always has a duty to perform. Like visiting neighbours, for instance, spending time talking to them in any free moments. Not quarrelling with neighbours since that sometimes causes bad feeling. And children don't have petty rows like grown-ups. They start fighting with other children, with their neighbours.

Well, at twelve, I joined in the communal work; things like harvesting the maize. I worked together with the others. It was also then that I began making friends, closer friends, in the community. I began taking over my mother's role too. My mother was the woman who coordinated certain things in the community. For instance: 'What shall we sow prior to the maize?' 'Should we only sow beans?' 'How shall we do it?' Most of this is our work – sowing beans, sowing potatoes, or any kind of vegetables which can be grown on the same land as the maize. Putting in little sticks for the beans so they don't harm the maize, or tying up the tendrils of the *chilacayotes* or whatever vegetables we've sown in with the maize. We define a task: what we have to do, step by step. Every *compañero*, every neighbour, has his little bit to tend, to harvest, to pick the crop. He tends it from the first day it is sown, looking after the plant right through until it bears fruit and he picks the fruit. We all make a promise to do this. It's a collective obligation, naturally.

It was during that time that I began to take on responsibility. The Catholic religion had already come to our region. The Catholic religion chooses, or at least the priests choose, people to become catechists. I was a catechist from the age of twelve. The priest used to come to our area every three months. He'd bring texts for us to teach the doctrine to our community. We did it on our own initiative as well, because my father was a dedicated Christian. By accepting the Catholic religion, we didn't accept a condition, or abandon our culture. It was more like another way of expressing ourselves. If everyone believes in this medium, it's just another medium of expression. It's like expressing ourselves through a tree, for example; we believe that a tree is a being, a part of nature, and that a tree has its image, its representation, its *nahual*, to channel our feelings to the one God. That is the way we Indians conceive it. Catholic Action is like another element which can merge with the elements which already exist within Indian culture. And it confirms our belief that, yes, there is a God, and, yes, there is a father for all of us. And yet it is something we think of as being only for what happens up there. As far as the earth is concerned, we must go on worshipping through our own intermediaries, just as we always have done, through all the elements found in nature. And this helped us a lot in becoming catechists and taking on the responsibility of teaching others; in the way we teach in our community, by being an example to others who are growing up. Many of the images of Catholic Action are similar to ours, although ours are not written down. A lot of it is familiar. For example, we believe we have ancestors, and that these ancestors are important because they're good people who obeyed the laws of our people. The Bible talks about forefathers too. So it is not something unfamiliar to us. We accept these biblical forefathers as if they were our own ancestors, while still keeping within our own culture and our own customs. At the same time, it often refers to leaders, to kings. For instance the Bible tells us that there were kings who beat Christ. We drew a parallel with our king, Tecún Umán, who was defeated and persecuted by the Spaniards, and we take that as our own reality. In this way we adjusted to the Catholic religion and our duties as Christians, and made it part of our culture. As I said, it's just another way of expressing ourselves. It's not the only, immutable way of keeping our ancestors' intermediaries alive. It's twice the work for us, because we have to learn the doctrine, and we have to learn to pray. We pray in our ceremonies in our own culture, so that's not so different. We just have to memorize the prayers they tell us to use and add them to our own. Everything has to be in our language. Well, sometimes it's something we do, not because we understand it, but because that's the way it has to be. Because I remember that at first the prayers weren't even in Spanish but in Latin or something like that. So although it's something we say and express with all our faith, we don't always understand what it means. Since the priests don't know our language and they say the prayers in Spanish, our job is to memorize the prayers, and the chants. But we didn't understand exactly what it meant, it was just a channel for our self-expression. It's very important for us, but we don't understand it.

My father was a choirboy in the church and then he got married and had children. He totally accepted what Catholic Action is all about. He used to teach us that God exists, and that one way of reaching him is by worshipping the saints. That doesn't mean actually worshipping the saints, the images, it's just a form of expression. For instance, the image of the earth, the mother, is very important. She is created by a father, our one God, and so are the saints, our ancestors. We express ourselves through our designs, through our dress – our *huipil* for instance, is like an image of our ancestors. They are like the saints of Catholic Action. This is where you see the mixture of Catholicism and our own culture. We feel very Catholic because we believe in the Catholic religion but, at the same time, we feel very Indian, proud of our ancestors.

At first, I really didn't understand what this whole 'Catholic' thing was, but I was ready to open myself to it all the same. So I began teaching the doctrine in our community. My work was mostly with the small children. The priest used to come and celebrate Mass, form groups of catechists and leave texts for them to study. But as we couldn't read or write, we usually had to learn them by heart. That's how we started learning a few things. My brothers learnt to read and write from my cousins about then. I've got cousins who were at primary school for six years but had to stop then because there was no possibility of continuing. These cousins taught my brothers to read. When my brothers were young they had lots of friends and they began to learn to read with them. But as for me, I was illiterate, and so were my friends. When I was with my friends, we don't talk about enjoying ourselves or that sort of thing, we talk about work and the things we have to do. Even more so when we have our little animals. While we watch the animals, we talk about the things we dream of, about what we want to do with our animals. We do talk about life a bit, but only very generally. We never talk about travelling to other places, or dancing, learning to dance. We don't talk about that. The boys do. They begin teaching each other the things they know and they start playing games. There's an Indian game which is a bit like a sport. There's this wax, it's not beeswax but comes from another kind of insect found in the mountains which makes a black wax. When these insects leave their nest to make another one, the wax is left behind in the trees. So whenever they've a free moment, the boys love going off to the mountain to collect the wax. They bring the wax back and make little balls out of it to play with. It's a bit like gambling. The one who wins is the one who knocks everyone else's wax to bits. He wins a *centavo* or they can give him something else. This game they play with the wax is a competition. They also play the game with a *centavo* piece which they put on something metal and flick another coin at it. If it hits it and turns it over, then that boy wins. If it doesn't flick over, then he doesn't win. You can get the hang of the game with a lot of practice. The boys talk to each other a lot when they have some spare time in the mountains and they also play together in a group in the village.

As a rule, we girls don't play, because our mothers find it hard to let a girl go off and play on her own. Girls have to learn to look after things in the home, they must learn all the little things their mothers do. Mothers never sit around at home with nothing to do. They're always busy. If they haven't any specific job to do, they've always got their weaving, and if they haven't any weaving, there's always something else. So our games are mostly weaving or things like that, but at least we can do it together. There's a place in the fields which is so wonderful and pretty and shady that all the girls get together – seven or eight of us – and sit under the trees and hang up our weaving. We talk and weave. It's how we enjoy ourselves with our friends. And also, when we go to fetch water, we call all the girls in the village, shouting to each other, and off we go in a line, chattering, to fetch water. We fetch the water in earthenware pots carried on our head, so on the way back we walk slowly and sometimes put the jars down and sit for a bit. When there's no water nearby, we have to walk a long way to fetch it. That is another way of enjoying ourselves, talking to our neighbours and friends. That's how we make friends. Whatever job the women have to do, they always call their neighbours. Especially the girls. We don't like mixing with the older women so much. While we have great respect for older women, we prefer to talk to friends of our own age. We're taught, for example, not to mix with girls of twenty-two if we're only twelve, because they are adults and won't understand what we're talking about. So we always go around with those of our own age, our own size. Another time to get together is when we want leaves from the plants which grow in the mountains to make our *tamales*. We call all the girls, one afternoon, to go and cut leaves up in the mountains. I used to like climbing to the tops of trees, but only when my mother wasn't looking. Mothers think it's scandalous for girls to climb trees. They scold us very badly if they see us. We used to climb trees, shouting and singing, calling to each other; happy. These amusements are enough for us. When there are fiestas, even a village fiesta, girls mustn't leave their mother's side. Even in our own village we have to stay with our mother, so that people will respect girls who are growing up. Our parents say that a girl who goes off on her own learns bad things and becomes a girl who hangs about the streets. She must stay with her parents. So in the fiestas, although we say hello to the others and so on, we always stay by our mother's side.

The boys are given much more freedom on the whole. It may not be out of *machismo*, but more because nothing that happens to a girl, when she gets involved with a man, happens to them. So boys are a bit freer, but they still respect their parents' rules. If their father says: 'I want you home at such and such a time', then they're home at that time. They can go off on their own to play with their friends, but when they get older, when they're fourteen or fifteen, they have more work and haven't the time to wander off. Going for a walk for us means going to get firewood or do another job. The boys call to each other too and go together to collect firewood, or clear some undergrowth, or some other job. They get together and off they go. Boys and girls have fun in almost the same ways. Mind you, our parents don't allow us to mix with groups of boys, be they our neighbours or cousins, uncles or whatever. We have to go with the girls, not the boys, because the boys are often very crude. They don't like girls going with them either. In this sense, there's a big division between us. We do sometimes chat about the boys or the boys about the girls.

At home I used to talk to my father a lot because I was his favourite daughter. My brothers and sisters were there too, but I don't know – my father was just very fond of me. And I loved him very, very much. Sometimes he'd let me speak to our community, so that they would be as fond of me as they were of him. It wasn't that I was more important because I was a catechist, it was more because of the part I played in the community. Parents are always concerned about your participation in the community, but not at an adult's level since adults get together to talk about more serious things. The thing is that Indians have secrets and it's not always a good thing for children to know them. Or not so much that it's not a good thing but because it's not necessary . . . We respect these different levels in the community. If we need to, we find out about adult matters. If they don't need to, children know how to respect adults' talk. For example, if a neighbour comes to talk to my father or mother and they say: 'Go and fetch some firewood,' that means that they don't want me to listen. In our case, however, my father wanted us to be a part of the community, and wanted us to take community matters and our involvement in the life of our people seriously. That's how I began teaching the doctrine.

A lot of people (in fact almost everyone in my village) are Catholics, devout Catholics. We have rosaries, *novenas*,* we celebrate God's word, the lot. I learned the rosary by heart and my neighbours used to ask me to go and pray for a little two-year-old boy on his birthday and things like that. So

---

* *Novenas*: a devotion to a particular saint or patron consisting of special prayers on nine successive days.

I began working as a catechist, as a Catholic missionary, in the community. And I wasn't the only one. My brothers and sisters and our neighbours' children did as well because we all have a small part to play in the community. That's when we started organizing ourselves and taking a collection every time we met. One *centavo*, two *centavos*, and soon we'd collected a large sum of money in our collecting box and we bought things for the community. And we set up a little shop selling salt, and other things the community can use. It's a village enterprise, helped by the priest. The priests always tell us that we must unite, that we must band together. And we are now united. What I did in this sense was to start my day's work an hour earlier than I'd been used to doing before. So if I usually started work at six a.m., I'd be up and setting off for work at four a.m. ready to start work at five a.m. because we always walk to work and this takes us an hour or an hour and a half. I used to leave work at five p.m. but I began leaving an hour earlier and getting home at five, ready to pray with the neighbours. We have a very nice atmosphere in our village, and we can call our neighbours to come and pray. The Lord doesn't ask us all to say our rosaries alone at home but to have a regular meeting. We have our meeting for the cultural matters of our people on a Friday. Our Catholic meeting was on Mondays. On Mondays those who want to say the rosary ask for it in our Monday meeting of catechists. Those who want a different ceremony from the Catholic one ask for it on Fridays. This way things don't get mixed up. I got really interested in learning to play the instruments of our ancestors. The *tún*, the *tambor*, the *sijolaj* which we still use, and the *chirimía*. My brothers and sisters and I started practising. We used to pray as Catholics with our neighbours while we played our instruments. We knew some Catholic hymns. The first songs our parents were taught, they taught them to us and we sing them most of the time, but we have a lot of problems playing new songs because we have to memorize them.

So we decided Monday was the Catholic day. Monday is reserved. We have to be at the meeting at four p.m. We do everything the Bible asks us. When someone is ill we resort to our Indian methods but, at the same time, we believe Catholic Action is a form of expression. If anyone asks us to say a rosary for the sick person, the neighbours come and we pray in this way. First, we say a prayer to open the ceremony. Then, since we know the litanies and the mysteries, we say them and the Creed. We use the Creed a lot. In the middle of the Creed, there is usually a place for the sick person, and then we finish the prayer. We usually pray for an hour and a half, or two hours with the sick person. When we've finished, everyone hopes that the invalid will get better. Everyone offers support to the family with the sick person so they'll carry on and not despair. We sing the Catholic Action hymns. And we practise the doctrine. We report to parents about their children's progress and we talk about everything to do with the Catholic religion. For example: the priest is coming on such and such a day, what we are going to prepare for him, where we are going to receive him and so on. We talk about things that concern all of us. Sometimes there are a lot of things to discuss because the priests also send us questionnaires which we have to answer and fill in altogether as a community. So we meet and discuss all the things the catechists need to talk about and even when there's not a lot to discuss, we don't waste our time because there are always village matters to talk about. For instance, someone might need a house because his son is setting up his own home. We discuss what we can do to help him, who is going to go and help him, whose turn it is. There's always some collective action to arrange, either on a Monday or a Friday. Then there's another meeting which is the meeting of the community's important men and women. This usually has to do with our land. Especially when they started taking our land away. Every Thursday the village meets to decide: Who is going to the capital? Who would accompany my father, the community's elected leader? How would he get there? All this means we have to put aside time to attend to all the community's affairs. We must have time for our ceremonies, our Indian festivities. We must have time for the Catholic religion. This is another means of expression and complicates our situation. But the whole village is ready to give the time. No-one disagrees, because most of our people are not atheists. We don't live like the *ladinos*.

XIII

DEATH OF HER FRIEND BY POISONING

'I'd always see my mother cry ... I was afraid of life and asked myself, what will it be like when I'm grown up?'
—Rigoberta Menchú

My community always loved me very much, right from when I was very little. They'd tell me all their sorrows and their joys, because my family had been there for a very long time. We never let the slightest opportunity pass – any little fiesta – to organize some sort of celebration using our customs. It was our way of fulfilling our obligation to the community.

I remember going down to the *finca* when I was just beginning my fourteenth year. We'd all go down as a group now, whereas before everyone used to go off to different *fincas* and we wouldn't see each other until we got back to the *Altiplano*. On that occasion, we went down with our neighbours and their children – all happy together. We arrived at the *finca* and a friend and I were sent picking cotton. She was a catechist too and we were always together because we were great friends. One day she died of poisoning when they were spraying the cotton. We all buried her in the *finca* and we decided not to work for two days. It wasn't a strike really, it was more out of respect for our grief. Her name was Maria. She was my friend. A group of about ten of us had come down to the *finca*.

There were boys, men and women among the catechists. There was a group of women who began organising themselves along Christian principles. My mother was the president of the group. Then there was a group of young people around my little brother, the one who was killed (the young people were all together, boys and girls). I had a group of children because I loved children. I had a lot of patience. There was also a men's group. We used to organise many things in the community, but there wasn't any proper formal organization as such. The women used to go mostly to learn the Gospel, to sing a bit and chat and then go home, and it was the same for the children, I'd teach them doctrine, a few other things and play for a while. Sometimes we arranged to study texts with my brothers who could read. We'd read a text and analyze the role of a Christian. This brought us together more and made us more concerned about each other's problems.

My friend was a very important person for the community. She was much loved. From then on, I was very depressed about life because I thought, what would life be like when I grew up? I thought about my childhood and all the time that had passed. I'd often seen my mother crying, although many times she'd hide because she'd never let us see when she was grieving. But I'd often find her crying at home or at work. I was afraid of life and I'd ask myself: 'What will it be like when I'm older?' And that friend of mine had left me with many things to think about. She used to say that she would never get married because marriage meant children and if she had a child she couldn't bear to see him die of starvation or pain or illness. This made me think a lot, I drove myself mad thinking about it. I remember thinking that I couldn't go on. One day I'd be a grown-up woman, and the older I got the more responsibilities I had. I was afraid. I decided I wasn't going to get married either. And when my friend died, I said: 'I'll never get married', because that's what she'd said. I didn't want to go through all the grief. My ideas changed completely; so many ideas came to me. 'What am I going to do?' I often thought I'd stay and work in the *Altiplano*. Even if I went hungry, I wouldn't go down and work in the *finca*. I hated it because my friend died there and two of my brothers died there. My mother told me that one of my brothers died of intoxication as well and I saw another of them die of hunger, of starvation. I remembered my mother's life; I saw her sweat and work but she never complained. She carried on working. She often had nothing. One month she said we hadn't got a single *centavo*: 'What were we to do?' This made me very angry and I asked myself what else could we do in life? I couldn't see any way of avoiding living as everyone else did, and suffering like they did. I was very anxious.

They didn't give us the sack that time because they saw that we were right. Well, the thing was that we got an overseer who was less criminal than the others. He tried not to throw us out for the two days we missed and he didn't dock our wages for it at the end of the month. I was mad with grief then. I said: 'Why don't we burn all this so that people can't come and work here any more?' I hated the people who sprayed the crops. I felt they were responsible. 'Why did they spray poison when people were working there?' I was very upset when I went back home that time. I was with my neighbours and my older sister because my father had stayed up in the *Altiplano*. When I got home I told my mother that my friend had died. My mother cried and I said: 'Mother, I don't want to live. Why didn't die when I was little? How can we go on living?' My mother scolded me and told me not to be silly. But to me it wasn't silly. They were very serious ideas. After that, I got to know some priests. I remember that I couldn't speak Spanish so I couldn't talk to them. But I saw them as good people. I had a lot of ideas but I knew I couldn't express them all. I wanted to read or speak or write Spanish. I told my father this, that I wanted to learn to read. Perhaps things were different if you could read. My father said, 'Who will teach you? You have to find out by yourself, because I can't help you. I know of no schools and I have no money for them anyway.' I told him that if he talked to the priests, perhaps they'd give me a scholarship. But my father said he didn't agree with my idea because I was trying to leave the community, to go far away, and find what was best for me. He said: 'You'll forget about our common heritage. If you leave, it will be for good. If you leave our community, I will not support you.' My father was very suspicious of schools and all that sort of thing. He gave as an example the fact that many of my cousins had learned to read and write but they hadn't been of use to the community. They try to move away and feel different when they can read and write. My father explained all this to me, but I said: 'No, I want to learn, I want to learn,' and I went on and on about it.

After that we went down to the *finca* for the last time. It was to a different one this time. One of the landowners asked my father to let me go and work as a maid for him. My father refused. 'That's a bad life. They will treat you badly, in ways which we never have. I couldn't bear my daughter to suffer somewhere far from us. It's better to suffer together.' So, there I was with this problem of how to find a way out of this life when this landowner offered me twenty *quetzals* a month to be his maid. But I said no, better not to. My elder sister had the same problem. Well, she said: 'I'm going.' She made up her mind. My father told her she'd be going to her ruin, that who knows where they'd take her. He was very worried because he'd never wanted us to go to the capital to be maids. He thought that our ideas would be all distorted afterwards. He was afraid that we would forget all the things he and my mother had taught us since we were little.

My sister left, but I stayed on with my parents. I used to wonder how my sister was getting on. At the end of the month my father went to see her and when he came back he told me: 'Your sister is all right. But she's suffering because the work isn't like our work and because rich people treat you like dirt.' I said it didn't matter if they treated her badly, if she could learn Spanish and learn to read. That was my ambition. But my sister couldn't stand it and came home. 'I wouldn't wait on a rich man again for anything in the world,' she said. 'Now I've learned that rich people are bad.' But I wondered how it could be harder than our work, because I always thought that it would be impossible to work harder than we did. So why put up with it? And that's when I went to be a maid in the capital. I wasn't yet thirteen, still very young.

XIV

A MAID IN THE CAPITAL

'I was incapable of disobedience. And those employers ex-
ploited my obedience. They took advantage of my innocence.'
—Rigoberta Menchú

When we left the *finca*, the landowner's guards travelled behind him. And they were armed. I was terrified! But I told
myself, 'I must be brave, they can't do anything to me.' My
father said: 'I don't know if anything will happen to you, my
child, but you are a mature woman.'

So we reached the capital. I remember that my clothes were
worn out because I'd been working in the *finca*: my *corte*
was really dirty and my *huipil* very old. I had a little *perraje*,
the only one I owned. I didn't have any shoes. I didn't even
know what wearing shoes was like. The master's wife was at
home. There was another servant girl to do the cooking and
I would have to do all the cleaning in the house. The other
servant was also Indian, but she'd changed her clothes. She
wore *ladino* clothes and already spoke Spanish. I didn't know
any; I arrived and didn't know what to say. I couldn't speak
Spanish but I understood a little because of the *finca* overseers who used to give us orders, bully us and hand out the
work. Many of them are Indians but they won't use Indian
languages because they feel different from the labourers. So
I understood Spanish although I couldn't speak it. The mis-

tress called the other servant: 'Take this girl to the room in the back.' The girl came, looked at me with indifference and told me to follow her. She took me to the other room. It was a room with a pile of boxes in the corner and plastic bags where they kept the rubbish. It had a little bed. They took it down for me and put a little mat on it, with another blanket, and left me there. I had nothing to cover myself with.

The first night, I remember, I didn't know what to do. That was when I felt what my sister had felt although, of course, my sister had been with another family. Then later the mistress called me. The food they gave me was a few beans with some very hard *tortillas*. There was a dog in the house, a pretty, white, fat dog. When I saw the maid bring out the dog's food – bits of meat, rice, things that the family ate – and they gave me a few beans and hard *tortillas*, that hurt me very much. The dog had a good meal and I didn't deserve as good a meal as the dog. Anyway, I ate it, I was used to it. I didn't mind not having the dog's food because at home I only ate *tortillas* with chile or with salt or water. But I felt rejected. I was lower than the animals in the house. The girl came later and told me to go to sleep because I had to work in the morning and they got up at seven or eight. I was in bed awake from three o'clock. I didn't mind about the bed either because at home I slept on a mat on the floor and we sometimes didn't even have anything to cover ourselves with. But I had a look at the other girl's bed and it was quite comfortable because she wore *ladino* clothes and spoke Spanish. Later on, however, we got to know each other well. She used to eat the masters' leftovers; what they left in the dish. They'd eat first and she'd get what was left. If there wasn't any left, she'd also get some stale beans and *tortillas* or some leftovers from the fridge. She ate that and later on when we knew each other she'd give me some.

At three in the morning, I said: 'My God, my parents will be working and I'm here.' But I also thought, I must learn, and then go home. I always said that I must go home. Three o'clock, five o'clock, six o'clock. At seven, the girl got up and came and told me: 'Come here and wash the dishes.' I went in my same clothes and the mistress came in and said; 'How filthy! get that girl out of here! How can you let her touch the dishes, can't you see how dirty she is?' The girl told me to leave the dishes, but she was upset too. 'Here's the broom, go and sweep up,' the mistress said. I went out to sweep the yard. 'Water the plants,' she said, 'that's your job. And then come here and do the washing. Here are the clothes, but mind you wash them properly or I'll throw you out.'

Of course, I was in the city but I didn't know the first thing about it. I knew nothing about the city even though I'd been there with my father. But then we'd only gone to one place and to some offices. I didn't know how to find my way around and I couldn't read the numbers or the streets.

So I did what the lady told me to do and afterwards, about 11 o'clock when they finished eating, they called me. 'Have you eaten?' 'No.' 'Give her some food.' So they gave me what was left of their food. I was famished. At home we don't eat as much as we should, of course, but at least we're used to eating tortillas regularly, even if it's only with salt. I was really worried. At about half past eleven, she called me again and took me into a room. She said: 'I'm going to give you two months' pay in advance and you must buy yourself a *huipil*, a new *corte*, and a pair of shoes, because you put me to shame. My friends are coming and you're here like that. What would that look like to my friends? They are important people so you'll have to change your ways. I'll buy you these things but you stay here because I'm ashamed to be seen with you in the market. Here's your two months' pay.' Well, I didn't know what to say because I didn't know enough Spanish to protest or say what I thought. But in my mind I insulted her. I thought, if only I could send this woman to the mountains and let her do the work my mother does. I don't think she'd even be capable of it. I didn't think much of her at all.

She went off to the market. She came back with a *corte*. It was about a couple of yards long. The simplest there was. She also brought a simple *huipil* which must have cost her two-fifty or three *quetzals*. She must have got the *corte* for fifteen *quetzals* or even less, perhaps only twelve *quetzals*. She didn't buy me another belt, I had my old one. And she said she didn't buy me shoes because two months' pay wasn't enough. Then she gave me the *corte*. I had to tear it into two so that I could keep one of them to change into. I tore it into two parts. Now, I'm one of those women who can weave, embroider, and do everything. When the other girl became more friendly, she asked me: 'Can you embroider?' 'Yes,' I said. 'Can you make blouses? I'll give you some material. I've got some thread and if you like you can make a blouse.' And she gave me some material to make a blouse. Anyway, I tore that *corte* in two and changed right away. The mistress said, 'When you've changed, go to my room and make my bed.' I went to change, and she made me have a bath. I came back and started making her bed. When I'd finished she came to check my work and said, 'Do this bed again, you didn't make it properly.' And she began scolding the other girl; 'Why didn't you show her how to do it? I don't want mobs of people here who can't earn their keep.' We started to make the bed again. I didn't know how to dust because I'd never done it, so the other girl taught me how to dust, and how to clean the toilets.

And that was when I discovered the truth in what my grandmother used to say: that with rich people even their plates shine. Well, yes, even their toilets shine. At home we don't even have one. I was really very distressed, remembering all my parents' and my grandparents' advice. I learned to dust, wash and iron very quickly. I found ironing the hardest because I'd never used an iron before. I remember how the washing and ironing used to pile up. The landowner had three children and they changed their clothes several times a day. All the clothes they left lying around had to be washed again, and ironed again, and then hung up in the right place. The mistress used to watch me all the time and was very nasty to me. She treated me like . . I don't know what . . . not like a dog because she treated the dog well. She used to hug the dog. So I thought: 'She doesn't even compare me with the dog.' They had a garden and I sowed some plants. I used to do this at home so I got on really well with that. That's what I saw every day. The time came when I was working really well. I did all my jobs in a trice. I didn't find it difficult. I had to work for the two months that the mistress spent on my clothes without earning a *centavo*.

I didn't go out either although on Saturdays the mistress said I had to go out: 'Come on, out of here. I'm fed up with servants hanging around.' That made me very angry because we worked, we did everything. We probably didn't work as hard for our parents as we did for that rich old woman. But on Saturdays, she'd say: 'Out of here. I don't want to see heaps of maids around.' That's what happens to Indian girls in the capital. On Saturdays we were allowed out in the evenings, but it was preparing their maids for prostitution because we were ordered out and then we had to find somewhere to sleep. We went out on Saturdays and came back on Sundays. Thank Heavens the other girl was really decent. She said; 'I've got some friends here. We'll go to their house.' I went with her. But what if I'd been on my own? I wouldn't have had anywhere to stay, only the street, because I couldn't even speak to the mistress to tell her not to throw me out. I couldn't find my way around the city either. So the other girl took me to her friend's house. We went there every Saturday to sleep. On Sundays, we'd go back at night because during the day we were allowed to go dancing, to the dance halls and all the places where maids go in the capital.

The sons of the house treated us very badly. One must have been about twenty-two, the next about fifteen, and the youngest about twelve. They were petty bourgeois youths who couldn't even pick a duster up, or clear anything away. They liked throwing their dishes in our faces. That was our job. They threw things at us, they shouted at us all the time, and treated us very badly. When the mistress came home – and goodness knows what she did all day – she'd do nothing but complain. 'There's dust on my bed, there's dust here too,

you didn't shake this properly . . . the plants . . . the books
. . .'. All she did every day was complain. She just inspected
everything and slept. Then at night she'd say, 'Bring me my
meal, I'm tired.' And the other girl, who she said was much
cleaner, took her her meal in bed, with hot water to wash her
hands. She took everything to her. In the morning, the father
and the sons all shouted from their beds for us to fetch their
slippers and all the other things they needed. At breakfast, if
any of their favourite food was missing, they'd make a terrible fuss. And they had talks about our wages: 'What a waste
of money, these girls can't do anything.' The mistress was
like a parrot. The other maid relied on me a lot. She realized
that I wasn't hostile to her but always helped her with lots of
things.

There were times when we'd really had enough. One day
the other maid and I agreed we'd start being difficult. She
said: 'If the mistress complains, let her complain.' And we
stopped doing certain things just to annoy her. So she got
up and shouted at us, but the more she shouted the more
stubborn we became and she saw that that wasn't any use.
The other maid said: 'Come on, let's leave and find another
job.' But I was worried because I couldn't just decide like
that; I didn't know the city and if I counted on her, she
might take me somewhere worse. What was I to do? Soon
I realized that the mistress spurned this girl because she
wouldn't become the boys' lover. She told me later: 'That
old bag wants me to initiate her sons. She says boys have
to learn how to do the sexual act and if they don't learn
when they're young, it's harder for them when they're
older. So she put in my contract that she'd pay me a bit
more if I taught her sons.' That was the condition she'd
imposed, and that was why she was so hard on the girl:
because she'd refused. Perhaps she nursed the hope that
one day I'd be clean – she always said I was dirty – so that
one day I'd be all right to teach her sons. That's what she
hoped, that lady. She mistreated me and rejected me, but
she didn't actually throw me out.

I remember that after I'd been in that rich man's house for two months, my father came to visit me. I'd been praying to God that my father wouldn't come, because I knew that if he did, what a dreadful reception he'd get! And I couldn't bear my father to be rejected by that old hag. My father was humble, poor, as I was. He came, not because he had any time to spare to visit me, but because he was left in the city without a single *centavo* in his pocket. He'd been to see about the business of our land. He said they'd sent him to Quetzaltenango, then to El Quiché, and then they'd asked to see him in the capital and the money he'd brought for the trip had run out. So he hadn't got a penny. When my father rang the bell, the other maid went to see who it was. He said who he was. She told him to wait a minute because she knew what her mistress was like. She told her: 'Rigoberta's father is here.' 'All right,' said the lady of the house and went out to see my father. She saw how poor he was, of course. He was all dirty. Well, he would be because he'd been travelling to many places. That's what it's like for the poor. She went out to look and came straight back. She told me: 'Go and see your father but don't bring him in here, please.' That's what she said and I had to see him outside. She told me plainly not even to bring him into the corridor. He had to stay out in the yard and I explained the situation to him. I said the mistress was very nasty and that it disgusted and horrified her to see my father and that he couldn't even come into the house. He understood very well. He was used to it because we're rejected in so many different places. My father said: 'My child, I need money. I've nothing for anything to eat or to get home with.' But I still hadn't finished the two months that I owed and hadn't a penny to my name. I said; 'The mistress had to buy clothes for me and docked me two months' pay for it. I haven't earned a single *centavo*.' My father began to cry and said: 'It can't be true.' 'Yes,' I said, 'everything I'm wearing the mistress bought for me.' So I went to the other maid and told her my father had no money and I didn't know what to do; I couldn't ask the mistress for money as I couldn't speak

Spanish. Then she spoke to the mistress for me and said: 'Her father hasn't got a single *centavo* and needs money.' The girl was very tough and would stand up to anyone and anything. She was really angry with our mistress and said: 'She needs money and must be given some money for her father.' Then the mistress started saying that we were trying to get all her money off her, trying to eat her money up, and we couldn't even do our jobs properly. All maids are the same. They've nothing to eat in their own homes, so they come and eat us out of ours. She opened her bag and took out ten *quetzals* and threw them into my face. I took the ten *quetzals* and told my father that I thought she'd take another month's pay. It will be another debt, but this is what I can give you. So my father went home with ten *quetzals*. But the other girl just couldn't stomach this. She was really hurt by it and she often said that if the mistress complained, she would stand up for me. She had a plan, because she was leaving anyway. She began a resistance campaign against the mistress.

I worked for more than four months, I think, and received no money. Then she paid me a little. She gave me twenty *quetzals* and I was very happy. I wanted to keep them for my father. But she told me that I had to buy shoes, because she was ashamed to have anyone in her house go barefoot. I had no shoes. But I said to myself: 'I'm not going to buy any. If she wants me to have some, let her buy them.'

I remember that we spent a Christmas together, this maid and I, in this rich house. They were very grand people. We couldn't address them as '*tu*' at all, we had to use '*usted*' all the time, out of respect. Anyway, once when I was just starting to learn and was finding Spanish very hard, perhaps I might have used '*tu*' to the mistress. She almost hit me. She said, 'Call your mother "*tu*". Me, you treat with respect.' Of course, this wasn't difficult to understand because I knew we're always treated like this. It made me laugh sometimes, but as a human being, these things hurt. I used to go out with the other maid but I tried to keep the little I was earning. I was pleased because I now understood Spanish very well.

But since nobody taught me to memorize word by word, I couldn't say a lot. I could say the main things I needed for my work but I couldn't start a conversation, or answer back, or protest about something. Five, six months I must have been working there. The mistress never talked to me, and as I knew how to do the work, I didn't need to speak to her. Sometimes I'd talk to the other girl but there wasn't much time to chat; we each got on with our own work. But one day I was told not to talk to her and if I did I'd be thrown out. The mistress thought that she was teaching me things, like how to protest, things which didn't suit her. But I told the other maid on the quiet what the mistress had said. 'Of course, that's right, because it annoys her when we answer back. But don't be silly. Don't let her push you around.'

After eight months Christmas came and we had a lot to do, because the mistress told us we were going to make two hundred *tamales*. We had to make two hundred because her friends were coming and she'd promised to make *tamales* for them all. So the other maid told her that if she wanted them she'd better set to work herself because we weren't going to do anything. I was anxious because she hadn't paid me for two months and she was capable of turning me out without paying me. I was anxious so I said to the girl: 'What happens if she doesn't pay me?' 'If she doesn't pay, we'll leave with one of her jewels,' she said. 'We have to leave with something, so don't worry. I'll stand up for you.' On December 23rd, I was very worried about whether or not to do what she asked. Then the master came and brought us some five-*centavo* earrings. It was our Christmas present. He told us we had to make the *tamales* because guests were coming. The master wasn't so violent towards us and he often didn't know what his wife did to us.

First they sent us to kill the turkeys. We were told to kill four of them. We killed them, but we had a plan. We'd kill them, and pluck them, but we wouldn't dress them. And if they rotted, well, they could rot and we'd see what the mistress would do. We were going to ask for two days holiday and if they didn't give it to us we'd go and spend Christmas somewhere else. But I was anxious. I couldn't do it then, perhaps because of the way my parents had brought me up. I was incapable of disobedience. And those employers exploited my obedience. They took advantage of my innocence. Whatever it was, I did it, as my duty. My friend had plans but the mistress realized that we were making a real fool of her and she threw her out. She threw her out just before Christmas. She also did it so that I couldn't leave; but even if I had left, I wouldn't have known where to go. I still didn't know anyone. I didn't know the city. So she threw the girl out, saying that if she caught her hanging round the house, she'd shoot her, she'd plug her with a couple of bullets. But the girl told her she could do the same: 'Don't think I wouldn't do the same.' They had a terrible row. My friend told me: 'One day I'll shoot her; one day I'll come back and she'll know what it is to face me.' Then she left. I had to do all the work. The mistress made me serve everything, and she had to work a bit too to make all the *tamales* she'd promised. I hardly slept. We made the *tamales* and we did all the other jobs in the house. But the washing piled up and the house was dirty because there wasn't time to clean it. It was a big house with lots of rooms. Oh, it was a mess.

December 25th arrived and I remember that they started to drink. They drank and drank. They got completely drunk. They sent me out at midnight on the 25th to get wine and *guaro* from the *cantinas*. I had to walk. I didn't go very far because I knew that they were all drunk inside but I didn't know what to do because if I went back, they'd throw me out. I was very worried. I went out but I didn't find anything. Everything round there was closed. I didn't go further afield; I just spent the time walking round the streets, thinking of my home. We might have had hard times because we had very little, but I'd never suffered like I was suffering in the house of those rich people. I went back and they said: 'Did you bring the guaro?' 'No I couldn't find any.' 'You never went. That girl has given you ideas. You used not to be like that, you weren't as badly behaved as most Indians are, not like the girl who left.' And they started discussing the Indians they had at home, saying: 'Indians are lazy, they don't work, that's why they're poor. They're always making trouble because they won't work.' They began talking, half drunk. I put up with it, listening to them in the other room. Then the mistress said: 'Here's a *tamal* for you so you can try out my handiwork.' And she left me a *tamal*. I was so angry I couldn't bear it, I didn't even bother to look at the *tamal* she'd left me on the stove.

A whole crowd of people came and they took out all the expensive china. I was worried about having to spend two days washing up because I always used to think about the work coming up. They got out all their china, all their most modern things. Everyone brought them shiny presents, everyone who came had big presents for them. They gave presents to their friends too. They were all delighted. But I was sad because my friend wasn't there. If she'd have been there, we might not have had to put up with all this. We might have found another solution, perhaps we'd have gone out. Later the mistress said: 'There are no more *tamales*. We'll buy you another one tomorrow.' And she took away the *tamal* she'd given me. She needed it for one of her friends who'd arrived later. I just couldn't bear that. I didn't say anything to her. It wasn't that I wanted to eat it. I didn't feel hurt because I hadn't eaten it but because they'd given it to me as if they rejected me, as if to say, this is what is left over for you. And even then she'd taken it away. That was very, very important for me. I told her I didn't even want to eat it.

The mistress left and I went to sleep. I shut myself up in my room saying, 'They make the mess, let's see how they deal with it. I'm not going to pick up any plates or do anything.' And the mistress started shouting for me: 'Rigoberta, come and pick up the plates,' but I didn't get up. I was really stubborn and went to sleep. Of course, I wasn't asleep. I was thinking of our humble way of life and their debauched life. I said, 'How pathetic these people are who can't even shit alone. We poor enjoy ourselves more than they do.'

So the day passed. They slept all through the 26th. So who had to pick up the plates? Who had to clean the house? Who had to do everything? Me. If I didn't do it the old bag would throw me out. I got up early. I picked up all the plates, I picked up all the skins of the *tamales* that they'd thrown away, and I piled it all up in one place. This took almost to midday. I didn't know where to start: whether to wash up or clean the house? I didn't feel much like doing anything, because of all the work in front of me and just thinking of me having to do it all. The mistress got up and asked: 'Have you prepared lunch?' I said: 'I don't know what we're having to eat,' because I didn't know anything about it. 'Ah, you're not like Cande,' she said. (The other maid was called Candelaria). 'Cande had more initiative. You're just here to eat. You can't do anything. Go to the market and buy some meat.' I didn't know where the market was. 'Excuse me, Señora, but I don't know where the market is.' I could say straightforward things like that, but I couldn't say a lot of other things. 'Oh really? You Indian whore. You know how to make trouble, but you don't know how to do or say anything else.' She was very foul-mouthed. I took no notice and didn't even stop. I went on working although she kept on talking all day long. Then she called a neighbour in to complain to. She said her maid was useless and robbed them blind. I knew I wasn't stealing their food but that I paid for my keep with my work. In the end, she could do nothing and had to send her neighbour to market to buy everything. They made their meal, I didn't make anything. I'd been suffering from not having eaten for about two or three days, because I hadn't even had one of the *tamales* we'd made with all that effort. I'd gone without sleep to make them. We'd take some out of the oven and put the next lot in, and so on. I told myself – I'll never forget this part of my life.

December passed. And I went on working. All the work from Christmas set me back by two weeks. All the new clothes and all the new china they'd got out just piled up. The house was dirty. I had to do everything. The mistress pretended she didn't notice. She'd get up and go out. She didn't even complain so much, because she knew she needed me to do it all. That's when I thought: 'I must get out of this house. I must go home to my parents.' She gave me two months' money. It was forty *quetzals*. With this and with what I'd already saved, I thought, I can go home to my parents satisfied. It wasn't very much, perhaps, but it would help them. I told the mistress: 'I'm leaving. I'm going home.' She said: 'No, how can you? We're so fond of you here. You must stay. I'll put your wages up, if you like. I'll give you a *quetzal* more.' 'No,' I said, 'I've made up my mind to go.' I was announcing my departure, unfortunately. I say unfortunately because a terrible thing happened: one of my brothers arrived and said: 'Papá is in prison.'

XV

CONFLICT WITH THE
LANDOWNERS AND THE
CREATION OF THE CUC*

*'Gather in your grain and seeds and collect the young shoots,
because times of drought and hunger are approaching. Sharpen
your weapons because it will not be long before enemies,
hidden behind mountains and hills, will espy with greed the
expanse and richness of these lands.'*

—Popol Vuh

This was the first time my father went to prison. My brother
said, 'We don't know what to do for him because the lawyers
say Papá will be in jail for eighteen years. We need money to
get educated people to help us.' In Guatemala this is what
happens with the poor, especially Indians, because they can't
speak Spanish. The Indian can't speak up for what he wants.
When they put my father in jail, the landowners gave large
amounts of money to the judge there. The judge in El Quiché,
that is. There are several levels of authority. First, there is
the military commissioner. He sometimes lives in the villages
or is based in the town, and he tries to impose his own law.
Then there is what we call the mayor who represents the authorities that administer justice when they say someone has

---

* Comité de Unidad Campesina – United Peasant Committee.

broken the law. Next come the governors who govern the whole region, each province. And finally, there are the deputies – God knows who they are! To get to see the military commissioner, you first have to give him a *mordida*, that's what we call a bribe in Guatemala. To see the mayor, you have to get witnesses, sign papers and then give him a *mordida* so he will support your case. To see the governor you need not only witnesses from the village, and money, but also lawyers or other intermediaries to talk for you. The governor is a *ladino* and doesn't understand the language of the people. He'll only believe something if a lawyer or educated person says it. He won't accept anything from an Indian. The mayor is a *ladino* too. But he's a *ladino* who's come from our people. The military commissioner is also a *ladino* although this varies a bit, because in some places the commissioners are Indians who have done military service and lived in the barracks. There comes a time when they return to their village, brutalized men, criminals.

My father fought for twenty-two years, waging a heroic struggle against the landowners who wanted to take our land and our neighbours' land. After many years of hard work, when our small bit of land began yielding harvests and our people had a large area under cultivation, the big landowners appeared: the Brols. It's said there that they were even more renowned criminals than the Martínez and García families, who owned a *finca* there before the Brols arrived. The Brols were a large family, a whole gang of brothers. Five of them lived on a *finca* they had taken over by forcibly throwing the Indians of the region off their land. That was what happened to us. We lived in a small village. We cultivated maize, beans, potatoes and all sorts of vegetables. Then the Garcías arrived and started measuring the land in our village. They brought inspectors, engineers and Heaven knows who else; people they said were from the government. In Guatemala if it's to do with the government, there's no way we can defend ourselves. So they came and started measuring our land. My father went round collecting signatures in the village, and they held meetings. Then he went to the capital, to the INTA, Institute Nacional de Transformación Agraria de Guatemala: Guatemalan National Institute for Agrarian Transformation. But the landowners and the government had made a deal to take the peasants' land away from them. When my father went to protest about the way the landowners were forcing us off our land, the people in the INTA asked the landowners for money to be allowed to go on measuring. On the other hand, they gave the peasants a piece of paper which, according to them, said they didn't have to leave their land. It was a double-sided game. They called my father in. Papá used to be . . . well, I don't mean foolish exactly because it's the thieves who steal our land who are foolish. . . . Well, they asked my father to sign a paper but he didn't know what it said because he'd never learned to read or write. In fact, the paper said that the peasants confirmed, once again, that they would leave their land. This gave the landowners power, since he, the community's representative, had signed the paper. My father went back again to protest, this time through some lawyers. The INTA people and the lawyers started getting fat off us. Many lawyers wanted to help us and offered us different sorts of help. They said we were doing the right thing. The peasants trusted them but realized afterwards that they made them pay through the nose, even for a simple signature. My father dedicated himself entirely to our community's problems. The INTA told my father: 'You must get engineers to measure the land and then you'll be the owners of the land you live on. Don't worry, grow what you want. Don't worry, go ahead and clear the undergrowth because the land is yours.' With this encouragement, my father went home and called meetings in the village.

We were very happy and went on working until the landowners arrived with their engineers again. Our little bit of land has probably been measured something like twenty times, if I'm not mistaken. Engineers after engineers. What I can't forgive, and this is something that has contributed to my hate for these people, is that they said they came to help us. My father, mother, all the community, were very distressed. They were *ladinos*. They couldn't eat our food, our *tortillas* with salt. If we didn't feed them well they would probably favour the landowners. So we treated them very well, out of fear. We gave them our best, our fattest animals. We'd kill chickens for them to eat. Our community, which never bought so much as a bottle of oil, had to buy them rice, oil, eggs, chickens, meat. We had to buy coffee and sugar, because they couldn't eat *panela*. Our community never ate these things. We all had to go to town. The village got together, gave in their ten *centavos* and with this collection we bought what was needed. Earning ten *centavos* is hard for us, it's earned by a lot of sweat. It was worse when the inspectors stayed a whole week. When they left, the village breathed a sigh of relief and we were much poorer. *We* didn't eat meat. *They* did. They got their information with no difficulty. They went to the further points of our land and, of course, needed someone to go with them. But our people have no time to spare. It was my father who gave up his time because he loved the community, even if it meant we often had nothing to eat at home. My mother felt responsible for looking after these men. She saw how in need our neighbours were. So my mother stayed at home and said to us, 'You children go and work because I have to attend to these men.' My parents attended to them because, as leaders of the community, it was their responsibility – they were the most important people in the village. They looked after them very well. My mother even made them small *tortillas* because they couldn't eat our large ones. She had to make ones to suit them. So neither of my parents could work while those men were there. Our neighbours contributed what they could, but they didn't have very much. We couldn't speak Spanish. My father spoke a little, just enough to understand the inspectors. The INTA used to send for him. They sometimes made him go to Quetzaltenango, Huehuetenango, El Quiché or to the capital just to sign a piece of paper. You can imagine the cost of those journeys in food and transport. And on top of all this, we had to pay the lawyers who shuffle the papers.

The government says the land belongs to the nation. It owns the land and gives it to us to cultivate. But when we've cleared and cultivated the land, that's when the landowners appear. However, the landowners don't just appear on their own – they have connections with the different authorities that allow them to manoeuvre like that. Because of this, we faced the Martínez family, the Garcías, and then the Brols arrived. This meant we could either stay and work as *peónes* or leave our land. There was no other solution. So my father travelled all over the place seeking advice. We didn't realize then that going to the government authorities was the same as going to the landowners. They are the same. My father was tireless in his efforts to seek help. He went to other sectors, like the workers' unions. He asked them to help because we were already being thrown off our land.

The first time they threw us out of our homes was, if I remember rightly, in 1967. They turned us out of our houses, and out of the village. The Garcías' henchmen set to work with ferocity. They were Indians too, soldiers of the *finca*. First they went into the houses without permission and got all the people out. Then they went in and threw out all our things. I remember that my mother had her silver necklaces, precious keepsakes from my grandmother, but we never saw them again after that. They stole them all. They threw out our cooking utensils, our earthenware cooking pots. We don't use those sort of . . . special utensils, we have our own earthenware pots. They hurled them into the air, and, oh God! they hit the ground and broke into pieces. All our plates, cups, pots. They threw them out and they all broke. That was the vengeance of the landowner on the peasants because we wouldn't give up our land. All the maize cobs they found in the *tapanco*, they threw away. Afterwards all the peasants had to work together to collect them up. We did it together and put them in another place. I remember it was pouring with rain, and we had nothing to protect ourselves from the rain. It took us two days to make a roughly built hut out of leaves. We only had those nylon sheets the peasants use to cover themselves in the rain. The first night we spent in the fields with streams of water running along the ground. It wasn't raining then but the ground was sodden.

Those few days confirmed my hatred for those people. I saw why we said that *ladinos* were thieves, criminals and liars. It was as our parents had told us. We could see that they were doing the same to us. They killed our animals. They killed many of our dogs. To us, killing an animal is like killing a person. We care for all the things of the natural world very much and killing our dogs wounded us very deeply. We spent more than forty days in the fields. Then the community held a meeting and said, 'If they throw us out again, we will die of hunger.' We had no utensils for cooking our *tortillas*, and no grinding stones. They'd been thrown away into the undergrowth. We organized ourselves, all of us, and said, 'Let's collect our things together.' We went looking for any of our things that were still more or less all right. My father said, 'If they kill us they kill us, but we'll go back to our houses.' Our people looked on my father as their own father, and so we went back to our houses. There was another village quite near ours and they helped us. People brought cooking pots and plates so that we could cook our maize and eat. So we went back to our houses. And the landowners came back again for what they called 'collective negotiations.' They told us we should resign ourselves to working as *peónes* because the land belonged to them. We could stay in our houses, but the land was not ours. If we didn't agree, they would throw us off again. But my father said: 'We were the first families to come and cultivate this land and nobody can deceive us into thinking that this land is theirs. If they want to be the owners of more land, let them go and cultivate the mountains. There is more land but it is not land where things grow.' Who knows, perhaps if the community had been alone, we would have become *peónes* and our land would now be part of a big *finca*. But my father would have none of it. He said, 'Even if they kill us, we will do it.' Of course, in those days we didn't have enough political clarity to unite with others and protest about our land. What we did, we did as an individual community. So we went back to our homes and did not accept the landowners' deal. They left us alone for a month or two. Then there was another raid. All our things were broken for a second time, all the things our neighbours in the other village had given us. We couldn't stand what they were doing to us any longer and decided to go to the *finca*, abandoning our land. But we couldn't live in the *finca* all the time. What were we going to do? What would happen to us if we went to the *finca*? That's when we united and said: 'We won't go!'

We love our land very much. Since those people tried to take our land away, we have grieved very much. My grandfather used to cry bitterly and say: 'In the past, no one person owned the land. The land belonged to everyone. There were no boundaries.' We were sadder still when we saw our animals going hungry because of us. If our animals went near our crops, they were killed by the Garcías' henchmen who were guarding them. (I remember that the wickedest landowner was Honorio García. The other was Angel Martínez.) My grandfather said, 'If they kill our animals, we must kill them.' That was the idea that came to my grandfather. We spent about fifteen days away from our house, after the second raid and our elders advised us to burn them and leave. But where to? We didn't know whether it was better to go to the *finca* or agree to be labourers on the landowners' estate. We couldn't decide. We discussed it with all our neighbours. Among the whole community. During all this time we couldn't celebrate our culture; none of our ceremonies. That's when my father took his stand. He said, 'If they kill me for trying to defend the land that belongs to us, well, they'll have to kill me.' The idea of life without a father, or that Papá would be shot by those guards, was terrible for us. Sometimes my mother was very distressed and begged my father not to put his life in danger with those guards.

My father went on travelling. He was hardly ever at home

now. He didn't pay us much attention, or talk to us like he used to. He'd arrive, call a meeting of the community, talk to them and then sometimes leave the next day. We began to lose contact with him. When the landowners saw my father working so hard to save our land, they started threatening him. So he said, 'The best guardians, the best protection a man has, are his animals. Our dogs must learn to defend us.' We had some good dogs, they were very fierce. We spent time teaching the dogs to bite those men when they came to our houses – sometimes in the middle of the night.

Our life was now such that we couldn't go down to the *finca* because if we did our houses probably wouldn't be there when we got back. The community decided to eat plants or whatever they could find in the fields rather than go down to the *finca*. Or part of a family would go and the other part would stay and watch over the house. We became much more united. When the landowners came we'd unite so that they either had to throw us all off, kill us all or leave us alone. We began teaching the children to keep watch and tell us when the landowners were coming. We lived for quite a while like this – with all this tension. I kept on going down to the *finca* with my brothers and sisters. My mother always stayed in the house. Or my father was there. My father never went down to the *fincas* because the landowners would take advantage of this and go into the village. Then they started trying other things. We had maize and beans but we had to carry all our produce down from the village to the town which was a long way away. So the landowners set up a temporary market, a place to sell produce, and tried to isolate us from the town even more, so that they could take over our land more easily.

Then the INTA came and told us that the problem was solved. They said: 'We're going to give you a title to the land for you to sign and the land will be yours. No-one will bother you on your land. You can sow your crops, clear the un-dergrowth and go further into the mountains. This proposal comes from the government.' We signed it. I remember even the children signed it. We can't sign with a pen or a pencil.

We signed it in ink with our fingerprints on the paper. My father insisted they read the paper out even though we didn't understand it all. We did understand some. But they didn't want to read it. The INTA inspectors said we could rely on the paper, it was the title to the land. So we signed it.

They left us alone for two and a half years, I think it was, to let us calm down. Our people went on working. We hardly ever went down to the *finca* now so that we could cultivate more land. We tried to clear large areas of the undergrowth, into the mountains. We had a dream, a real dream. In five or eight years our land would yield its fruit. Two and a half years went by when we saw the engineers on our land again, shouting, measuring, with the landowners' guards. Now, not only the Martínez and the Garcías, but the Brols were all measuring part of our land. This time the problem was more complicated because they brought with them the document we had signed, which said we had agreed to stay on the land and live off its produce for two years only; that when the two years were up, we had another place to go to and would leave the land. This wasn't true. We didn't know what it was we had signed. My father said, 'This is unjust, because we were deceived.'

This is how my father started getting more deeply involved with the unions. I remember my father asked some unions in the FASGUA, Federación Autónoma Sindical de Guatemala – Guatemalan Federation of Independent Unions – to help us because they were unions for workers, for labourers, and we were peasants – agricultural labourers. The unions helped us a lot. They said they would denounce the fact that we were being thrown off our land. My father was continually going to see the unions, the INTA, the lawyers. It nearly drove him mad. He told us, 'My children, you must get to know the places I go to because otherwise, if they kill me the community will lose its land.' Very well. One of my older brothers began to travel with my father and began learning Spanish. The community had to contribute to my father's fares. He very often had no money at all and my mother had to sell our animals to pay for his trips. But at least we didn't leave our land. My mother thought about us more and more because, of course, they were growing up. They wondered how much their children would suffer afterwards. The whole community wondered.

When my father started going to the unions and getting their support, the landowners offered a great deal of money to the judge who dealt with land claims, and my father was arrested. They accused him of 'compromizing the sovereignty of the state.' He was endangering the 'sovereignty and the well-being of the Guatemalans'! They put him in prison. I remember that I'd been working as a maid for a year. I'd saved a little money to take home as a surprise for my family, especially my mother. I'd saved it so that my mother wouldn't have to go to the *finca* for a couple of months. My brother told me: 'They're asking for money. We don't know what to do.' I decided to leave my job and go back to the *finca*. From the money I'd saved and my brothers' wages in the *finca*, we had to pay for witnesses, lawyers, documents, secretaries. There were so many things we had to pay for to be able to get to see the authorities. Since we didn't speak Spanish, we had to find an intermediary to translate my mother's statements. The lawyer was a *ladino* and didn't understand our language, so we had to get an intermediary to interpret for him. From the beginning the landowners paid the interpreter not to say what we said. The interpreter 'sold himself' to the landowners and, instead of our statements, he said something else. They played so many tricks on us. The result was that our lawyer had nothing to do because, according to the interpreter, we ourselves acknowledged that the land belonged to those landowners. They had paid us to cultivate the land. That wasn't true. We were very afraid that they would send my father to the state prison. As long as he was in the local prison, his case wasn't so serious, but once he got to the state prison, the one in El Quiché, we'd have no way of preventing him from having to carry out the sentence he'd been given. If he went to the criminals' prison, as the authorities in Quetzaltenango said, it meant he would be in jail for eighteen years or more.

We had enormous trouble getting my father out of prison. My mother had to go and work as a maid in Santa Cruz del Quiché, and the rest of us . . . in the *finca*. All our earnings went towards paying lawyers, intermediaries, everything we needed for my father's case. I remember that the year my father was in prison, I didn't get home even once. I didn't stop working. My brother went up to the *Altiplano* once a month to give my mother the money. She and the community worked for my father. For a whole year, we went back again and again to the law courts. The whole community helped get my father out. The landowners thought that my father was the king, the village chief, and that if they defeated the chief, they could defeat the whole community. But they soon realized that it wasn't like that. My father carried out the wishes of the community. He didn't make the laws. The most distressing thing for us was not being able to speak. That was when I told myself: 'I must learn to speak Spanish, so that we don't need intermediaries.' They asked the village for nineteen thousand *quetzals* to buy the land. The government asked for it through the INTA. They were just making fun of us, like saying peasants aren't worth a shit. They knew that peasants couldn't even dream of nineteen thousand *quetzals*. We had barely ten *centavos*. Saying nineteen thousand was like saying, 'Get off that land quick.' So my father came out of prison. He came out with such courage and such joy.

I remember when I left my maid's job, I said: 'Before I go and work in the *finca*, I'm going to visit my father in prison.' I went to the Santa Cruz prison. I'd never been in this prison in Santa Cruz del Quiché before. My father was there with the other prisoners. They were hitting each other, biting each other, and most of them were mad. He was there among all these people. Some of them had fleas. They ate with their hands and were constantly fighting. You could see blood on all their faces. I said: 'How can he be made to live here? If he's here for eighteen years, he'll go mad too.' I thought this was an enormous punishment, a cruel punishment to give my father. I said: 'I'll do everything I can to get him out, even if it means my mother has to suffer as a maid and all her work goes to pay for lawyers.' We were all willing to do it. I worked willingly, so did my brothers and sisters, waiting to hear about my father's case, to hear that he wouldn't have to go to the state prison. 'What could it possibly be like there,' I said, 'if the local prison is already hell?' My father, humble as he was, found a friend in prison. He was a man who'd been in prison for thirty years, I think. I don't know what he'd done. He did all his own things in prison, made his own food and everything. He was in charge of the prisoners' work. They made bags, typical *morrales*, baskets, all sorts of things, and this man paid them for their work. My father made friends with him and started eating well. He ate what his friend ate. He did his work, making *morrales* and other things, and he was paid for it. So from inside prison my father was helping us with money to pay to get him out. They made my father make an endless stream of statements. Every five days they took him before the judge and asked him the same things to see if he'd changed his mind or changed the statement justifying his case. That is to say, the judges had no valid justification, so they were looking for something to appease the landowners. The landowners arrived with more and more money to pressurize the judges into 'selling' my father and keeping him in prison like a criminal. We were very unhappy because we didn't see our mother or our father as we were working all the time in the *finca*.

In the end, we managed to get him out. Papá was in prison for a year and two months. His enemies were furious when he came out. He came out so happy and determined to fight. He said: 'Our ancestors were never cowardly. And prison doesn't eat people. Prison is a punishment for the poor, but it doesn't eat people. I must go home and go on fighting.' He didn't rest for a minute. That's how he maintained his contacts with the unions and gained their support.

We were very sad each time he said goodbye and went away. He said: 'Children, look after yourselves because if I don't come back, you have to continue my work. I don't do it alone: you are all part of it too. We'll never give the landowners satisfaction. I am very hopeful. We must go on fighting.' My father was away travelling for three months after he got out of prison. Then they kidnapped him and we said, 'They'll have finished him off.' In those days, they were criminals, but a different sort. The landowners' henchmen kidnapped my father near our house on the path going to town. One of my brothers was with him as we hardly ever let him go alone after they'd threatened so often to kill him. We were worried. So even if it meant less work, it was better for the community if someone went with him. He always went with a neighbour or one of his children. My brother escaped and immediately mobilized the whole village. They couldn't take him very far because we cut off the paths right away. We used weapons, our everyday weapons, for the first time. The people took machetes, sticks, hoes and stones to fight the guards. They would have beaten or killed any of them, they were so angry. Around midday we found my father. He'd been tortured and abandoned. There was no sign of the torturers but we knew they were the landowners' guards. My father was on the ground. They had torn off the hair on his head on one side. His skin was cut all over and they'd broken so many of his bones that he couldn't walk, lift himself or move a single finger. He looked as if he was dying. It was almost unbearable for us. The community made him one of those chairs the people use for carrying their wounded and we took him down to the town. He was almost cold. He was almost dead when we arrived at the health centre but they wouldn't attend to him there because the landowners had got there before us and paid them not to look after my father. They'd given the doctors money so none of them would see my father. All the doctors were *ladinos*. So my mother had to call an ambulance from Santa Cruz del Quiché, which took him to a hospital called San Juan de Dios in El Quiché. He arrived there half dead. They gave him serum and said he'd have to stay there for about nine months for some of the very badly damaged parts of his body to heal. They'd broken many of his bones and he was an old man so they wouldn't mend quickly. More bitterness for my mother. She had to go to El Quiché and look after my father. She worked there to pay for his medicine and some special care.

My brothers and sisters decided not to go down to the *finca* now. They said: 'From now on we'll stay here, even if we starve to death, because we have to cultivate our land. We'll try and grow enough crops to live on and not go to the *finca*.' My mother used to come once every fifteen days perhaps. She'd stay a day and then go back. We had a little sister and we looked after her so that my mother didn't have to take her with her. Some neighbours had a little goat which gave milk. We gave her goat's milk because we didn't have any cows. My little sister was about one and a half then.

Later on we received another threat. A message came saying that they were going to kidnap my father from the hospital. The community was frightened and said it would be better for him to come home and be looked after here where they couldn't kidnap him. We told my mother straight away. One of my brothers went to El Quiché to warn her about the message we'd received. With the help of the priests and nuns, who gave us money, we put my father in a secret place where the landowners couldn't find him. He was in the hospital of San Juan de Dios for six months and in the other place for another five months. After that he came home but he was in so much pain that he was never his old self again. He couldn't carry things; he couldn't walk very well and it was a big effort for him to walk to the town. At night he couldn't sleep because his bones ached and all the parts where he'd been beaten hurt him.

He returned home with a greater hate for his enemies. If before they'd been enemies of the community, now they were even more the enemies of my father. We hated all those people. We weren't only angry with the landowners, but with all the *ladinos*. To us, all the *ladinos* in that region were evil. In the hospital my father had talked to many people and found that we had many things in common with the Indians in other areas. This gave us a different view; another way of seeing things. After this my father went on working with the help of the unions. When he couldn't go to the capital, the unions looked after his affairs there. Whatever my father was organizing was done by one of the unions helping us.

Then in 1977, my father was put in prison again. They wouldn't leave us in peace. After my father came out of hospital and returned home, they kept on threatening him because they knew as long as the community was united they couldn't send their engineers to the villages. We would use machetes or stones. So they went on threatening my father and said they were going to catch him on the road again and kill him. But my father said: 'They are cowards, they just talk, they never do it.' But it worried us a lot because it would be very difficult for us if they did. That was when my father started advising us not to put our trust in him alone but in the whole community. 'I'm your father now,' he said, 'but afterwards the community will be your father.' He went on travelling and refused to keep quiet. He went on doing his work. It was in 1977 that they arrested him again and sent him to prison.

I was learning some Spanish at the time with the priests and nuns. I used to travel too. The priests helped me to go to the capital and stay with the nuns in a convent for a few days. When my father came out of hospital, I started travelling with him too, to get to know the circles he moved in. We were already thinking about my father's death. They could kill him any minute, so we needed to know where it was he went. I began accompanying him all the time. The community, the priests and some friends of my father helped us. Some Europeans were helping us too. They sent us a lot of money. They were people who had worked for a time teaching the peasants how to farm. But the way they plant isn't the way we do it. Indians reject the chemical fertilizers they tried to teach us about. They weren't really welcomed so they left, but they were very good friends of my father and helped us. They knew the problems of our village. They went back to their country but they still love Guatemala and help my father. We saved the money we received for my father's trips, all our trips, so that the village wouldn't have to contribute. At that time the INTA was asking for forty-five *quetzals* a month for papers and expenses. They never gave us a receipt. Who knows where all that money has gone!

When my father was arrested the second time, they considered him a political prisoner. The case against him was much worse this time. Now that he was a political prisoner, he was sentenced to life imprisonment. He was a communist, a subversive, they said. The same military commissioners as the first time came and got him from our house with clubs and took him to prison. They beat him and tied him up. He was a political prisoner. This was much worse for him. But by now the community was more aware of all these things. They had their own means of self-defence against the landowners. My brothers now spoke a bit of Spanish and my mother had also learned something from all the suffering, all the knocks, all the responsibility she'd had. We also had the support of the priests, the nuns, the unions and our community. It wasn't just my father now, it was a whole people behind him. My father was well known and well loved in many places so there was a big protest against my father's arrest. The unions especially pressed for his release. They still wanted witnesses, lawyers and all those things of course, but my father was soon out of prison. They started threatening him again even before he was out. They said if he continued his work, he would be assassinated and this time if they couldn't kill him they'd kill one of his children. This was his death sentence from the authorities. Of course, the authorities didn't exactly say that *they* would kill him, but they said the landowners would take care of it.

He was in prison for fifteen days. Then he came home. He was very proud and very happy because in prison he'd met another prisoner who really *was* a political prisoner. He was someone who defended the peasants and he told my father the peasants should unite and form a peasants' league to reclaim their lands. He said it wasn't our problem alone: our enemies weren't the landowners but the whole system. This man saw things more clearly than my father. So my father came back very proudly and said, 'We must fight the rich because they have become rich with our land, our crops.' That was when my father started to join up with other peasants and discussed the creation of the CUC with them. A lot of peasants had been discussing the committee but nothing concrete had been done, so my father joined the CUC and helped them understand things more clearly. My father didn't have to be told how to organize. Many peasants had been thinking of how they would form the CUC, so, in fact, the peasants had already shown they were unhappy with their situation. My father was in clandestinity from 1977 onwards; that is, he was in hiding. He left our house so he wouldn't involve us. He left his family and went to work with the peasants in other regions. He came back now and again but had to come via the mountains because if he passed through the town the landowners would know he was at home.

It was very sad for us that he couldn't live with us at home. He came at night and left at night. Or he spent several days at home but didn't go out. Our community suffered a great deal because they loved him as if he were their own father. Everything in our life is like a film. Constant suffering. We began thinking, with the help of other friends, other *compañeros*, that our enemies were not only the landowners who lived near us, and above all not just the landowners who forced us to work and paid us little. It was not only now we were being killed; they had been killing us since we were children, through malnutrition, hunger, poverty. We started thinking about the roots of the problem and came to the conclusion that everything stemmed from the ownership of land. The best land was not in our hands. It belonged to the big landowners. Every time they see that we have new land, they try to throw us off it or steal it from us in other ways.

XVI

PERIOD OF REFLECTION ON THE ROAD TO FOLLOW

'An obscure vision, obscure because he dared not free it from his consciousness and examine it; he was content to half look at it, and seek no explanation.'
—Miguel Angel Asturias, *Men of Maize*

I'd like to say here, that I wasn't the only important one. I was part of a family, just like all my brothers and sisters. The whole community was important. We used to discuss many of the community's problems together, especially when someone was ill and we couldn't buy medicine, because we were getting poorer and poorer. We'd start discussing and heaping insults on the rich who'd made us suffer for so long. It was about then I began learning about politics. I tried to talk to people who could help me sort my ideas out. I wanted to know what the world was like on the other side. I knew the *finca*, I knew the *Altiplano*. But what I didn't know was about the problems of the other Indians in Guatemala. I didn't know the problems other groups had holding onto their land. I knew there were lots of other Indians in other parts of the country, because I'd been meeting them in the *finca* since I was a child, but although we all worked together, we didn't know the names of the towns they came from, or how they lived, or what they ate. We just imagined that they were like us. Well, I started thinking about my childhood, and I came to the conclusion that I hadn't had a childhood at all. I was never a child. I hadn't been to school, I hadn't had enough food to grow properly, I had nothing. I asked myself: 'How is this possible?' I compared it to the life of the children of rich people I'd seen. How they ate. Even their dogs. They even taught their dogs only to recognize their masters and reject the maids. All these things were jumbled up in my mind, I couldn't separate my ideas. That's when I began making friends from other villages in Uspantán. I asked them: 'What do you eat? How do you make your breakfast? What do you have for lunch? What do you eat for supper?' And yes, they said the same: 'Well, in the morning we eat *tortillas* with salt and a little *pinol*. At midday, our mother brings *tortillas* and any plants she finds in the fields.' 'At night we eat *tortillas* with chile,' they said, 'chile with *tortillas*, and then we go to sleep.' So everything was the same. It gave me a lot to think about. I have to tell you that I didn't learn my politics at school. I just tried to turn my own experience into something which was common to a whole people. I was also very happy when I realized that it wasn't just my problem; that I wasn't the only little girl to have worried about not wanting to grow up. We were all worried about the harsh life awaiting us.

The CUC started growing; it spread like fire among the peasants in Guatemala. We began to understand that the root of all our problems was exploitation. That there were rich and poor and that the rich exploited the poor – our sweat, our labour. That's how they got richer and richer. The fact that we were always waiting in offices, always bowing to the authorities, was part of the discrimination we Indians suffered. So was the cultural oppression which tries to divide us by taking away our traditions and prevents unity among our people. The situation got worse when the murderous generals came to power, although I didn't actually know who was the president at the time. I began to know them from 1974 on, when General Kjell Laugerud came to power. He came to our region and said: 'We're going to solve the land problem.

The land belongs to you. You cultivate the land and I will share it out among you.' We trusted him. I was at the meeting when Kjell Laugerud spoke. And what did he give us? My father tortured and imprisoned. I know it was because he'd discovered all their underhand tricks. He hated those people. He used to say: 'What do they know about hunger when they suck the blood of our people every day?' It angered me too not to have my elder brothers with us, not to know them, because they'd died of hunger, of malnutrition, of not having enough to eat in the *finca*. I said: 'If they'd had enough to eat, my brothers would still be alive with us today. They didn't die because they wanted to.'

Later I had the opportunity of meeting other Indians, Achi Indians, the group that lives the closest to us. And I got to know some Mam Indians too. They all told me: 'The rich are bad. But not all *ladinos* are bad.' And I started wondering: 'Could it be that not all *ladinos* are bad?' I used to think they were all bad. But *they* said that they lived with poor *ladinos*. There were poor *ladinos* as well as rich *ladinos*, and they were exploited as well. That's when I began recognizing exploitation. I kept on going down to the *finca* but now I really wanted to find out, to prove if that was true and learn all the details. There were poor *ladinos* in the *finca*. They worked the same, and their children's bellies were swollen like my little brother's. So I said: 'It must be true, then, that not all *ladinos* are bad.' I was just beginning to speak a little Spanish in those days and I began to talk to them. I said to one poor *ladino*: 'You're a poor *ladino*, aren't you?' And he nearly hit me. He said: 'What do you know about it, Indian?' I wondered: 'Why is it that when I say poor *ladinos* are like us, I'm spurned?' I didn't know then the same system which tries to isolate us Indians also puts up barriers between Indians and *ladinos*. I knew that all *ladinos* rejected us but I didn't know why. I was more confused. I still thought all *ladinos* were bad. Soon afterwards, I was with the nuns and we went to a village in Uspantán where mostly *ladinos* live. The nun asked a little boy if they were poor and he said: 'Yes, we're poor but we're not Indians.' That stayed with me. The nun didn't notice, she went on talking. She was foreign, she wasn't Guatemalan. She asked someone else the same question and he said: 'Yes, we're poor but we're not Indians.' It was very painful for me to accept that an Indian was inferior to a *ladino*. I kept on worrying about it. It's a big barrier they've sown between us, between Indian and *ladino*. I didn't understand it.

In our village, we went on working. I still didn't have a clear idea of who exactly our enemies were. We began putting safety measures into practice in our village. We used the methods our forefathers had used, and which our own grandparents told us about. Our forefathers passed them down to us. We said that if the landowners' soldiers come, we'll kill them right here. That's when we decided to use violence. I remember that it was my job to explain to the children of the community that our situation had nothing to do with fate but was something which had been imposed on us. I taught them that they had to defend themselves against it, to defend our parents' rights. I'd have a sort of political chat with the children, although I wasn't very clear about our situation politically. But my experiences told me what I needed. I didn't need speeches or courses or anything like that. I didn't have to read books because my experiences were born of suffering. I, who'd hardly had a pair of shoes by the time I was fifteen. Shoes: they protected feet against the heat and the stones. But, all the same, I didn't really know what to do with them.

I didn't sleep much during this period, thinking about the future. What would it be like if all the Indians rose up and took the land and the crops away from the landowners? Would they get weapons and kill us? I had incredible dreams. But, in fact, they weren't just empty dreams. My dreams came true when we started organizing. Children had to behave like grown-ups. We women had to play our part as women in the community, together with our parents, our brothers, our neighbours. We all had to unite, all of us together. We held meetings. We began by asking for a community school. We didn't have a school. We collected signatures. I was involved in this. I played a key role because I was learning Spanish and because the priests knew me and so did some of my father's other friends. I asked for help wherever I could, and I got it. We had a *ladino* friend in the town who gave us a little money, both for my father and us at home. But we didn't use this money for ourselves: we shared it with the community. We were now getting organized. We already had various organisations: children's groups, young people's groups, women's groups, catechists' groups, and we began strengthening these groups. We wanted to make plans for us all to learn Spanish. I spent one afternoon teaching the children the bit of Spanish I knew. Not to write, of course, because I couldn't write. I couldn't read or write. But to teach them to speak as we spoke in our language.

At the end of 1977, I decided to join a more formal group – a group of peasants in Huehuetenango. It was a clandestine group and we'd go down to the *finca* and work among the workers in the *finca*. The *compañeros* of the CUC worked among them too. And yet, I still hadn't reached the rewarding stage of participating fully, as an Indian first, and then as a woman, a peasant, a Christian, in the struggle of all my people. That's when I started being more involved.

My father went on with his work. He used to say: 'My children, there are rich people and there are poor. The rich have become rich because they took what our ancestors had away from them, and now they grow fat on the sweat of our labour. We know this is true because we live it every day, not because someone else tells us. The rich try to obstruct us. The rich come from over there, where the *ladinos*' government is. It's the government of the rich, the landowners.' We began seeing things more clearly and, as I said, it was not difficult for us to understand that we had to join together in the struggle, because for us this was something real, something we'd all experienced.

I began travelling to different areas, discussing everything. I must say one thing, and it's not to denigrate them, because the priests have done a lot for us. It's not to undervalue the good things they have taught us; but they also taught us to accept many things, to be passive, to be a dormant people. Their religion told us it was a sin to kill while we were being killed. They told us that God is up there and that God had a kingdom for the poor. This confused me because I'd been a catechist since I was a child and had had a lot of ideas put in my head. It prevents us from seeing the real truth of how our people live. I tried to get rid of my doubts by asking the nuns: 'What would happen if we rose up against the rich?' The nuns tried to avoid the question. I don't know if it was intentional or not, but in any case no-one answered my question. I was very disturbed. In my community's terms, I was already a grown woman, and I was very ashamed at being so confused, when so many of my village understood so much better than I. But their ideas were very pure because they had never been outside their community. *We'd* been down to the *fincas*, but *they* hadn't known anything different. Going to the capital in a lorry brings about a change in an Indian, which he suffers inside himself. That's why my little brothers and my brothers and sisters understood more clearly than I did.

XVII

SELF-DEFENCE IN THE VILLAGE

*'... They began to fulfil the destiny which was concealed in
the marrow of their bones ...'*

—Popol Vuh

My time working as a maid, my long stay in the *finca* without going home, and my parents' problems, made me very confused. Yes, I was very confused. I went through a sort of painful change within myself. It wasn't so difficult for the rest of them at home to understand what was real and what was false. But I found it very hard. What did exploitation mean to me? I began to see why conditions are so different. Why do they reject us? Why is the Indian not accepted? Why was it that the land used to belong to us? Used our ancestors to live here? Why don't outsiders accept Indian ways? This is where discrimination lies! Catholic Action too submitted us to tremendous oppression. It kept our people dormant while others took advantage of our passivity. I finally began to see all this clearly. And that's when I started working as an organizer. No-one taught me how to organize because, having been a catechist, I already knew. We began forming groups of women who wanted to join the struggle. And I saw that teaching the children how to act when the enemy came was part of the struggle too. The moment I learned to identify our enemies was very important for me. For me now the landowner was a big enemy, an evil one. The soldier too was a criminal enemy. And so were all the rich. We began using the term 'enemies', because we didn't have the notion of enemy in our culture, until those people arrived to exploit us, oppress us and discriminate against us. In our community we are all equal. We all have to help one another and share the little we have between us. There is no superior and inferior. But we realized that in Guatemala there was something superior and something inferior and that *we* were the inferior. The *ladinos* behave like a superior race. Apparently there was a time when the *ladinos* used to think we weren't people at all, but a sort of animal. All this became clear to me.

I threw myself into my work and I told myself we had to defeat the enemy. We began to organize. Our organization had no name. We began by each of us trying to remember the tricks our ancestors used. They say they used to set traps in their houses, in the path of the *conquistadores*, the Spaniards. Our ancestors were good fighters, they were real men. It's not true what white people say, that our ancestors didn't defend themselves. They used ambushes. Our grandparents used to tell us about it, especially my grandfather when he saw that we were beginning to talk about defending ourselves against the landowners, and wondering if we had to rid ourselves of the landowners before we'd be left in peace. We said: 'If they threaten us, why don't we threaten the landowner?' My grandfather gave us a lot of support. There was always a lot of discussion in our house, because my brothers reached their own conclusions, I reached mine, and everyone came to their own conclusions. My grandfather said: 'Yes, my children, you have to defend yourselves. Our ancestors defended themselves. The white men are telling lies when they say we are passive. They fought too. And we, why don't we fight with the same arms the landowners use?' If an elderly person tells us this, then it must be true.

The first step the community took was to have my father, the village leader, living in the centre of the community. Everyone felt my father should live in the centre. When Kjell Laugerud divided our small pieces of land into plots, some people had to go and live on one side of the village, some on the other, in different plots. So we were some way away from our neighbours. What my brothers and I decided (my father happened to be with us at the time too) was that we would share the piece of land we had on the flat ground, on the plain. All the members of the community who lived some way off could come down and we'd live together, or with our houses close together so that we could call to each other when the landowners' people came. This was the first step we took. But what were we going to tell people? They knew we had to defend ourselves against the landowners, but they didn't understand that one day the repression would reach us and large numbers of us would be killed. We held a meeting and discussed it with everybody. We talked about sharing out the piece of land behind our house so that our neighbours could live closer. We also asked other neighbours to share their land too. We said that in two months we could have all our neighbours' houses near ours. This proposition was put to the community: 'Are you willing to leave your houses and live near us so that when the landowners come, we'll all be together?'

We were making these plans when a village near ours got a taste of the repression. The repression reached San Pablo, a village nearby. They kidnapped the community's leaders – the elected representatives, the chief catechist, and their families. They took away some other catechists too. Men, women and children were taken. They too were fighting a landowner, but they weren't organized yet. This served as an example for us, and my brothers and I, and our neighbours began dividing up the work to be done. Everyone went to cut palm leaves to build the new houses. Some prepared the ground for the houses, others collected leaves, and others cut poles for the walls. We shared the work out. We built the houses close together.

And one day a troop of soldiers arrived. It was the first time we'd seen so many troops in the village; there were ninety of them. We couldn't resist but we did nothing to provoke them either. The community knew more or less what to do if any one of us was taken. The idea from the beginning was that they either left us alone or they'd have to kill all of us. We wouldn't let a single *compañero* be taken away from the village. That's what we did. The soldiers stayed for two weeks and used the community house where we carried out all our ceremonies, and held our meetings. They lived there. At night they went into our maize fields to dig up our potatoes, cut off the maize cobs and young beans, and ate very well. They cut any cobs they wanted. For us this was violating our culture, because we Indians have to perform a ceremony before picking the cob, the fruit of the earth and of the peasants' labour. We were very angry but we didn't show our anger because there were ninety of them, capable of massacring us all. They were armed.

One night around ten o'clock, we were getting ready to go to sleep when my mother saw something black moving around at the back of our house, where we have a little patch of potatoes. She thought it was one of our neighbour's animals and began throwing sticks at it. It was a soldier stealing potatoes. That was the first time my mother got aggressive with any of the soldiers; without a thought to whether she'd be killed or not. She had all our dogs with her. We had a lot of dogs then because all our neighbours had decided to buy another dog each to defend themselves with. So my mother went out with her dogs and her sticks. The soldier said: 'No, no, don't, I'm a person.' And my mother said: 'If you want to eat, why don't you go and work? You're protecting the rich and they don't even feed you. Here we've worked hard for our crops, young man. Leave my things alone or I'll beat you with this stick.' So the soldier left the potatoes and went running off in a hurry. The next day they left. They went away.

After they left, the village got together to decide what to do with our maize fields. We would forget our customs, our ceremonies, for a while, and plan our security first. Afterwards we'd go back to the things we want to do. The community decided: 'No-one must discover our community's secret now, *compañeros*. It's secret what we are doing here. The enemy must not know, nor must our other neighbours.' Everyone agreed. We began teaching our children to be discreet. They're usually discreet anyway, but we advised them not to say a single word to any children who weren't from our village about what their parents were doing. We prepared our signals. Our signals were to be all the everyday things we use, all natural things. I remember that we performed a ceremony before beginning our self-defence measures. It was a village ceremony where we asked the Lord of the natural world, our one God, to help us and give us permission to use his creations of nature to defend ourselves with. The ceremony was conducted with a lot of feeling, because, well, we knew that it was up to the community, up to our measures of self-defence, whether two, three, four or five of our members would be kidnapped, tortured or murdered. The following day everyone came with ideas of how to defend themselves. Some brought stones, others machetes, others sticks, others their work tools. The women brought salt, hot water, etc. We put all our ideas together. How would we use them? One *compañero* would say: 'I think that this is useful for defence. How can we use it?' Another would say: 'This is what I have in mind . . .'. And he explains what *he* would do if they came. Each person contributed something. Then we organized very carefully who would plan the best ways to use the community's ideas and who would teach them. How would we teach the children? Which duties would the children have? Who would be in charge of seeing that the women played their special part? When would we hold a general assembly to evaluate all this? We began to get a much better idea of how to organize our community.

I was enthralled by all this. As I said before, when the government parcelled the land out and tried to create divisions within the community – everyone with their own plot, their own bit of land – there wasn't enough land for us all to live in one place together. They gave us plots which were very separate, a long way from each other, and many neighbours lived quite a distance away, and the houses were very far apart. We lived like this with the land divided up for about two or three years. They used this method to separate us but the little plots of land weren't big enough to work. We had barely a *manzana* of land each. It was all divided up. What all the neighbours did was to give some of their land to the community as a whole, but even so our houses were still very far apart. So when the repression started coming closer, we realized we had to put our houses together to confront the soldiers when they came to repress our village. It wasn't only the villages nearest to us that had been attacked, there'd been massacres in other communities too. Chajul, Bebaj, Cotzal, were the first to suffer the repression.

We had to build houses for our neighbours between us, and it took about two or three months before everyone was living together. We did it so as to make our self-defence measures more effective. When they were finished, we started developing our security system and each member of the community had special duties to carry out. The children, the women, the young people, the adults, and even the old people had their role to play. Our animals, especially the dogs, help us with our defences too. That's when we started preparing things we had to do secretly, like the traps. No-one must know about the traps in our villages. But we all had to know where our neighbours' traps were, otherwise they might capture one of us instead of a soldier or a landowner's bodyguard. One of our *compañeros*, or perhaps a group, took charge of checking the traps which were already there and putting them in working order. These traps were initially meant for catching the mice that eat the cobs, and for the mountain animals which come down and eat our maize. We gave these traps another use – catching the army. They were usually large ditches with invisible nets so that neither animals nor soldiers could see them. They might also be something metal to stop the army. In any case, we know the army can't come in lorries, or bicycles or cars because there are no roads as far as our village. They have to come on foot along the one path. We'd already seen that the army was cowardly and didn't dare come too far into the mountains. They're frightened because they think there are guerrillas there. Those poor soldiers, they don't even know what a guerrilla is, so they imagine he is a monster, like a fierce bird or a sort of animal. This makes them afraid of going into the mountains. They have to come along paths and we set traps on all the main paths leading to our village. We don't set only one trap, we set several because one might fail. This was our first experience with traps so we had to set three or more on every path. In addition to the traps on the path, there were more traps in each house, so that if the army gets as far as the village by another path, he will still get a shock in each *compañero*'s house. Each house also had an emergency exit for every *compañero*, every one of us.

I was helping with the security measures, by setting traps and all the other things for our defence. But at the same time I was involved in organizing and educating the *compañeros*. We had to do whatever work the community wanted, what was most needed at the time. And that was teaching many of the *compañeros* to do the same job we did. We tried to avoid all working at the same thing and changed round all the time so that everyone got experience of the different duties. We began organizing the children, the women, the men. We started using our safety measures, the emergency exits for example. We decided who'd leave first, who second, third and last, if the army took the village. At first, when we hadn't much experience and hadn't much idea of how to confront the enemy, we planned that the women should leave first with their children – all the kids – and that the men should stay until the last. But we found that in practice that system proved not to be very effective and we were constantly changing our ways of escaping. What happened was that the women and children were safer than the men because the army showed them a bit more respect. It was usually the men they kidnapped, especially the village leaders. So because of this, our men would leave first and the women would stay behind to take the beatings. It wasn't that we had a set plan, with a theory and each role worked out, and that was that. No, we were putting new ideas into practice the whole time and practising the things we had to do together. And then, when people were least expecting it, we'd cause some confusion in the village to see how we'd react. We tested our traps and our emergency exits. We realized that, when the army arrived, it wouldn't be very sensible to escape into the mountains in single file along the paths. So we dug large ditches and underground paths. Whenever a village leader gave the signal, we'd all leave and gather in one place. We broke with many of our cultural procedures by doing this but we knew it was the way to save ourselves. We knew what to do and most of the village was ready to follow us. The community elects its leader but everything he does has to be approved by the others. What the community does not approve cannot be carried through. Everyone plays an equal part: men, women, and the children as well. One of the first decisions taken was that there should be a signal for when we were to leave the village. That is a very serious signal. It's only given when the enemy is close by. And the signal will change according to which side the enemy is approaching from. There is one signal for the day and another for night-time, because at night we can't see where the enemy is coming from. We got together with other villages and built a house at each of the four corners from which the enemy could approach. Some of us would take it in turns to keep watch at night and others would keep watch during the day.

This is something that happened while I was in the village; it was the first time we put our self-defence measures into practice. The soldiers who'd stayed in our village for fifteen days left, but they left with the idea that we were organized. They were already suspicious of certain things while they were in the village, in spite of the fact that our organization was totally secret. They came back one night and our whole network of information was already in operation. We'd built a camp for the village so that if, at any time, we couldn't live in the village, we could go to the camp. That's when we found our friends from the natural world even more useful – the plants, the trees and the mountains. Our community began getting used to an even harder life in case we couldn't go back to the village for fifteen or twenty days. It was better than being massacred. We began practising going to the camp to sleep at night whether there were any enemies or not. Our *compañeros* would give us the signal, from far away. So, we'd set traps on the path, and the traps in the houses, and get all the preparations ready. And also on each path, one *compañero*'s house was empty, except for the dogs. If the soldiers came at night, the dogs would bark and follow them. As long as the dogs kept on barking, we knew that the soldiers were still there. That's how our dogs helped us. We knew when the army was in the village. They barked at whatever time of day the army left. That was the signal that the army had left the village.

That first night they arrived, they went into the houses and found no-one. They beat the dogs, killed some of them, and left. We said to ourselves: 'They went into our houses and they are going to go on looking for us. So now we have good cause to find new methods.' That's how the community itself looks for ways of improving certain things that weren't any good. We did everything together because there were no longer specific tasks for men and others for women. Now, going to the fields or building a neighbour's house, or anything, was all done communally. We didn't have our own individual things, because this would disperse the community and when the enemy came, he'd be able to kidnap some of us. So we worked together. The women took turns with the men to keep watch at night. Before doing any of these tasks, we had to be sure how we were going to do them. We thought of what would happen if at any time, we couldn't use our traps, or rather that they didn't work. If we couldn't use our escape route or any other of our security measures, we should at least have our weapons ready – the weapons of the people: machetes, stones, hot water, chile, salt. We found a use for all these things. We knew how to throw stones, we knew how to throw salt in someone's face – how to do it effectively. This could only work against the paramilitary forces, from the regiment, because we knew that we had no answer for machine guns. But if the police came with their guns, our weapons can be effective. We've often used lime. Lime is very fine and you have to aim it in a certain way for it to go into someone's eyes. We learned to do it through practice; we practised taking aim and watching where the enemy is. You can blind a policeman by throwing lime in his face. And with stones for instance, you have to throw it at the enemy's head, at his face. If you throw it at his back, it will be effective but not as much as at other parts of the body. These are things we're practising the whole time in our village. And if we're stuck in our homes, we can resort to throwing hot water at them. The whole village must be prepared, in one place and with all their materials for self-defence ready. The whole family must know where an uncle's or a neighbour's things are in case they can't use their own. We need to be on the constant lookout for new techniques. But everything must have a reason or we might do things we want to, but without knowing why we're doing them. Our main weapon, however, is the Bible. We began to study the Bible as a text through which to educate our village. There are many wonderful stories in the Bible.

XVIII

THE BIBLE AND SELF-DEFENCE: THE EXAMPLES OF JUDITH, MOSES AND DAVID

'... when the strangers who came from the East arrived, when they arrived; the ones who brought Christianity which ended the power in the East, and made the heavens cry and filled the maize bread of the Katún with sadness ...'
—Chilam Balam

'Their chief was not defeated by young warriors, nor wounded by sons of Titans. It was Judith, the daughter of Marari, who disarmed him with the beauty of her face.'
—Book of Judith

We began to study the Bible as our main text. Many relationships in the Bible are like those we have with our ancestors, our ancestors whose lives were very much like our own. The important thing for us is that we started to identify that reality with our own. That's how we began studying the Bible. It's not something you memorize, it's not just to be talked about and prayed about, and nothing more. It also helped to change the image we had, as Catholics and Christians: that God is up there and that God has a great kingdom for we the poor, yet never thinking of our own reality as a reality that we were actually living. But by studying the scriptures, we did. Take Exodus for example, that's one we studied and analyzed. It talks a lot about the life of Moses who tried to lead his people from oppression, and did all he could to free his people. We compare the Moses of those days with ourselves, the 'Moses' of today. Exodus is about the life of a man, the life of Moses.

We began looking for texts which represented each one of us. We tried to relate them to our Indian culture. We took the example of Moses for the men, and we have the example of Judith, who was a very famous woman in her time and appears in the Bible. She fought very hard for her people and made many attacks against the king they had then, until she finally had his head. She held her victory in her hand, the head of the king. This gave us a vision, a stronger idea of how we Christians must defend ourselves. It made us think that a people could not be victorious without a just war. We Indians do not dream of great riches, we want only enough to live on. There is also the story of David, a little shepherd boy who appears in the Bible, who was able to defeat the king of those days, King Goliath. This story is the example for the children. This is how we look for stories and psalms which teach us how to defend ourselves from our enemies. I remember taking examples from all the texts which helped the community to understand their situation better. It's not only now that there are great kings, powerful men, people who hold power in their hands. Our ancestors suffered under them too. This is how we identify with the lives of our ancestors who were conquered by a great desire for power – our ancestors were murdered and tortured because they were Indians. We began studying more deeply and, well, we came to a conclusion. That being a Christian means thinking of our brothers around us, and that every one of our Indian race has the right to eat. This reflects what God himself said, that on this earth we have a right to what we need. The Bible was our principal text for study as Christians and it showed us what the role of a Christian is. I became a catechist as a little girl and I studied the Bible, hymns, the scriptures, but only very superficially. One of the things Catholic Action put in our heads is that everything is sinful. But we came round to asking ourselves: 'If everything is sinful, why is it that the landowner kills humble peasants who don't even harm the natural world? Why do they take our lives?' When I first became a catechist, I thought that there was a God and that we had to serve him. I thought God was up there and that he had a kingdom for the poor. But we realized that it is not God's will that we should live in suffering, that God did not give us that destiny, but that men on earth have imposed this suffering, poverty, misery and discrimination on us. We even got the idea of using our own everyday weapons, as the only solution left to us.

I am a Christian and I participate in this struggle as a Christian. For me, as a Christian, there is one important thing. That is the life of Christ. Throughout his life Christ was humble. History tells us he was born in a little hut. He was persecuted and had to form a band of men so that his seed would not disappear. They were his disciples, his apostles. In those days, there was no other way of defending himself or Christ would have used it against his oppressors, against his enemies. He even gave his life. But Christ did not die, because generations and generations have followed him. And that's exactly what we understood when our first catechists fell. They're dead but our people keep their memory alive through our struggle against the government, against an enemy who oppresses us. We don't need very much advice, or theories, or documents: life has been our teacher. For my part, the horrors I have suffered are enough for me. And I've also felt in the deepest part of me what discrimination is, what exploitation is. It is the story of my life. In my work I've often gone hungry. If I tried to recount the number of times I'd gone hungry in my life, it would take a very long time. When you understand this, when you see your own reality, a hatred grows inside you for those oppressors that make the people suffer so. As I said, and I say it again, it is not fate which makes us poor. It's not because we don't work, as the rich say. They say: 'Indians are poor because they don't work, because they're always asleep.' But

I know from experience that we're outside ready for work at three in the morning. It was this that made us decide to fight. This is what motivated me, and also motivated many others. Above all the mothers and fathers. They remember their children. They remember the ones they would like to have with them now but who died of malnutrition, or intoxication in the *fincas*, or had to be given away because they had no way of looking after them. It has a long history. And it's precisely when we look at the lives of Christians in the past that we see what our role as Christians should be today. I must say, however, that I think even religions are manipulated by the system, by those same governments you find everywhere. They use them through their ideas or through their methods. I mean, it's clear that a priest never works in the *fincas*, picking cotton or coffee. He wouldn't know what picking cotton was. Many priests don't even know what cotton is. But our reality teaches us that, as Christians, we must create a Church of the poor, that we don't need a Church imposed from outside which knows nothing of hunger. We recognize that the system has wanted to impose on us: to divide us and keep the poor dormant. So we take some things and not others. As far as sins go, it seems to me that the concept of the Catholic religion, or any other more conservative religion than Catholicism, is that God loves the poor and has a wonderful paradise in Heaven for the poor, so the poor must accept the life they have on Earth. But as Christians, we have understood that being a Christian means refusing to accept all the injustices which are committed against our people, refusing to accept the discrimination committed against a humble people who barely know what eating meat is but who are treated worse than horses. We've learned all this by watching what has happened in our lives. This awakening of the Indians didn't come, of course, from one day to the next, because Catholic Action and other religions and the system itself have all tried to keep us where we were. But I think that unless a religion springs from within the people themselves, it is a weapon of the system. So, naturally, it wasn't at all difficult for our community to understand all this and the reasons for us to defend ourselves, because this is the reality we live.

As I was saying, for us the Bible is our main weapon. It has shown us the way. Perhaps those who call themselves Christians, but who are really only Christians in theory, won't understand why we give the Bible the meaning we do. But that's because they haven't lived as we have. And also perhaps because they can't analyze it. I can assure you that any one of my community, even though he's illiterate and has to have it read to him and translated into his language, can learn many lessons from it, because he has no difficulty understanding what reality is and what the difference is between the paradise up above, in Heaven, and the reality of our people here on Earth. We do this because we feel it is the duty of Christians to create the kingdom of God on Earth among our brothers. This kingdom will exist only when we all have enough to eat, when our children, brothers, parents don't have to die from hunger and malnutrition. That will be the 'Glory', a kingdom for we who have never known it. I'm only talking about the Catholic Church in general terms because, in fact, many priests came to our region and were anti-communists, but nevertheless understood that the people weren't communists but hungry; not communists, but exploited by the system. And they joined our people's struggle too, they opted for the life we Indians live. Of course many priests call themselves Christians when they're only defending their own petty interests and they keep themselves apart from the people so as not to endanger these interests. All the better for us, because we know very well that we don't need a king in a palace but a brother who lives with us. We don't need a leader to show us where God is, to say whether he exists or not, because, through our own conception of God, we know there is a God and that, as the father of us all, he does not wish even one of his children to die, or be unhappy, or have no joy in life. We believe that, when we started using the Bible, when we began studying it in terms of our reality, it was because we found in it a document to guide us. It's not that the document itself brings about the change, it's more that each one of us learns to understand his reality and wants to devote himself to others. More than anything else, it was a form of learning for us. Perhaps if we'd had other means to learn, things would have been different. But we understood that any element in nature can change man when he is ready for change. We believe the Bible is a necessary weapon for our people. Today I can say that it is a struggle which cannot be stopped. Neither the governments nor imperialism can stop it because it is a struggle of hunger and poverty. Neither the government nor imperialism can say: 'Don't be hungry,' when we are all dying of hunger.

To learn about self-defence, as I was saying, we studied the Bible. We began fashioning our own weapons. We knew very well that the government, those cowardly soldiers . . . perhaps I shouldn't talk of them so harshly, but I can't find another word for them. Our weapons were very simple. And at the same time, they weren't so simple when we all started using them, when the whole village was armed. As I said before, the soldiers arrived one night. Our people were not in their homes. They'd left the village and gone to the camp. They made sure that we hadn't abandoned the village altogether but thought it would be better to occupy it in the daytime. So sometime later, when we weren't expecting them, about fifteen days later, our lookouts saw the army approaching. We were in the middle of building houses for our neighbours. We needed some more huts there. We had two lookouts. One was supposed to warn the community and the other had to delay or stop the soldiers entering. They were aware that they might have to give their lives for the community. At a time like this, if someone can't escape, he must be ready to accept death. The army arrived, and the first two to enter wore civilian clothes. But our children can easily recognize soldiers, by the way they walk, and dress, and everything about them, so the lookouts knew they were soldiers in disguise. They asked the names of certain *compañeros* in the community so they could take them away, kidnap them. One of the lookouts got away and came to warn the village that the enemy was nearby. We asked him if he was sure and he said: 'Yes, they are soldiers, two of them. But as I was coming up here I saw others coming, further off, with olive-green uniforms.' The whole community left the village straight away and gathered in one place. We were very worried because the other lookout didn't appear. They were capable of having kidnapped him. But he did turn up in the end and told us how many soldiers there were, what each one was like, what sort of weapons they had, how many in the vanguard and the rearguard. This information helped us decide what to do, because it was daytime and we hadn't set our traps. We said: 'What are we going to do with this army?' They came into the village and began beating our dogs and killing our animals. They went into the houses and looted them. They went crazy looking for us all over the place. Then we asked: 'Who is willing to risk their lives now?' I, my brothers and some other neighbours immediately put up our hands. We planned to give the army a shock and to show them we were organized and weren't just waiting passively for them. We had less than half an hour to plan how we were going to capture some weapons. We chose some people – the ones who'd go first, second, third, fourth – to surprise the enemy. How would we do it? We couldn't capture all ninety soldiers who'd come to the village, but we could get the rearguard. My village is a long way from the town, up in the mountains. You have to go over the mountains to get to another village. We have a little path to the village just wide enough for horses . . . and there are big rivers nearby so that the path isn't straight. It bends a lot. So we said, 'Let's wait for the army on one of those bends and when the soldiers pass, we'll ambush the last one.' We knew we were risking our lives but we knew that this example would benefit the village very much because the army would stop coming and searching the village all the time. And that's what we did.

We chose a *compañera*, a very young girl, the prettiest in the village. She was risking her life, and she was risking being raped as well. Nevertheless, she said: 'I know very well that if this is my part in the struggle, I have to do it. If this is how I contribute to the community, I'll do it.' So this *compañera* goes ahead on another path to a place that the army has to pass on their way to the village. That's where we prepared the ambush. We didn't have firearms, we had only our people's weapons. We'd invented a sort of Molotov cocktail by putting petrol in a lemonade bottle with a few iron filings, mixed with oil, and a wick to light it. So if the army got one of us, or if we couldn't do anything else, we'd set fire to them. This cocktail could burn two or three soldiers because it could land on them and burn their clothes. We had catapults too, or rather, they were the ones we'd always used to protect the maize fields from the birds that would come into the fields and eat the cobs when they were growing. The catapults could shoot stones a long way and if your aim is good it lands where you want it to. We had machetes, stones, sticks, chile and salt – all the different people's weapons. We had none of the weapons the army had. The community decided that the young girl who went on ahead would try to flirt with the last soldier and try to make him stop and talk to her. We all had numbers: who would be the first to jump, who would get him off balance, who would frighten him and who would disarm him. Each of us had a special task in capturing the soldier.

First came the ones without weapons – they were members of the secret police, soldiers in disguise. Then came the others. The whole troop. They were about two metres away when the last one came. Our *compañera* came along the path. She paid no attention to the others. It was a miracle they didn't rape her, because when soldiers come to our area they usually catch girls and rape them – they don't care who they are or where they're from. The *compañera* was ready to endure anything. When she came to the last soldier, she asked him where they'd been. And the soldier began telling her: 'We went to that village. Do you know what's happened to the people?' The *compañera* said: 'No, I don't know.' And he said: 'We've been twice and there's no-one, but we know they live there.' Then one of our neighbours jumped onto the path, another came up behind the soldier. My job was to jump onto the path as well. Between us we got the soldier off balance. One of us said: 'Don't move, hands up.' And the soldier thought there was a gun pointing at his head or his back. Whatever he thought, he did nothing. Another *compañero* said: 'Drop your weapon'. And he dropped it. We took his belt off and checked his bag. We took his grenades away, his rifle, everything. I thought it was really funny, it's something I'll never forget, because we didn't know how to use it. We took his rifle, his big rifle, and a pistol, and we didn't even know how to use the pistol. I remember that I took the soldier's pistol away and stood in front as if I knew how to use it but I didn't know anything. He could have taken it off me because I couldn't use it. But, anyway, we led him away at gunpoint. We made him go up through the mountains so that if the others came back they wouldn't find the path. If they had it would have been a massacre. Two *compañeras* of about forty-five and a fifty-year-old *compañero* had taken part in the ambush. The little *compañera* who'd attracted the soldier was about fourteen.

We took the disarmed soldier to my house, taking all the necessary precautions. We blindfolded him so that he wouldn't recognize the house he was going to. We got him lost. We took him a round-about way so that he'd lose his sense of direction. We finally arrived back. I found it really funny, I couldn't stop laughing because we didn't know how to use the gun. We were very happy, the whole community was happy. When we got near the camp, the whole community was waiting for us. We arrived with our captured soldier. We reached my house. He stayed there for a long time. We took his uniform off and gave him an old pair of trousers and an old shirt so that if his fellow soldiers came back – we tried to keep him tied up – they wouldn't know he was a soldier. We also thought that those clothes could help us confuse the other soldiers later on. Then came a very beautiful part when all the mothers in the village begged the soldier to take a message back to the army, telling all the soldiers there to think of our ancestors. The soldier was an Indian from another ethnic group. The women asked him how he could possibly have become a soldier, an enemy of his own race, his own people, the Indian race. Our ancestors never set bad examples like that. They begged him to be the light within his camp. They explained to him that bearing a son and bringing him up was a big effort, and to see him turn into a criminal, as he was, was unbearable. All the mothers in the village came to see the soldier. Then the men came too and begged him to recount his experience when he got back to the army and to take on the role, as a soldier, of convincing the others not to be so evil, not to rape the women of our race's finest sons, the finest examples of our ancestors. They suggested many things to him. We told the soldier that our people were organized, and were prepared to give their last drop of blood to counter everything the army did to us. We made him see that it wasn't the soldiers who were guilty but the rich who don't risk their lives. They live in nice houses and sign papers. It's the soldier who goes around the villages, up and down the mountains, mistreating and murdering his own people.

The soldier went away very impressed, he took this important message with him. When we first caught him, we'd had a lot of ideas, because we wanted to use the gun but didn't know how. It wasn't that we wanted to kill the soldier because we knew very well that one life is worth as much as many lives. But we also knew that the soldier would tell what he'd seen, what he'd felt and what we'd done to him, and that for us it could mean a massacre – the deaths of children, women, and old people in the village. The whole community would die. So we said: 'What we'll do with this man is execute him, kill him. Not here in the village but outside.' But people kept coming up with other ideas of what to do, knowing full well the risk we were running. In the end, we decided that, even though it might cost us our lives, this soldier should go and do what we'd asked him, and really carry through the role he had to play. After about three hours we let him go, in his new disguise. His comrades, the troop of ninety soldiers, hadn't come back for him because they thought he'd been ambushed by guerrillas and they were cowards. They ran off as fast as they could back to town and didn't try to save the soldier left behind. We didn't kill the soldier. The army itself took care of that when he got back to camp. They said he must be an informer, otherwise how could he possibly have stayed and then returned. They said the law says that a soldier who abandons his rifle must be shot. So they killed him. This was the village's first action and we were happy. We now had two guns, we had a grenade, and we had a cartridge belt, but we didn't know how to use them, nobody knew. We all wanted to find someone who could show us but we didn't know where or who, because whoever we went to, we'd be accused of being guerrillas using weapons. It made us sad to open the rifle and see what was inside, because we knew it killed others. We couldn't use it but it was the custom always to keep anything important. A machete that's not being used for instance, is always smeared with oil and wrapped in a plastic bag so it doesn't rust with the damp or the rain. That's what we had to do with the weapons because we didn't know how to use them. From then on the army was afraid to come up to our villages. They never came back to our village because to get there they would have to go through the mountains. Even if they came by plane they had to fly over the mountains. They were terrified of the mountains and of us. We were happy. It was the most wonderful thing that had happened to us. We were all united. Nobody went down to the *finca*, nobody went to market, nobody went down to any other place, because they would be kidnapped. What we did was to go over the mountains, go to other towns where they sell local salt, or rather some black stones which are really salt. I don't know if you only get this type of black stone in Guatemala, it's black and it's salt. It tastes very good, delicious. So we got very large stones and cooked with these so we didn't have to buy salt in the market. The *compañeros* got salt by other means. You find these stones in Sacapúlas, a town in El Quiché. It's rather strange there because it's up on the *Altiplano* where it's cold and yet when you go down a bit, it's warm. It's on a hillside which produces all the fruits you get on the south coast. You get mangoes, watermelon, bananas. And that's where you get this salt stone. They sell it but it's very cheap because nobody wants to buy. In Guatemala it's called 'Indian salt'. We don't eat sugar, we're not used to drinking coffee. Our drink is *atol*, ground maize made into *atol*. We produce the maize in our own areas and we do it collectively to grow things better and make better use of the land. The landowners were frightened to come near our village because they thought they would be kidnapped now that our village was organized. So they didn't come near us. The landowners went away, and didn't threaten us like before. The soldiers didn't come any more. So we stayed there, the owners of our little bit of land. We began cultivating things so we wouldn't have to go down to town. It was a discipline we applied to ourselves in the village to save lives and only to put ourselves at risk when we had to. My village was organized from this moment on.

I couldn't stay in my village any longer because, now that it could carry on its struggle, organize itself and take decisions, my role was not important. There was no room for a leader, someone telling others what to do, any more. So I decided to leave my village and go and teach another community the traps which we had invented and which our own neighbours had used so successfully. It's now that I move on to teach the people in another village.

XIX

ATTACK ON THE VILLAGE BY THE ARMY

'Don't wait for strangers to remind you of your duty, you have a conscience and a spirit for that. All the good you do must come from your own initiative.'

—Popol Vuh

I was free in those days. My father told me: 'You are independent, you must do what you want to, as long as you do it for our people.' That was my father's idea. I was absolutely free to decide, to leave for another village. So I said: 'I'm going away.' I went because they hadn't kidnapped anyone, nor raped anyone, in our village. But in other villages they had, and I couldn't bear so many women – hundreds of women, young girls, widows – being pregnant because the soldiers had used them sexually. I was ashamed to stay safely in my village and not think about the others. So I decided to leave. My father knew and he said: 'Where you are going, you may not have control over your life. You can be killed at any time. You could be killed tomorrow, the day after tomorrow, or any time.' But I knew that teaching others how to defend themselves against the enemy was a commitment I had to make – a commitment to my people and my commitment as a Christian. I have faith and I believe that happiness belongs to everyone, but that happiness has been stolen by a few. That was what motivated me. I had to go and teach others. That's why I went to the villages most in need, the one most threatened. I had friends there already, I'd met many *compañeras* from that community down in the *fincas*. I'd also met them when we went to the river to collect these little animals – *jutes* – to sell in the town. Those girls were collecting them as well. The animals are like little snails. We sell them in the market and people like eating them very much because they come from the mountains. So every Saturday, my mother used to go to the river and fish for *jutes*, and the next day she'd take them to market to sell. Women do it more than men because on Saturdays they are fixing the animal pens or doing other little jobs around the house, things that they don't have time for the rest of the week. So we spent a lot of time fishing for *jutes*. At the same time, we women felt a lot of affection for the river. It's a lovely feeling down by the river, even if we have to spend the whole day in the river looking for *jutes* among the stones. I enjoyed it very much. I made these friends there and we became closer friends later on when we worked together down in the *fincas* picking cotton. They were still only little. Cotton picking has three 'hands', as we say in Guatemala. Cotton is like sponge, like snow. The first 'hand' is picked by adults, and they pick the second 'hand' too. But the third 'hand' is picked by children because they can get in underneath the bushes. A cotton bush is not very tall, only about three feet high. The tallest ones would be only five or six feet. So the children get in under the bush to pick the bits which are left; we mustn't miss a single bit or they don't pay us what they owe us. So with these friends, because I was big and they were little, we'd agreed that I'd pick the second 'hand' and they would do the third 'hand'. They went underneath and I went on top. So we'd talk to each other while we were picking cotton. We became friends.

When I heard from neighbours the news that so-and-so and so-and-so had been raped by the army, I was very angry thinking about my friends – pretty, humble girls. That's really what made me decide to go. I said, 'I can't possibly stay here at home while that is happening there.' Of course, our region hadn't been liberated and we were still in constant fear of the enemy, with its more and more modern machines, modern weapons, and there could be a massacre in my village at any time. Nevertheless, I felt a greater need to be in the other village and I moved over there to be close to my friends. They told me of their despair at having been raped. There were four of them. Two of them were pregnant by soldiers and the other two not. But they were ill too because they'd been raped by five soldiers who'd come to their house. While I was living in the house of one of my friends who was pregnant, she told me: 'I hate this child inside me. I don't know what to do with it. This child is not my child.' She was very distressed and cried all the time. But I told her: 'You must love the child. It was not your fault.' She said: 'I hate that soldier. How can I feed the child of a soldier?' The *compañera* aborted her child. She was from a different ethnic group than ours. Her community helped her by telling her that it wasn't unusual, that our ancestors did the same when they were raped, when they had children without wishing to, without any love for the child. But my two friends suffered very much. I didn't know what to do, I felt helpless.

I spoke the same language as they did in that village. What happens in Guatemala is that the Quiché language is the most common. The main languages are Quiché, Cakchiquel and Mam, and from these three mother languages spring all the other languages found here. However one ethnic group doesn't all speak the same language. For instance, the Ixiles are Quichés but they don't speak Quiché and their customs differ from those of the Quiché. So there's a conglomeration of ethnic groups, languages, customs and traditions, and even though there are three mother languages, that doesn't mean we all understand each other. We don't. It was the same with my four *compañeras*. They were from another people, another community, and we just understood each other but with many deformations of the same language. I must say it's unfortunate that we Indians are separated by ethnic barriers, linguistic barriers. It's typical of Guatemala: such a small place but such huge barriers that there's no dialogue between us. We Indians say: 'This is my group and this is where I must be.' The government takes more and more advantage of these barriers. The two who'd been raped but weren't pregnant must have been about fourteen. They were very ill, but I didn't really know what was the matter with them. One couldn't walk very well and the other had very bad stomach pains. She said her stomach hurt but, honestly, I had no knowledge of things like that. The two who were pregnant rejected their babies and didn't want to mother soldiers' children. It made me feel so helpless. I didn't know what to do. I felt so much pity for them. Their situation was very difficult. But my staying with them did them a lot of good because I spent time with them and talked to them as we'd done when we were young, when we were little girls.

We started setting traps in that village, the same traps as ours but in slightly different ways. The community had many things hidden that they hadn't used out of respect for those objects. But we decided that we needed to use them, because life is worth more than objects even if it means revealing many of our Indian secrets. We started to use them. Another community nearby, the village of Cotzal, was very persecuted. It had been very badly repressed in 1960. From then on there'd been many massacres, many women raped, many men tortured. While I was in the village, a woman arrived, a very old woman. As my father said, unfortunately we don't live very long in Guatemala these days. We usually live to about sixty, that's the life expectancy. People die early because of the conditions we live in. But this woman was extraordinary. She was an exceptional case in this village. She must have been about ninety. They had just killed her last son. First they'd killed her husband. He'd gone to town and hadn't come back. One of her sons went to look for him and he didn't come back. Another went and didn't come back either. The others were all kidnapped from their house. So this woman was left all alone. She was looking for a refuge. I was in the village and

my *compañeros* said there was a very old woman who wanted
to join our community. She thinks she should stay here. I said:
'Of course, she must. We must all help each other and defend
ourselves to the very last person.'

With all the *compañeros*, we'd installed a self-defence system like the one in my village, using this village's own traps.
We said that if the army were to arrive during the night it was
good for the very old woman to be with us. We decided that
before it got dark, we'd all go and sleep in the mountains.
We kept combined watches during the night – a young girl
with a boy or a man. This way we'd protect the community
throughout the night. That was different from the way we'd
done it, but the village wanted to combine the duties for a
reason. Keeping watch at night meant turning ourselves into
tree trunks, without moving, or else we'd be cannon fodder
for the army. The girl would be on another side making herself look like something different from the man. That was this
village's idea. Their traps were different and their weapons
were different. Everything was the way the *compañeros* of
the village were used to doing things. Nevertheless, they accepted me. We set to work and I was accepted because of all
the help I gave the village.

The army raided the village at night. When they heard the
dogs, they fired wildly into the air. They fired everywhere but
there was no-one at home. The whole village had taken all
their belongings out of their houses and carried them to the
camp. So even though the army wanted to steal things, there
was nothing there. And even though they burned the houses, it didn't matter very much because the mountains were
sheltering the community. We spent two, three, four nights
like this. The old lady got really fed up. She couldn't stand
the cold. It rained and rained. When it started to pour with
rain during the night, the water gushed down through the
camp and we got soaking wet. That old lady couldn't bear
the cold and one day decided: 'Let them kill me if they want,
but I'm not going with you to the mountains.' It was hard
for us to accept the idea of leaving that dear old lady there.

She'd taught us many things and often helped us through the experience of her years. The community said they wouldn't agree to her staying in her hut. But she said: 'No, I'm staying. I must stay here. If they kill me, they kill me. Anyway, I've no children, no grandchildren, all my grandchildren have been taken away and I've nobody left. If I have helped in any way, it was only my duty.' So, with a great deal of sadness, and pain, we had to leave her in her house.

When night came, we all left for the mountains. We left one by one and met up in the mountains. We'd left traps at the doors of all the houses. The trap consisted of a pole and a big, big pit, about as deep as the distance between the floor and the roof. We put the pole across the pit and a board on the pole so that whoever stood on it would fall in. We take it off during the day and set it at night. Everyone in the village knew each others' traps so none of us would fall in. The old lady set her trap. She set the trap and prepared her axe, her machete, her hoe and her stones. She got everything she needed to defend herself ready and went to sleep. We saw our lookout giving the signal from far away and we left. We always have *compañeros* on watch at the main entrance to the village. They signal with their torches. They light it and indicate the number of soldiers approaching by the number of times they wave it. And when the soldiers leave, the *compañero* also has to tell us if they've all gone or not. Everyone was distressed, and I most of all, because I was sure they were going to kill the old lady or rape her. I knew those murderers were so criminal they didn't respect anyone's life, neither old people nor children. They like raping old people and children. At around two in the morning the dogs began to bark and there was shooting and everything, but we didn't hear any shouts from the old woman. We were quite a way away from the village but, all the same, we could pick up all the noises from there. But we didn't hear anything. We thought they'd killed the poor woman. At about half past three, the lookout gave the signal that the army had left the village. He indicated how many had left. Some were still there. We

didn't know what to do. So we waited until dawn to see if
we should go back to the village or stay in the mountains. At
about half past five, when dawn was just breaking, we saw
the old woman coming towards us. How could she possibly
have escaped death? She stopped and said: 'I have a surprise
for you,' and she was laughing and crying at the same time.
But she was crying with joy. There was also anxiety written
on her face, however, and we immediately thought that she
was an 'ear'.

There have been 'ears' in a lot of villages – people who
sell themselves to the government. But I think it's not always
their fault. They have to, they are forced to sell themselves,
because they are threatened and see no alternative. The government uses them to get information from the community
and this causes many deaths. So we thought this old lady
was an 'ear' although we could hardly believe it of such an
honest person. But we took it very seriously because at that
time we were very clear about what we had to do. We didn't
like violence but if it was the only way of saving our lives, we
would use it with justice. Although it hurt us, if this woman
had sold herself, we would have to execute her. But she says:
'I've got a surprise for you. I've killed a soldier'. 'I've killed a
soldier,' she says. But nobody believed her. Well, how could
we believe it because, first of all, she was very old and, second, she could hardly see, and third, she didn't have the sort
of arms the enemy did. But she kept saying: 'I'm so happy. I
don't want to die, I want to live again. I killed a soldier.' Still
no-one believed her. 'I'm telling the truth,' she said, 'look,
here are his guns.' She was carrying the soldier's rifle and his
pistol. She was happy. 'Show me, show me how to use it,'
she said. To me it was like a dream, like a comic strip, hardly
believable. She told us: 'What happened was that they came
into my house, they all managed to jump over the trap, all of
them. I hid and crept out of the house on the other side, trying to get away from the house because I thought they'd catch
me. The only thing I had with me was my axe. There was a
soldier standing at the door looking in, I hit him on the head

with my axe and he fell to the ground. The others thought it was guerrillas. They were in such a rush to get out that one of them fell in the trap and the other was rolling around on the ground. The other soldiers shot their wounded comrade. He was trying to escape.'

He was old, and afterwards we saw that the wound wasn't serious, not enough for them to have to kill him. But the other soldiers had killed him and left. And that's why we'd been sent the signal that they weren't all there, and why we were so suspicious when the old lady arrived at the camp. We knew that not all the army had left the village. I was so overjoyed, so overjoyed. I said: 'This is a great victory for our secrets, no-one has discovered them. We must go on doing this because it is not right that our lives should be worth less than a bird or anything else, and that they can kill us as they wish.' The old lady deserved a big reward. But we didn't know what to give really, just our thanks for what she had done. The old lady made a promise: 'I want to live, I want to go on with you.' She was almost dancing. 'Now we have something to defend ourselves with. If we learn to use this, we'll have a weapon like theirs. This is what killed my children,' she said. Well, it was something special for her. But it was for us too.

What should we do with the soldier? He'd fallen into the trap with his guns and everything. He had grenades as well. He was very well equipped. We carried the dead body out of the village and put him on a path where they could see him, but which didn't put the community at risk (although they knew he had been there anyway). The other one wasn't dead. He was alive in the trap. We didn't know what to do with him because if we went up to the trap, he'd probably shoot us. In the end, we told him to give up his weapons. We threw a rope down into the pit, talking to him from some way away, telling him that if he sent his weapons up, we'd let him live but that if he refused, he'd die. The soldier must have been pretty miserable in that hole and he said yes, and tied his guns to the rope and we pulled them up. But who could be sure he didn't have another gun? That was very worrying, but some of the community said: 'Even if he has a gun, he can only kill one of us, not all of us.' So we threw the soldier a rope and we all pulled. He came out and it was true he was unarmed. He'd given up all his weapons.

We did the same with this soldier as we'd done with the one in the village. Here they asked him as well: 'How could a soldier be like that?' The *compañeras* who were pregnant told him they were carrying a soldier's child but that they couldn't give birth to a child with blood like a soldier's blood. For an Indian it was like a monster, something unbearable. The soldier began to cry and said: 'It's not my fault. They give me orders. They forced us to come here and if we don't obey, they kill us.' He said: 'We take orders from a captain, and we do what this captain says. If I go into the army, I'm an enemy of the people anyway, and if I lay down my arms, I'm the army's enemy. If one side doesn't kill me, the other will. I don't know what to do.' So we told him that if it was difficult for him, from now on he should hide or find something else to do, but that he must stop being evil, like the army. And he told us a lot about how they tortured in the barracks. He said: 'From the first day I arrived in the barracks, they told me that my parents were stupid,' – he was an Indian too – 'that they were stupid because they couldn't speak and that they'd teach me how people should speak. So they started teaching me Spanish. They gave me a pair of shoes which I found very hard to wear but they beat me into wearing them anyway. They hit me until I got used to them. Then they told me I had to kill the communists from Cuba and Russia. I had to kill them all and then they gave me a gun.' But we asked him: 'And who do you kill with this gun? Why are you hunting us? Do they say that if your father or mother are on the other side, you must use this gun to kill them too?' 'I use this gun the way they tell me to use it. I'm not to blame for all this, they just grabbed me in the town.' He cried and we felt sorry for him, because we are all human.

By that time I understood the position very well. I knew it wasn't the fault of the soldiers. The government force our people to be soldiers too. That soldier talked and told us everything they did. This time we were a bit more aware because, as I said, the first time we only begged the soldier to help us, we didn't even ask him the things he did. Now the second time we got a lot of information from him about how they treat the soldiers in the army. 'We have to obey the captain. The captain is always behind us and if we don't obey, he shoots us.' We asked him: 'And why don't you get together then if there's only one captain.' 'Well, not all of us think the same,' he said, 'many have come to believe in what we're doing.' And we asked him: 'And what are you defending? Where are these communists?' The soldier didn't even know what communists were. We asked him: 'What do communists look like?' And he said: 'Well, they tell us they're in the mountains, that they don't look like people, and things like that.' He had no idea of what he was doing. Then we said to him: 'You are defending the rich. You are defending authority. You're not defending your own people.' 'It's true,' he said, 'from now on I'm not going back. I promise you, I swear, I'm not going back to the barracks.' And we said to him: 'If you are a true son of your people, if you really remember the advice of our ancestors, you must go and make a life where you can, but stop being a criminal. Don't go on killing.' The soldier went away convinced. And we heard that he didn't go back to the barracks but went and hid. Perhaps they've killed him now or he might be alive, but anyway that soldier didn't go back to his camp.

That was my second experience of organizing work in my people's struggle. My dream was to go on fighting and getting to know my people more closely. At the same time I was very concerned that everything handed down from our ancestors should still be practised. And even though the tortures and kidnappings had done our people a lot of harm, we shouldn't lose faith in change. This is when I began working in a peasant organisation and went on to another stage of my life. These are other things, other ways.

XX

THE DEATH OF DOÑA PETRONA CHONA

'Inhuman are their soldiers, cruel their fierce mastiffs.'
—*Chilam Balam*

There is something I didn't say before when I spoke about the landowners in my area – the Garcías and the Martínez. I think I should say it now. I remember something I saw, now that I'm remembering things about other people's lives. In 1975, the Garcías had a market near where I lived and they tried to make all the Indians sell their maize and beans there so that they could buy it cheap, transport it to other places and sell it dear. They had a *finca* where I used to work a lot when I was a child since it was near our house. I used to pick coffee. It was mostly coffee there. There were banana trees to shade the coffee but the landowner didn't let us pick the bananas because they were there for shade. The bananas rotted on their stalks while we were all hungry but couldn't pick them.

I had a friend called Petrona Chona. She had two children, the little boy would be about two and the little girl about three. She had a husband. Petrona was very young and so was her husband. They both worked in the Garcías' *finca*. Then one day the son of the landowner, his name was Carlos García, began courting my friend. I hate him in the very depth of my being. He asked her if she'd be his mistress. She was an Indian. She said, 'How can I, I'm a married woman.' He said that he loved her, that he really loved her, that he adored her and all that. Then he started threatening her. The landowner's son came to the fields every day, and as he didn't have anything else to do, he kept after her. One Friday she didn't go to work because her little boy was ill and she had to stay at home. They lived in the *finca*. They paid rent and worked as *peones* but they weren't paid. What they earned went for the rent of the land and the little house. She told me she was in despair because they had nothing to eat even though they worked all the time. One Friday she stayed at home and the landowner's son came to her house. He'd been to the fields and hadn't found her, so he went to the house, to her hut. And he began again asking her to be his mistress and to let him have his way with her. She was very worried about her little boy and kept saying no, and no. They argued for a long time but unfortunately we were all working a long way away. There were some *peones* near the house but they were working too. In the end she refused, and the landowner's son went away. But what that murderer Carlos García did was to send his father's bodyguard to kill the woman in her house. But he told the bodyguard not to shoot her but to hack her to death with a machete. Naturally the bodyguard did as he was told and went to the woman's house and, catching her by surprise, hacked her up with his machete.

It was the first dead body I'd ever seen, and that's why I was saying that I'll have to talk about a lot more corpses, but this was the first one I'd ever touched. He hacked her to pieces and cut one of her baby's fingers off because she was carrying her on her back. The other child came running out of the house in fright. He took the baby off her back, put her on one side and hacked her into twenty-five pieces, if I'm not mistaken. She lay there in pieces. I won't forget it because my friend had talked to me earlier that morning and told me that they were leaving the *finca*. But they didn't have time. The woman had shouted, but none of the workers went near because they saw that first the landowner's son had been there and then the bodyguard arrived. Which of them was going to interfere? He'd only be killed himself or dismissed from his job. So the woman was left in pieces. That same Friday afternoon, I went to see her body lying on the ground. The parts of her body were all there on one side. I couldn't believe it was Petrona lying there. There she stayed. No-one could bear to lift her up. Not even our community. A lot of people came. But since many different people worked there, from many different areas, no-one went near the young woman's body. Then my father came. He cried when he saw her. He said: 'Petrona was such a good person.' No-one could believe it. We picked her little boy up and bandaged his finger so it wouldn't bleed so much. But we didn't know what to do. She stayed there all night. And all Saturday morning. Saturday night came and Sunday. No-one would pick her up. Then my father said: 'Well, it's up to us.' She was already smelling very bad. The smell of her body carried a long way. My father said: 'Yes, it's up to us to move her. We must do it.' There is a law in Guatemala that you can't move a dead body until the authorities have been so we'd told the authorities immediately. They are in town and don't come until they have time, so they wouldn't get there until Monday. By Sunday the body was already covered with flies and everything. It's a very hot place, so there was the smell and all that. My father said: 'Well, it's up to us to move the body even if they think that we have committed the crime.' We collected Doña Petrona up in baskets and her blood was congealed on the ground. Her hands, her head, every bit of her, all cut off. We picked her up in baskets, we put her in a box and buried her on Sunday. Many people came afterwards, but a lot didn't come at all because it was a crime and nobody wanted to get involved in case the authorities accused them as well. We knew the landowners were capable of anything.

The mayor arrived on Monday. It was the first time that I felt, well, I don't know how to explain – like an invalid. I couldn't do anything. Just before the mayor arrived, the landowner talked to him and they were laughing. We didn't understand what they were saying. They didn't ask us to tell them what had happened, when it had happened, or at what time. Nothing. The mayor arrived as if it was nothing at all, and calmly went away again. They put the bodyguard into prison for fifteen days, just to smooth things over, so our people would say nothing. After fifteen days, he went back to work. Every time I remember it I get the same feeling. The first time I picked up a dead body. All in pieces. For about six years afterwards perhaps, I dreamed about Doña Petrona. There wasn't a single night I didn't feel I'd dreamed about Doña Petrona. For a long time I couldn't go to sleep for thinking about her.

XXI

FAREWELL TO THE COMMUNITY: RIGOBERTA DECIDES TO LEARN SPANISH

'Our people will never be scattered. Our destiny will triumph over the ill-fated days which are coming at a time unknown. We will always be secure in the land we have occupied.'
—Popol Vuh

My father came out of prison in 1977. He used to come and visit us now and again but, as I was saying before, he could no longer walk along the paths or travel by bus. He had to go across the high mountains to reach our house because the army or the landowners would see to it he was killed. That same year he joined the CUC. It was just being formed. Actually, the CUC already existed as an underground organisation but it came out into the open in May 1978, when it was strong enough. My father was with many *compañeros*, with Emeterio Toj Medrano and others who've since been murdered, and some who are still alive. They began to think about the future of the CUC and what its objectives were. But the government wouldn't recognize the CUC, so it had to be a spontaneous organisation and a clandestine one at the same time. Later on we joined it too, first as helpers and then as members.

So my father came home in 1978, and I went home too. That's when we said goodbye. Those were the last moments our whole family spent together. It was the time when my father might never get home again. He was already a wanted man. Although he used to come furtively sometimes, it was getting too risky for him to continue. In addition, one of my brothers was in danger. That was my little brother, the one who was burned to death. He'd been a catechist since he was a child too and he'd become secretary to our community. I don't mean secretary in the sense of a grand person who can read and write, but someone who put into practice the little he had learned. We arrived at the village. All our neighbours were overjoyed, because we hadn't been back for such a long time. They said they were going to have a village fiesta and get out all the Maya instruments we kept in our villages. The *tún*, the *sijolaj*, the *chirimía*, the *marimba*. They had a fiesta. They invented a special fiesta because those weren't times for ceremonies. Nor were they times for fiestas. They said it would be a fiesta for saying goodbye to us, because they thought the day would come when we wouldn't see each other again. Many of them had already gone off to fight in the mountains. Some had come down and were present then. It was a great honour for the community.

The fiesta began. We were the guests. I remember we had it in the house which had for so long been used for our meetings. We all sat in there. The Guatemalan Indian custom for a very important fiesta is to make *atol* and *tamales*, and it's the only time we eat meat. The whole village contributed a pig. They killed the pig. We made food for everyone, and then, quite late, about seven or eight o'clock, the music began. In my village they always set off bombs that they make themselves out of gunpowder. I'd forgotten about those bombs. It's a very old custom. It's in a mortar – you put it in a mortar and light the fuse. The bomb shoots up and explodes with a loud bang. When we started practising self-defence, we sometimes used to use these bombs to throw at the army. We made a lot of bombs to set off that night. It was a real party, with dancing. When midnight came, a lot of people danced. That's another custom in our community: that when a fiesta is rather special for us, we wait until midnight to celebrate. Midnight because, as our forefathers say, that's when we say goodbye to the old day and the new day begins. It meant a lot to the community, that midnight celebration, and it gave us a moment at midnight to express a little of what we felt and thought about our community. The fiesta began, we ate until nearly midnight and around half past eleven we were given a chance to speak. My father spoke. He said he felt very happy to be leaving the community and going to other areas, because now in our community the children were mature and could look after themselves. Now he was needed to educate other children, in other places. 'I may not return, so you must take care of yourselves,' he said. That was his farewell. And my mother said, 'I am here now, but I feel that I'm needed in other areas.' Each one of us said our farewell to the community. They all cried and sometimes they laughed because they were happy but couldn't express their joy. My father was very happy. He said that a man's head wasn't just for wearing a hat (we Indians all wear hats). It wasn't only for a hat but was for thinking about what the community should do to try and change things, and for that change to bring about other changes in society at every level. We wanted change so that we could express our feelings and conduct our ceremonies again the way we used to, because at that time there was no possibility of doing so. My father spoke a lot and he said goodbye to us in front of the community because he was going to one area, I had to go to another, and my mother to another again. We would all be scattered, so that if I was caught I wouldn't be able to tell where my parents were. It was very hard for us to think of our father and mother in one area and their children in another. But that was our reality and we had to accept it. So our father began to say goodbye. I remember him saying: 'My children, from now on the people will be your father. The enemy will perhaps take our small lives, but we must try to protect them and defend them to the last. But if there is no other way, have faith and hope in your father the people, because the people will look after you as I do.' My father often used to say: 'I didn't do enough for you because I had to nourish the INTA, because the INTA sapped all my strength, because the landowners were threatening us. I was not to blame. They were to blame. It is right to tell our people this, it is our small contribution.' Then my father told us girls who weren't married that we had absolute freedom to do as we wished, that we should be independent, and give everything we could to the struggle without anyone behind us ordering us about or forcing us to do anything. He said he gave us total freedom, but that he would like us to use that freedom for the good of the people, to teach the people what he had taught us. He said: 'They can kill me, but they can't destroy my children. And if they kill any of you, I will carry on until my last moments.' It was a very sad farewell.

Of course, it was the start of a new commitment too, it was to commit ourselves more deeply to our work. The ceremony ended with many tears from our community, our neighbours, our uncles and aunts, and our cousins. It was also a farewell to many of the community because many elders, many of the men, had to go up into the mountains. They couldn't live in the village because their lives had been threatened, and the village considered them important people who could contribute to the change. Even if they are not there when victory comes, through their example many others will be. So we had to say goodbye to many people that night. It wasn't only us. The next day my father left for El Quiché and I stayed at home for another week. I remember it was the last time my brothers and sisters and I were together. Eight days later I left for another area on a specific task for the CUC. My job was to organize people. I had to learn Spanish and to read and write. At the farewell fiesta I decided to do many things and, in fact, I began to get them under way.

XXII

THE CUC COMES
OUT INTO THE OPEN

*'They've always said, "Poor Indians, they can't speak," so
many speak for them. That's why I decided to learn Spanish.'*
—Rigoberta Menchú

When General Kjell came to power, he set the agrarian reform in motion. But first he set his electoral campaign in motion. The landowners on the south coast forced many of the
peasants to vote for Kjell. The overseers made them. They
said anyone who didn't vote would be thrown out of work.
It was the same as it had always been, but before I didn't
understand. Kjell campaigned in the provinces and the mu-
nicipalities, and I remember him coming to Uspantán at that
time. It was a Sunday and we were in the town. Kjell talked
a lot about giving us bread and sharing out the land. They
have to say bread, they can't even say *tortilla*. Most of them
don't know what Indians eat. We eat maize and vegetables,
our food is the *tortilla*. But they, when they come to the
countryside, they offer us more than *tortillas*, they offer us
bread. Yes, they were going to give us bread, health services,
schools, roads and a whole load of things they told us about
then. And land. They told us: 'The land is yours.' That is,
from then on, we would own the land. That was in 1974.
And so, many people voted at that time. I didn't vote because

I was still a minor but my parents, my brothers and sisters, even my mother, voted, believing that it was true, that this would solve our problem. After Kjell took power, he began to divide the land into small plots. What happened was that the struggle had previously been between the *finca* owners and the communities. I already told the story of how they took our land away. But when Kjell came to power, he solved that problem by dividing our lands into small plots and saying we were the owners. Oh yes, that man was more intelligent than the previous ones. He gave each neighbour a plot. We all had our own plots. Our plots measured one *manzana*.

Soon enough he started getting money in other ways. That's when they set up the INAFOR (Instituto Nacional de Forestación de Guatemala: Guatemalan Forestry Commission), an institution looking after trees and forests in Guatemala. What were we going to do then? I remember that my father and all of us were very worried. We couldn't cut down trees because we each had our own plot and no-one could go outside his plot. We had to apply to a judge for permission to buy so many trees through a letter to the INAFOR. Each tree cost five *quetzals*. And we used practically to eat wood – we have no stoves, no gas, nothing. Many of the peasants cut trees down and the INAFOR arrived and took them prisoner because they'd killed a tree. That was when our big problems with the land division started in the *Altiplano*. But there were also big problems in the *fincas* when Kjell came to power, as we shall see. In the *Altiplano*, especially in the region of El Quiché where the CUC was born, most of the peasants began to unite and protest against the INAFOR and the agrarian reform because it tried to divide us. We survive because of our communities. Even though the government or the foreigners, whoever it is, divides our land up to keep us separate, the community knows that it must live in a communal way. So what we did in our village was to set aside an area to grow our maize and an area for our animals, even though the agrarian reform had allocated us our own plots. We decided to put them all together in spite of the sub-divisions – the ones they imposed on us.

Many peasants started protesting about this, and about the bad conditions in the *fincas* as well. Labourers were brutally treated in those days, and once people had begun protesting about the agrarian reform, they also found reasons to protest about other things. *They* had the law. And *we* were so humble. But the answer they gave us, well, it wasn't very humble. We wrote documents and sent letters signed by the whole community to the INAFOR begging them, apologetically, to let us cut down trees to be able to eat. The INAFOR said 'no'. We had to pay for them. What made us really angry was that in my village we had two large trees and when we asked the INAFOR for permission to cut one down, they made us beg for permission, and still pay for it. But when big businessmen come to cut, I don't know, huge quantities of wood to sell, to export, of course they were free to cut five hundred, six hundred trees. This made our people even more conscious of their situation. We collected signatures to send a protest to the president of the republic and ask him not to leave us without wood. There was no reply. We protested against our little plots; we wanted to grow crops on our own land but not have it divided up. We had no reply to that either. That's when the peasants, most of us, went down to the coast. The majority of people from the *Altiplano* had to go to the coast because there we earned a little money. We couldn't use the wood and we had nothing to sow. Many, many people went down to the coast.

When nearly all the people from the *Altiplano* had gone to the coast, there were unemployment and sackings there because the *finca* owners could impose whatever conditions they fancied. Since there were so many people looking for work, the landowners had no problem getting rid of two hundred, three hundred peasants at the same time. Others were waiting to do the work. Then they began to mistreat the peasants as far as food was concerned. They fed them when they wanted to, and when they didn't want to, they didn't. Ill treatment in the *fincas* was more open and widespread now. That's how the CUC began to form as such. It organized the peasants both in the *Altiplano* and on the coast. It wasn't a formal organization with a name and all that: more like groups of communities, at the grass roots, that sort of thing. The time came when the CUC asked for legal status; it asked the president to recognize it as a union which defended peasants' rights. But the government did not reply – it did not accept the CUC's representativity as an institution defending peasants' rights. Nevertheless, the CUC went on with its work. It said, well, if they don't recognize our organisation legally, it's they who make us illegal. And the CUC worked clandestinely. The repression of its leaders began, especially in El Quiché. They started picking up the CUC's organizers.

Kjell left the presidency in 1978 and Lucas García took over. Lucas, well, he did the same thing. He came to the villages in the different regions and offered us everything. He offered us roads, schools, teachers, doctors, etc., just as Kjell had. But the people didn't believe him at all. Because they'd received nothing. We said: 'They come with more lies, they're still liars.' And no-one wanted to vote. But behind the promises were threats; they said that if we didn't vote, our villages would be repressed. The people were forced to vote. All the same, most people spoilt their votes; that is, they put in blank votes or voted for everyone. The votes were void. So Lucas came to power.

But before that, under Kjell, there was a massacre of one hundred and six peasants in Panzós, an area of Cobán. It was the 29th of May, 1978. Panzós is a town where they discovered oil and began throwing peasants off their land. But since the peasants didn't know where to go, they all came down in an organized fashion with their leaders. They were Kekchi Indians and the army massacred them as if they were killing birds – men, women and children died. Blood ran in the main square in Panzós. We felt this was a direct attack on us. It was as if they'd murdered us, as if we were being tortured when they killed those people. It all came out in the newspapers.

But nobody paid much attention, they were more interested in the government which had just come to power. So the story died. Nobody was interested in the death of all those peasants. The CUC condemned this act, and that's when it was recognized under the name of Comité Unidad Campesina, as an organization defending peasants' rights. Our objectives were: a fair wage from the landowners; respect for our communities; the decent treatment we deserve as people, not animals; respect for our religion, our customs and our culture. Many villages in El Quiché were unable to perform their ceremonies because they were persecuted or because they were called subversives and communists. The CUC championed these rights. It came out into the open. Then the repression against it began. We held a huge demonstration to herald the CUC with the participation of Indian men, women and children, although the CUC also recognizes that it is not only Indians who are exploited in Guatemala but our poor *ladino compañeros* as well. The CUC defends all peasants, Indians and *ladinos*. And within the framework of the organization, we began having contacts between *ladinos* and Indians.

So the CUC comes into the open; it calls strikes, demonstrations and demands for a fair wage. We obtained a wage of three-twenty *quetzals*. That was the bare minimum, really. For a family which has to feed nine or ten children three-twenty is not a fair wage. The *finca* owners said yes. They signed an agreement to pay a minimum wage of three-twenty *quetzals*. They agreed. It was a victory for us obtaining three-twenty but, in practice, the landowners didn't pay that. They kept on paying their *peones* the same: one-twenty *quetzal*. What the landowners actually did was to supervise the work more closely, raise the work quotas and, at the same time, charge for every tiny error the peasants make. Now we couldn't let even the tiniest fly alight on a leaf, or walk on it, because we'd have to pay for the plant. This was very hard for the peasants. We kept up our demands but we didn't know how to act. It was a bitter blow when our first *compañeros* fell. But we carried on working.

It was in 1978, when Lucas García came to power with such a lust for killing, that the repression really began in El Quiché. It was like a piece of rag in his hands. He set up military bases in many of the villages and there were rapes, tortures, kidnappings. And massacres. The villages of Chajul, Cotzal and Nebaj suffered massacres as the repression fell on them again. It fell above all on the Indian population. Every day new clandestine cemeteries, as they call them, would appear in different parts of the country. That is, they'd kidnap people from a village, torture them, and then some thirty bodies would appear in one place. On a hillside for example. Then they'd tell the people to go and get their relatives there. But they didn't dare look for the bodies because they knew they'll be taken away too. So the bodies just stayed there. Then what they did was dig a pit for the bodies and put them all in: so it was a secret cemetery. About this time, the peasants joined up with the industrial workers and the unions. There was a miners' strike in Ixtahuacán in 1977. It was a workers' strike and agricultural labourers and industrial workers were all mixed up on the march. The last strike we had was a big one, very big. It was the strike of seventy thousand peasants organized by the CUC on the south coast.

When I joined the CUC in 1979, I was given various tasks to do and I became one of the organization's leaders. I travelled to different areas and slept in the houses of different *compañeros*, and what I found most distressing was that we couldn't understand each other. They couldn't speak Spanish and I couldn't speak their language. I felt so helpless. I'd ask myself how was this possible? It's a division which they have kept up precisely so that we Indians cannot unite, or discuss our problems. And how effective a barrier it has been! But I understood why now. I began learning Mam, I began learning Cakchiquel and Tzutuhil. I decided to learn these three languages as well as Spanish. I didn't speak very well. Oh, I made so many mistakes! And of course I couldn't read or write, so learning Spanish meant listening and memorizing, like a cassette. The same with the other languages; I couldn't write them either. So for a while I got everything mixed up. Learning to read and write, learning Spanish and three other languages – and my own as well – was all very confusing. I began to wonder whether it wasn't better to learn first one and then another. Since Spanish was a language which united us, why learn all the twenty-two languages in Gautemala? It wasn't possible, and anyway this wasn't the moment to do it.

It was at this period that I was travelling all over the place. I also went down to the coast. I had some political work to do, organizing the people there, and at the same time getting them to understand me by telling them about my past, what had happened to me in my life, the reasons for the pain we suffer, and the causes of poverty. When you know there is work to do and you are responsible, you try and do it as well as you can because you have suffered so much and you don't want your people to go on suffering. I knew all the contacts, and I had many jobs to do; carrying papers, machines, leaflets, texts for teaching people. I remember that the texts for learning Spanish and learning to read and write were full of drawings, figures and designs. That is, it wasn't only writing because writing didn't mean much to me and I didn't understand what it said. At the same time, I was going to a convent where the nuns taught me to read and write. They also taught me Spanish. As I was saying before, not all priests are people who can't see the reality and suffering of the people. Many of them love the people and, through this love for the people, they love each one of us and help us show our people the way. I have many good memories of many nuns who have helped me. They took me by the hand like a child who, well, who needed to learn many things. And I was anxious to do my best, to learn a lot. Because I believe my life has taught me many things but human beings are also made to learn many more. I learned Spanish out of necessity.

XXIII

POLITICAL ACTIVITY IN OTHER COMMUNITIES. CONTACTS WITH LADINOS

'*We have revealed our secrets to those who are worthy. Only they should know the art of writing and no-one else.*'
—Popol Vuh

We went on organizing our people in 1979. I remember that I hadn't heard anything of my parents since the farewell in the community. I didn't know where they were. They had no news of me either. We didn't see them for a long time. I went to the *fincas*, I went to other areas, but I couldn't go back to my village because I was a fugitive like my parents. We lived with other people, with *compañeros* from other Indian groups, and with the many friends I made in the organization. It was almost as if I were living with my brothers and sisters, with my parents. Everyone showed me so much affection. So we organized the majority of workers on the south coast, in the sugar, coffee and cotton plantations. And they agreed to carry on the political work when they returned to the *Altiplano* so that everybody would be organized. Most of the workers were Indians and poor *ladinos*, and we didn't need to hold courses explaining the situation since it was all around us. Our work went very well. And soon there just wasn't enough time for everything; we had to rush from one place to another, carrying documents, carrying everything. The reason for this was so that others wouldn't put themselves at risk; we were already in danger, the enemy knew us. I travelled from region to region, sleeping in different houses. All this gave me a lot to think about, a lot, because I came across the linguistic barriers over and over again. We couldn't understand each other and I wanted so much to talk to everybody and feel close to many of the women as I was to my mother. But I couldn't talk to them because they didn't understand me and I didn't understand them. So I said: 'We can't possibly go on like this. We must work to help people understand their own people, and be able to talk to one another.' From then on I concentrated on getting to know my *compañeros* closely and teaching them the little I knew, so that they too could become leaders of their communities. I remember we talked of many things: of our role as women, our role as young people. We all came to the conclusion that we hadn't had a childhood, nor had we ever really been young because, as we were growing up we'd had the responsibility of feeding little brothers and sisters – it was like having a lot of children ourselves. I sometimes stayed with other Indians in their houses.

I remember the village of Huehuetenango very well, where I stayed in the house of a *compañero* who had ten children. I made a mistake there, it was something that I hadn't realized, thinking that we'd all had the same experiences. The mistake was not to have brought a blanket with me for this journey. I only had a sheet with me for the night. I arrived at that village in the *Altiplano*, and it was so cold, so incredibly cold. You can't believe how cold it was. So I hoped these people would lend me some clothes or a shawl to put over me. But at night I saw that they didn't even have anything for themselves and it made me very sad. How were we going to sleep? It was so cold! The dogs came in and out of the little house all the time because it was open. I asked: 'Tell me, are we going to stay here?' I thought we could get leaves from the mountain to warm ourselves with. It was rather late to think of that but they collected quite a lot of leaves . . . And so they all lay down round the fire; they were all sleeping and I wondered, well, where should I go. And I lay down next to them. By midnight it was so cold that we were almost frozen! The cold woke the parents up. 'How cold it is,' they said. 'Yes,' I said, and my jaw was almost stiff with cold. I'd never felt so cold before. Although my home is in the *Altiplano* too, the cold there doesn't compare with this. The parents got up for a while and then went to sleep again. I began to wonder how human beings can stand so much. We often say we can't bear something but we do bear it. The children were all right, quiet on the floor. Since the parents were very fond of me and thought of me as a leader, they said: 'Look, here is a mat. Sit on this.' But for my part, I couldn't use the mat because I was too ashamed, and also because I felt we were all equal and that they had as much right to the mat as I had. I told my host that I was ashamed by the special treatment they gave me because I was poor too, I was from the mountains too, from the same conditions, and that if we are fighting for equality for everyone, we must begin by sharing everything we have. I didn't mind sharing the mat with the children but I didn't deserve the mat for myself. It made me think a great deal, because I said: 'In our house we have a mat each.' This meant that I'd never suffered as they had here. And I began to discover many things that I hadn't experienced but that many others had. And this made me really angry. I thought, so many rich people wasting even whole beds – one mattress isn't enough for them, they have two or three on their beds. And here there isn't even a mat to sleep on. This gave me a lot to think about. This happened with many people. I used to sleep one, two, three nights in one place, then I'd move on to another place for my work. I was happy.

Something I want to tell you, is that I had a friend. He was the man who taught me Spanish. He was a *ladino*, a teacher, who worked with the CUC. He taught me Spanish and helped me with many things. We used to meet secretly because we couldn't meet openly where he lived. That *com-*

pañero taught me many things, one of which was to love *ladinos* a lot. He taught me to think more clearly about some of my ideas which were wrong, like saying all *ladinos* are bad. He didn't teach me through ideas, he showed me by his actions, by the way he behaved towards me. At that time, we used to talk through the night. It was when we began supporting the struggle of peasants in general, and carrying out coordinated actions. For instance, if we call a strike, it's for all workers. If we call an assembly, we listen to the views of all the masses. It was my job to sound out the views of all the *compañeros* I was in contact with in the area I happened to be in, and send them to the regional coordinating body. Then they'd be sent to the national coordinating body to be discussed by the *compañeros* there. Anyway, the example of my *compañero ladino* made me really understand the barrier which has been put up between the Indian and the *ladino*, and that because of this same system which tries to divide us, we haven't understood that *ladinos* also live in terrible conditions, the same as we do.

That's when I became very attached to my *compañeros ladinos* and we began to talk a lot. Our organization includes Indians and poor *ladinos*, so we began putting this into practice. I remember having lengthy discussions with *ladinos*. I especially remember the times for criticism and the self-criticism which, I think, all revolutionary struggles go through to make the change more profound. The first time I pointed out an error by one of the *ladinos*, I felt terrible. Well, I'd never ever criticized a *ladino* before. I know deep inside what it is to feel humiliated, to have always been called 'dirty Indian'. 'She's an Indian', they'd say as an insult. So for me criticizing a *ladino* was like putting on a mask and doing something shamelessly. Nevertheless, my criticism was constructive. I criticized the *compañero* but accepted his criticism too. These were the first things I found difficult to accept in our struggle.

As I was saying, I'm an Indian*ist*, not just an Indian. I'm an Indianist to my fingertips and I defend everything to do with my ancestors. But I didn't understand this in the proper way, because we can only understand when we start talking to each other. And this is the only way we can correct our ideas. Little by little, I discovered many ways in which we had to be understanding towards our *ladino* friends and in which they had to show us understanding too. Because I also knew *compañeros ladinos* with whom we shared the worst conditions, but who still felt *ladino*, and as *ladinos* they didn't see that our poverty united us. But little by little, both they and I began discussing many very important things and saw that the root of our problems lay in the ownership of the land. All our country's riches are in the hands of the few.

My friend was a *compañero* who had taken the side of the poor, although I have to say that he was middle class. He was someone who'd been able to study, who had a profession and everything. But he also understood clearly that he had to share these things with the poor, especially his knowledge. He preferred to help the CUC rather than become a member because he said: 'I don't deserve to be called a peasant. I'm an intellectual.' He recognized his inability to do or know many things that peasants know, or the things poor people know. He said: 'I can't talk about hunger the way a peasant can.' I remember that when we said the root of our problems was the land, that we were exploited, I felt that being an Indian was an extra dimension because I suffered discrimination as well as suffering exploitation. It was an additional reason for fighting with such enthusiasm. I began thinking about my childhood, when we used to go to the market. They used to cheat us when they bought our things because we didn't speak Spanish. Sometimes they'd say they'd paid for our beans or our plants in the market but when we got home and did our sums, the money didn't add up. So in this sense, they exploited us but, at the same time, they discriminated against us because we were ignorant.

So I learned many things with the *ladinos*, but most of all to understand our problem and the fact that we had to solve it ourselves. Sometimes we'd have very heated discussions because the Indians and *ladinos* didn't understand each other. In Guatemala the division between Indians and *ladinos* has contributed to our situation. And it's certain that in our hearts this has affected us very badly. *Ladinos* are *mestizos*, the children of Spaniards and Indians who speak Spanish. But they are in the minority. There is a larger percentage of Indians. Some say it is sixty per cent, others that it's eighty per cent. We don't know the exact number for a very good reason – there are Indians who don't wear Indian clothes and have forgotten their languages, so they are not considered Indians. And there are middle-class Indians who have abandoned their traditions. They aren't considered Indians either. However this *ladino* minority thinks its blood is superior, a higher quality, and they think of Indians as a sort of animal. That's the mark of discrimination. The *ladinos* try to tear off this shell which imprisons them – being the children of Indians and Spaniards. They want to be something different, they don't want to be a mixture. They never mention this mixed blood now. At the same time, there are differences between *ladinos* too; between rich *ladinos* and poor *ladinos*. The poor are considered lazy, people who don't work, who only sleep and who have no enjoyment in life. But between these poor *ladinos* and Indians there is still that big barrier. No matter how bad their conditions are, they feel *ladino*, and being *ladino* is something important in itself: it's *not* being an Indian. That's how they have separated the way they act, the way they think. The *ladinos* want to improve their situation, they're looking for a way out of their shell, because even though the *ladino* is poor, even though he's exploited as we are, he tries to be something better than an Indian. In the market, for example, no *ladino* would steal from another *ladino* as he would from an Indian. A *ladino* would even insult a lady but an Indian could never do that. The *ladino* has many ways of making his voice heard – if he goes to a lawyer, he doesn't need an intermediary. He has more channels of access. And so that's why the poor *ladino* rejects the Indian. If a *ladino* gets on a bus, that's normal. If an Indian gets on, everyone is disgusted. They think we are dirty, worse than an animal or a filthy cat. If an Indian goes near a *ladino*, the *ladino* will leave his seat rather than be with the Indian. We feel this rejection deeply. If you examine the conditions of poor *ladinos* and our conditions, you'll see they are the same. There is no difference. When I was little I used to think about this a lot. What is it? What does the *ladino* have that we don't? I compared myself with them. Is it that some parts of his body are different? And the system feeds this situation. It separates the Indian from the *ladino*. The radio, all the radio stations speak Spanish. Indians have no access to radio. So although we were all poor, we did not understand each other.

That's when I started being more aware of the situation. I understood that my bitter experiences, my affection for my *compañeros*, for my people, had made it difficult for me to accept certain things. I identified certain of my attitudes – very rigid ones. Discrimination had made me isolate myself completely from the world of our *compañeros ladinos*. I didn't express certain of my attitudes but they were nevertheless there, like a thorn in my heart, from having repeated so many times: 'They are *ladinos*, they can't understand because they are *ladinos*.' But slowly, through our discussions, we understood each other. There came a time when the two of us had to carry out tasks together. A *compañero ladino* and me, an Indian. For me it was unbelievable to walk with a *ladino*. I'd been told that Indians were separate for so long. It was like a dream for me, and it made me very reserved with the *compañero*. But that was in the early days and, little by little, as we talked we learned more. To bring about change we had to unite, Indians and *ladinos*. What they valued most in me was my knowledge of self-defence, my knowledge of our traps and escape routes. I could teach other *compañeros*. And later on, through my involvement in the struggle – through my participation as a woman, as a Christian, and as an Indian – I was given responsibilities which recognized my abilities as well. So I had a lot of responsibility.

It was the same with my father. On the rare occasions we saw each other he used to tell me of his experiences and say:

'Now I'm in charge of a whole town. I'm responsible for *ladinos* and Indians. I can't read or write. And my Spanish isn't very good. I've often felt inadequate. Nevertheless, I know my experience is valuable and that I must share it with others.' And this confirmed my certainty that the justification for our struggle was to erase all the images imposed on us, all the cultural differences, and the ethnic barriers, so that we Indians might understand each other in spite of different ways of expressing our religion and beliefs. Our culture is still the same. I discovered that all Indians have a common culture in spite of the linguistic barriers, ethnic barriers and different modes of dress. The basis of our culture is maize. I was by now an educated woman. Not in the sense of any schooling and even less in the sense of being well read. But I knew the history of my people, and the history of my *compañeros* from other ethnic groups. I'd got to know many of the groups closely and they'd taught me a lot, including some things which I'd forgotten.

So we come to 1979. We carried out important tasks on the south coast and in the *Altiplano*, directing the people's struggle. Our organization was no longer a tiny seed. It had won the hearts of the majority of Guatemalans: Indian peasants or poor *ladino* peasants. We travelled all over the *Altiplano*, we went down to the south coast, and we also began working in the east. The important thing to remember is that in the east there are no Indians now. The Indians there have forgotten their costumes, their languages. They no longer speak Indian languages. Just a few old folk speak a little Chorti. It made me very angry that they should forget their customs and culture. They were workers in the *fincas* too. Or else they were overseers, administrators, soldiers or police. I thought about this a lot. They didn't want to do that but they'd been brutalized. I remember my father telling us: 'My children, don't aspire to go to school, because schools take our customs away from us.' These people in the East had more access to lower schools but not to any further training. A few have money but the majority only reach second, third or sixth grade in primary school. But they already think differently: although they are still poor they think differently since we Indians have never even seen a teacher. So I thought: 'Thank God our parents didn't accept teachers or schools in our community to wipe out what is ours.' Sometimes I'd hear how those teachers taught and what education was like in the villages. They said that the arrival of the Spaniards was a conquest, a victory, while we knew that in practice it was just the opposite. They said the Indians didn't know how to fight and that many of them died because they killed the horses and not the people. So they said. This made me furious, but I reserved my anger to educate other people in other areas. This taught me that even though a person may learn to read and write, he should not accept the false education they give our people. Our people must not think as the authorities think. They must not let others think for them.

We can select what is truly relevant for our people. Our lives show us what this is. It has guaranteed our existence. Otherwise we would not have survived. We have rejected all the aims governments have tried to impose. It wasn't only me who did this, of course. I'm saying we did it together. Those are the conclusions my whole community came to. It was the community who taught me to respect all the things which must remain secret as long as we exist, and which future generations will keep secret. That is our objective anyway. When we began to organize ourselves, we started using all the things we'd kept hidden. Our traps – nobody knew about them because they'd been kept secret. Our opinions – whenever a priest came to our village we all kept our mouths shut. We women covered ourselves with our shawls and the men kept their heads bowed. We pretend we're not thinking of anything. But when we're all together, amongst ourselves, we discuss, we think, we give our views. What happens is that, since we've never been given the opportunity to speak, express our opinions, or have our views considered, we haven't bothered to make ourselves heard just for the fun of it. I think as far as this is concerned, we have selected what is relevant for us and have fought for this. As I said before, the life of any single animal means a lot to us. And so much more so the life of a human being. And so when we have to protect our lives, we are ready to defend them even if it means revealing our secrets.

This is why Indians are thought to be stupid. They can't think, they don't know anything, they say. But we have hidden our identity because we needed to resist, we wanted to protect what governments have wanted to take away from us. They have tried to take our things away and impose others on us, be it through religion, through dividing up the land, through schools, through books, through radio, through all things modern. This is why we maintain the rites for our ceremonies. And why we don't accept Catholic Action as the only way to God, and why we don't perform only Christian ceremonies. We don't want to because we know that they are weapons they use to take away what is ours.

XXIV

THE TORTURE AND DEATH
OF HER LITTLE BROTHER,
BURNT ALIVE IN FRONT
OF MEMBERS OF HIS
FAMILY AND THE COMMUNITY

'My mother said that when a woman sees her son tortured,
burnt alive, she is incapable of forgiving, incapable of getting
rid of her hate.'
—Rigoberta Menchú

'. . . but next winter the requital will come [they thought],
and they fed the blaze with branches of the great thorn trees,
because in the fire of warriors, which is the fire of war, even
the thorns weep.'
—Miguel Angel Asturias, *Men of Maize*

It was in 1979, I remember, that my younger brother died,
the first person in my family to be tortured. He was sixteen
years old. After the family's farewell, each of us went their
own way: he stayed in the community since, as I said, he
was secretary of the community. He was the youngest of my
brothers, though I have two little sisters who are younger.
One of them went with my mother and the other stayed in the
community, learning and training in self-defence. My moth-

er, unable to find any other solution, had gone off somewhere else. My brothers too, because they were being hunted, and so as not to expose the community to danger. . . . The thing is that the government put about this image of us, of our family, as if we were monsters, as if we were some kind of foreigners, aliens. But my father was Quiché, he was no Cuban. The government called us communists and accused us of being a bad influence. So, in order not to expose the community to danger and to weed out this 'bad influence', we had to go away to different places. But my young brother had stayed there in the community.

On 9 September 1979 my brother was kidnapped. It was a Sunday, and he'd gone down to another village – he worked in other villages as well as his own. His name was Petrocinio Menchú Tum – Tum is my mother's name. Well, my brother had a job to do. He was very fond of organizing work. So he went round organizing in various places, and the army discovered him and kidnapped him. After 9 September my mother and the rest of us began to worry. At that time – and I still thank God they didn't kill all of us – my mother nonetheless went to the authorities to enquire after him. If they kill me because of my son, she said, let them kill me. I wasn't there at the time; I was in Huehuetenango when my brother was captured. They say that the day he fell, my mother was at home and my other brothers were not far away. Mother went into the village to find out where her son was, but nobody could give her any news of his whereabouts. However, he had been betrayed by someone in the community. As I said before, there are people who'll turn their hand to anything when you least expect it. Out of pure necessity, often they'll sell their own brothers. This man from the community had been a *compañero*, a person who'd always collaborated and who had been in agreement with us. But, they offered him fifteen *quetzals* – that's to say fifteen dollars – to turn my brother in, and so he did. The army didn't know who he was. That day my brother was going to another village with a girl when they caught him. The girl and her mother followed along after him.

From the first moment they tied his hands behind his back, they started to drive him along with kicks. My brother fell, he couldn't protect his face. The first part of him to begin to bleed was his face. They took him over rough ground where there were stones, fallen tree trunks. He walked about two kilometres being kicked and hit all the time. Then they started to threaten the girl and her mother. They were risking their lives by following my brother and finding out where he was being taken. Apparently they said to them: 'Do you want us to do the same to you, do you want us to rape you right here?' That's what this thug of a soldier said. And he told the *señora* that if they didn't go away they'd be tortured just like he was going to be because he was a communist and a subversive, and subversives deserved to be punished and to die.

It's an unbelievable story. We managed to find out how he died, what tortures they inflicted on him from start to finish. They took my brother away, bleeding from different places. When they'd done with him, he didn't look like a person any more. His whole face was disfigured with beating, from striking against the stones, the tree trunks; my brother was completely destroyed. His clothes were torn from his falling down. After that they let the women go. When he got to the camp, he was scarcely on his feet, he couldn't walk any more. And his face, he couldn't see any more, they'd even forced stones into his eyes, my brother's eyes. Once he arrived in the camp they inflicted terrible tortures on him to make him tell where the guerrilla fighters were and where his family was. What was he doing with the Bible, they wanted to know, why were the priests guerrillas? Straight away they talked of the Bible as if it were a subversive tract, they accused priests and nuns of being guerrillas. They asked him what relationship the priests had with the guerrillas, what relationship the whole community had with the guerrillas. So they inflicted those dreadful tortures on him. Day and night they subjected him to terrible, terrible pain. They tied him up, they tied his testicles, my brother's sexual organs, they tied them behind with string and forced him to run. Well, he couldn't stand that, my little brother, he couldn't bear that awful pain and he cried out, he asked for mercy. And they left him in a well, I don't know what it's called, a hole with water and a bit of mud in it, they left him naked there all night. There were a lot of corpses there in the hole with him and he couldn't stand the smell of all those corpses. There were other people there who'd been tortured. He recognized several catechists there who'd been kidnapped from other villages and were suffering as badly as he was. My brother was tortured for more than sixteen days. They cut off his fingernails, they cut off his fingers, they cut off his skin, they burned parts of his skin. Many of the wounds, the first ones, swelled and were infected. He stayed alive. They shaved his head, left just the skin, and also they cut the skin off his head and pulled it down on either side and cut off the fleshy part of his face. My brother suffered tortures on every part of his body, but they took care not to damage the arteries or veins so that he would survive the tortures and not die. They gave him food so that he'd hold out and not die from his wounds. There were twenty men with him who had been tortured or were still undergoing torture. There was also a woman. They had raped her and then tortured her.

As soon as she heard, my mother got in touch with me and I came home. My brother had been missing for three days when I got home. Most of all it was a matter of comforting my mother, because we knew that our enemies were criminals and, well, we wouldn't be able to do anything. If we went to claim him, they'd kidnap us at once. Mother did go, the first days, but they threatened her and said that if she came again she'd get the same treatment as her son was getting. And they told her straight out that her son was being tortured, so not to worry.

Then, on 23 September, we heard that the military were putting out bulletins around the villages. They didn't come to my village because they knew the people were prepared, ready for them at a moment's notice. In other villages, where we also had *compañeros*, they handed out bulletins and propaganda announcing punishment for the guerrillas. Saying they had such and such a number of guerrillas in their power and that they were going to carry out punishment in such and such a place. Well, when we got this news – it must have been about eleven in the morning, I remember, on the 23rd – my mother said: 'My son will be among those who are punished.' It was going to be done in public, that is, they were calling the people out to witness the punishment. Not only that, a bulletin said (we'd managed to get hold of a copy) that any who didn't go to witness the punishment were themselves accomplices of the guerrillas. That was how they threatened the people. So my mother said: 'Come along then, if they're calling out everyone, we'll have to go.' My father also came home at once, saying it was an opportunity we couldn't miss, we must go and see. We were in a frenzy. My brothers arrived. We were all together at home, my brothers, my little sisters, Mother, Father and me. We were preparing the midday meal when we heard the news and we didn't even finish preparing it or remember to take a bit of food to eat on the way. We just went.

We had to cross a long mountain ridge to get to another village – Chajul, where the punishment took place. Mother said: 'We've got to be there tomorrow!' We knew it was a long way off. So we set out at eleven in the morning on the 23rd for Chajul. We crossed long stretches of mountain country on foot. We walked through some of the night, with pine torches, in the mountains. About eight o'clock the next morning we were entering the village of Chajul. The soldiers had the little village surrounded. There were about five hundred of them. They'd made all the people come out of their houses, with threats that if they didn't go to watch the punishment they'd suffer the same punishment, the same tortures. They stopped us on the road, but they didn't know we were relatives of one of the tortured. They asked us where we were going. My father said: 'To visit the saint at Chajul.' There's a saint there that many people visit. The soldier said: 'No chance of that, get going, go over there. And if you get there, you'll see that no-one leaves this village.' We said, 'All right.' About twenty soldiers, it must have been, stopped us at different points before we reached the village. They all threatened us the same way. They were waiting for the men whom they hadn't found when they emptied the houses, in case they'd gone to work, to make them come back to the village to see the punishments. When we reached the village there were many people who'd been there since early morning: children, women, men. Minutes later, the army was surrounding the people who were there to watch. There were machines, armoured cars, jeeps, all kinds of weapons. Helicopters started to fly over the village so that the guerrilla fighters wouldn't come. That's what they were afraid of. The officer opened the meeting. I remember he started by saying that a group of guerrillas they'd caught were about to arrive and that they were going to suffer a little punishment. A little punishment, because there were greater punishments, he said, but you'll see the punishment they get. And that's for being communists! For being Cubans, for being subversives! And if you get mixed up with communists and subversives, you'll get the same treatment as these subversives you'll be seeing in a little while. My mother was just about a hundred per cent certain her son would be amongst those being brought in. I was still not sure, though, because I knew my brother wasn't a criminal and didn't deserve such punishments.

Well, a few minutes later three army lorries came into the village. One went a little ahead, the middle one carried the tortured people and the third one brought up the rear. They guarded them very closely, even with armoured cars. The lorry with the tortured came in. They started to take them out one by one. They were all wearing army uniforms. But their faces were monstrously disfigured, unrecognizable. My mother went closer to the lorry to see if she could recognize her son. Each of the tortured had different wounds on the face. I mean, their faces all looked different. But my mother recognized her son, my little brother, among them. They put them in a line. Some of them were, very nearly, half-dead, or they were nearly in their last agony, and others, you could see that they were; you could see that very well indeed. My brother was very badly tortured, he could hardly stand up. All the tortured had no nails and they had cut off part of the soles of their feet. They were barefoot. They forced them to walk and put them in a line. They fell down at once. They picked them up again. There was a squadron of soldiers there ready to do exactly what the officer ordered. And the officer carried on with his rigmarole, saying that we had to be satisfied with our lands, we had to be satisfied with eating bread and chile, but we mustn't let ourselves be led astray by communist ideas. Saying that all the people had access to everything, that they were content. If I remember aright, he must have repeated the word 'communist' a hundred times. He started off with the Soviet Union, Cuba, Nicaragua; he said that the same communists from the Soviet Union had moved on to Cuba and then Nicaragua and that now they were in Guatemala. And that those Cubans would die a death like that of these tortured people. Every time he paused in his speech, they forced the tortured up with kicks and blows from their weapons.

No-one could leave the meeting. Everyone was weeping. I . . . I don't know, every time I tell this story, I can't hold back my tears, for me it's a reality I can't forget, even though it's not easy to tell of it. My mother was weeping; she was looking at her son. My brother scarcely recognized us. Or perhaps . . . My mother said he did, that he could still smile at her, but I, well, I didn't see that. They were monstrous. They were all fat, fat, fat. They were all swollen up, all wounded. When I drew closer to them, I saw that their clothes were damp. Damp from the moisture oozing out of their bodies. Somewhere around half-way through the speech, it would be about an hour and a half, two hours on, the captain made the squad of soldiers take the clothes off the tortured people, saying that it was so that everyone could see for themselves what their punishment had been and realize that if we got mixed up in communism, in terrorism, we'd be punished the same way. Threatening the people like that, they wanted to force us to do just as they said. They couldn't simply take the clothes off the tortured men, so the soldiers brought scissors and cut the clothes apart from the feet up and took the clothes off the tortured bodies. They all had the marks of different tortures. The captain devoted himself to explaining each of the different tortures. This is perforation with needles, he'd say, this is a wire burn. He went on like that explaining each torture and describing each tortured man. There were three people who looked like bladders. I mean, they were inflated, although they had no wounds on their bodies. But they were inflated, inflated. And the officer said, that's from something we put in them that hurts them. The important thing is that they should know that it hurts and that the people should know it's no easy thing to have that done to your body.

In my brother's case, he was cut in various places. His head was shaved and slashed. He had no nails. He had no soles to his feet. The earlier wounds were suppurating from infection. And the woman *compañera*, of course I recognized her; she was from a village near ours. They had shaved her private parts. The nipple of one of her breasts was missing and her other breast was cut off. She had the marks of bites on different parts of her body. She was bitten all over, that *compañera*. She had no ears. All of them were missing part of the tongue or had had their tongues split apart. I found it impossible to concentrate, seeing that this could be. You could only think that these were human beings and what pain those bodies had felt to arrive at that unrecognizable state. All the people were crying, even the children. I was watching the children. They were crying and terrified, clinging to their mothers. We didn't know what to do. During his speech, the captain kept saying his government was democratic and gave us everything. What more could we want? He said that the subversives brought foreign ideas, exotic ideas that would only lead us to torture, and he'd point to the bodies of the men. If we listened to these exotic slogans, he said, we'd die like them. He said they had all kinds of weapons that we could choose to be killed with. The captain gave a panoramic description of all the power they had, the capacity they had. We, the people, didn't have the capacity to confront them. This was really all being said to strike terror into the people and stop anyone from speaking. My mother wept. She almost risked her own life by going to embrace my brother. My other brothers and my father held her back so she wouldn't endanger herself. My father was incredible; I watched him and he didn't shed a tear, but he was full of rage. And that was a rage we all felt. But all the rest of us began to weep, like everyone else. We couldn't believe it, I couldn't believe that had happened to my little brother. What had he done to deserve that? He was just an innocent child and that had happened to him.

After he'd finished talking the officer ordered the squad to take away those who'd been 'punished', naked and swollen as they were. They dragged them along, they could no longer walk. Dragged them along to this place, where they lined them up all together within sight of everyone. The officer called to the worst of his criminals – the *Kaibiles*, who wear different clothes from other soldiers. They're the ones with the most training, the most power. Well, he called the *Kaibiles* and they poured petrol over each of the tortured. The captain said, 'This isn't the last of their punishments, there's another one yet. This is what we've done with all the subversives we catch, because they have to die by violence. And if this doesn't teach you a lesson, this is what'll happen to you too. The problem is that the Indians let themselves be led by the communists. Since no-one's told the Indians anything, they go along with the communists.' He was trying to convince the people but at the same time he was insulting them by what he said. Anyway, they lined up the tortured and poured petrol on them; and then the soldiers set fire to each one of them. Many of them begged for mercy. They looked half dead when they were lined up there, but when the bodies began to burn they began to plead for mercy. Some of them screamed, many of them leapt but uttered no sound – of course, that was because their breathing was cut off.

But – and to me this was incredible – many of the people had weapons with them, the ones who'd been on their way to work had machetes, others had nothing in their hands, but when they saw the army setting fire to the victims, everyone wanted to strike back, to risk their lives doing it, despite all the soldiers' arms. . . . Faced with its own cowardice, the army itself realized that the whole people were prepared to fight. You could see that even the children were enraged, but they didn't know how to express their rage.

Well, the officer quickly gave the order for the squad to withdraw. They all fell back holding their weapons up and shouting slogans as if it were a celebration. They were happy! They roared with laughter and cried, 'Long live the fatherland! Long live Guatemala! Long live our president! Long live the army, long live Lucas!' The people raised their weapons and rushed at the army, but they drew back at once, because there was the risk of a massacre. The army had all kinds of arms, even planes flying overhead. Anyway, if there'd been a confrontation with the army, the people would have been massacred. But nobody thought about death. I didn't think that I might die, I just wanted to do something, even kill a soldier. At that moment I wanted to show my aggression. Many people hurried off for water to put out the fires, but no-one fetched it in time. It needed lots of people to carry the water – the water supply is in one particular place and everyone goes there for it – but it was a long way off and nothing could be done. The bodies were twitching about. Although the fire had gone out, the bodies kept twitching. It was a frightful thing for me to accept that. You know, it wasn't just my brother's life. It was many lives, and you don't think that the grief is just for yourself but for all the relatives of the others: God knows if they found relatives of theirs there or not! Anyway, they were Indians, our brothers. And what you think is that Indians are already being killed off by malnutrition, and when our parents can hardly give us enough to live on, and make such sacrifices so that we can grow up, then they burn us alive like that. Savagely. I said, this is impossible, and that was precisely the moment for me, personally, when I finally felt firmly convinced that if it's a sin to kill a human being, how can what the regime does to us not be a sin?

Everyone set to work, so that in two hours there were coffins for all the bodies. Everyone busied themselves with finding a blanket to put over them. I remember they picked bunches of flowers and put them beside them. The people of Guatemala are mostly Christian. They express their faith one way or another; they went to fetch the priest (I suppose that priest's since been murdered as well) to ask him, since he was a long way from the village, to bless the blanket to put over the corpses. When the fires died out, for a while nobody knew what to do: it was both terrifying to see the burned, tortured bodies and at the same time it gave you courage, strength to keep on going. My mother was half dead with grief. She embraced her son, she spoke to him, dead and tortured as he was. She kissed him and everything, though he was burnt. I said to her: 'Come, let's go home.' We couldn't bear to watch, we couldn't bear to keep looking at the dead. It wasn't through cowardice, rather that it filled us with rage. It was intolerable. So, all the people promised to give all the dead and tortured a Christian burial. Then my mother said, 'I can't stay here.' So we had to go, to leave it all behind and leave off looking. My father and my brothers were there, grieving. We just saw that the people . . . there were flowers, there was everything. The people decided to bury them there, not to take them home. There would have been a wake in one of the houses, but the people said, they didn't die in a house, it's fitting that this place should be sacred to them. We left them there. And it started to rain; it rained heavily. There they were getting wet, the people watching over the corpses. None of them left that spot. They all stayed.

But we went home. It was as though we were drunk or struck dumb; none of us uttered a word. When we got home Father said: 'I'm going back to work.' Then he started to talk to us. He said, rightly, that if so many people were brave enough to give their lives, their last moments, their last drop of blood, then wouldn't we be brave enough to do the same? And my mother, too, said: 'It's not possible that other mothers should suffer as I have suffered. The people cannot endure that, their children being killed. I've decided too to abandon everything; I shall go away.' And we all said the same: there was nothing else you could say. Though, for myself, I didn't know what would be the most effective: to take up arms, to go to fight – which was what I most wanted to do – or to go to some other village and continue consciousness-raising among the people. My father said: 'I may be old, but I'm joining the guerrillas. I'll avenge my son with arms.' But I also considered that the community was important, since I had experience in organizing people. We concluded that the most important thing was to organize the people so that they wouldn't have to suffer the way we had, see that horror film that was my brother's death.

The next day my father sorted out his things and left the house without delay. 'Whether I return or not,' he said, 'I know the house will remain. I'll try to attend to everything in the community; that's always been my dream. Well, I'm going now.' And my father left. Mother stayed in the house, not knowing what to do. She couldn't bear it, she remembered the whole thing. She cried from moment to moment, remembering. But most of the time she didn't cry; she tried to be cheerful. She said that her son was the one who had been a lot of trouble to bring up, because he'd nearly died as a little child. She had to go into a lot of debt to cure him. And then for this to happen to him. It made her very sad. But there were times when she cheered up. I remember that during this time Mother was very close to the *compañeros* in the mountains. Since we still had my brother's clothes – his trousers and shirts – my mother gave them away to one of the *compañeros* in the mountains, saying it was only just that they should be used by the *compañeros* because they were her son's clothes and her son had always been against the whole situation we were facing. And since the *compañeros* were against it too, they should use the clothes. Sometimes my mother was mad. All the neighbours would come and look. And mother thought: 'If I start crying in front of the neighbours, what sort of example will that be?' 'No crying; fighting's what we want,' she'd say, and she'd act tough, and in spite of the fact that she was always a little ill and felt very tired, she'd battle on.

I stayed in the house a week longer. Then I made up my mind and said: 'I must go.' So I left, keener than ever to work. I knew that my mother also had to leave home. There was hardly any communication between us, either about where we were going or what we were going to do. I had the chance to say goodbye to my brothers, but I didn't know what they were going to do either. Each of us took our own decision. And so I left.

XXV

RIGOBERTA'S FATHER DIES IN THE OCCUPATION OF THE SPANISH EMBASSY. PEASANTS MARCH TO THE CAPITAL

'My father said: *"Some have to give their blood and some have to give their strength; so while we can, we'll give our strength."*'

—Rigoberta Menchú

In November of that same year, 1979, I saw my father quite by chance. I'd gone to El Quiché for a meeting. It was a meeting of leaders of the Committee from many different areas. I'd been invited. When I saw my father, I was delighted. And in front of all the *compañeros*, he said: 'This badly brought up daughter has always been a good daughter,' and he asked them to be a father to me, to all of us, if one day he was killed. The meeting lasted a long time and a lot of things happened with regard to our work. After the meeting I was able to talk to my father for two days. We talked about our experiences in our work. He was pleased and said that as our people became able to organize by themselves, as new *compañeros* were coming up to lead the struggle, he was ready to take up arms. Because he said: 'I am a Christian and the duty of a Christian is to fight all the injustices committed against our people. It is not right that our people give their blood, their pure lives, for the few who are in power.' His views were as clear as any theoretician, as if he'd studied and all that. All his concepts were clear. Then he gave me some encouragement for us to go on with our work. 'We may not see each other for a long time but remember that, alive or not, I will always help you in whatever way I can.' Then he told us to look after my mother. He said we should look for her and find her so that she shouldn't put her life in such danger because – 'Some people give their blood and some people give their strength. So while we can, we must give our strength. In this hour of need, we must look after our little lives very well so that they provide a source of strength for our people.' And he said clearly: 'We want no more dead, we want no more martyrs, because we already have too many in our land, in our fields, through too many massacres. What we must do is protect our lives as much as we can and carry on with our struggle . . .'

Then I said goodbye to my father. He recommended I be in the capital in January because there was going to be some action calling on the government to do something about the situation. The situation would only improve if many of us were willing to risk our lives. It was going to be another demonstration with students, workers, unions, peasants, Christians, all protesting about the repression in El Quiché. Soldiers were kidnapping people all the time in El Quiché. We'd hear news of ten, fifteen people who'd disappeared somewhere but they never said who they were. We'd get news like that every day. So my father said it was very important for me to be there. He would be there, and my brothers, and I should be there too if I could. I was determined to be there.

I arrived in the area where I was to work. They were being repressed too and needed to organize. What should we do? We got a course of self-defence under way. My father sent me word of the date of the demonstration but I had a commitment. I remember this peasant *compañero* there saying: 'No, *compañera*, this course is important. You can't go to the capital.' I thought about it a lot. It was perhaps my only chance of seeing my father. I loved my father very much. But our situation wouldn't allow me to go. The course was very important too. We had to support the peasants there right away. So I stayed to do my work.

The march on the capital was organised to demand that the army leave El Quiché. They brought many orphaned children with them as proof of the repression. They took over several radio stations to tell people about our plight. At the same time, they thought they should make it known internationally by occupying an embassy where the ambassadors would be spokesmen. Unfortunately most of us were too poor to think of going on a tour of other countries. We were very poor and our organization didn't have the resources to fight the army. The people wanted arms to defend themselves. And so first they occupied the Swiss embassy in Guatemala. Others took over radio stations. The peasants came from many different areas. From the south coast, from the east, but most of them were from El Quiché because that's where the repression was concentrated. Almost all the leaders in the struggle were peasants. My father was, so were many other *compañeros* who died that day. The last action was to occupy the Spanish embassy. Before the occupation – it was a miracle – I heard that my mother was willing to go, and so were my brothers. But the organization said no, because they were afraid something might happen; the *compañeros* were all prepared to put themselves in any kind of danger. So they occupied the Spanish embassy.

But what happened afterwards was something we could never have imagined. First, because they were important people; and second because government officials were there and they died in the fire together with the peasants. Of course we knew there would be tension, but we thought that they would give all the ones who occupied the embassy permission to leave the country as political refugees, and they would be able to spread the news of our struggle abroad. The objective was to tell the whole world what was happening in Guatemala and inform people inside the country as well.

They were all burned to death. The only thing left was their ashes. This was a tremendous blow for us. For me, it wasn't mourning my father so much. It was easy for me to concede that my father had died, because he had been forced to lead the same brutal, criminal life that we all had. My father was prepared, it was clear that he had to give his life. So for me it wasn't painful accepting my father's death, I was happy because I knew he hadn't suffered as I imagined he would have suffered if he'd fallen into the enemy's hands alive. That was what I dreaded. No, what hurt me very, very much was the lives of so many *compañeros*, fine *compañeros*, who weren't ambitious for power in the least. All they wanted was enough to live on, enough to meet their people's needs. This reinforced my decision to fight.

But I had to face some terrible moments. First, when the news came that the bodies were unrecognizable and I thought that my mother and my brothers were there. What I couldn't bear was the idea of them all dying together. We must all give our lives, I know – but not all together. Let it be one at a time so that someone is left, even if it's only one of our family. I couldn't bear it. I couldn't bear to be the only one left. I actually wanted to die. These are things which happen to you as they do any human being. But we face them and bear them. I desperately wanted to go to the city. Even if only just to see my father's grave. There will be many *compañeros* to bury, and my love will be for all of them, not just for my father. I didn't go to the capital.

The burned bodies were buried. It was something extraordinary for the whole of Guatemala. Never in all its history had the people been so militant, on every level. Thousands of people buried the *compañeros* who died. The people were moved by resistance to and hatred of the government. People at all levels – poor, middle class, professional – all risked their lives by going to the funeral of the *compañeros* from the Spanish embassy. They'd occupied the Spanish embassy perhaps because of our relationship with Spain. The good thing was that Spain broke off relations with Guatemala immediately. Although if you think about it, Spain has a lot to do with our situation. They have a lot to do with the origins of the suffering of the people, especially of the Indians. Some of the versions they gave out were, that the peasants were armed, that they burned themselves, etc. Neither we nor any of our *compañeros* can say what the real truth is because no-one from the Spanish embassy siege survived. All of them, every single one – died; the *compañeros* who coordinated the action and the *compañeros* who were keeping watch. Some were gunned down in other places after the embassy events. The G2 and the police stormed the embassy. There were a lot of journalists there, in fact, because of the solidarity work of other *compañeros*. They say that the police threw bombs, or I don't know what, at the embassy and it started to burn. The only clues we had were that the bodies were stiff, rigid and all twisted. From the study made by our *compañeros* afterwards and the opinion of other people who know about explosives and bombs that kill people, they could have used sulphur bombs so that they only had to breath in the smoke to become stiff straight away. But it is incredible, because my father had five bullet holes in the head and one in the heart, and he was very stiff. It's thought that the grenades thrown into the embassy were what punctured the bodies.

Endless versions have been offered. But, in fact, one of our *compañeros*, Gregorio Yuja Xona, was still alive among the bodies. We managed to rescue him and take him to a private hospital for medical attention. He was the only one who might have told what really happened. But later he was kidnapped from the hospital by armed men, men in uniform who just calmly took him away. The next day he was left in front of San Carlos University: tortured, with bullet wounds, dead. So the government itself had not allowed this *compañero* to live. We weren't able to talk to him because he was dying. The real truth is that we know the peasants couldn't have had firearms. They'd have had weapons like machetes and stones with them. That was all they ever used in the places they took over. However, as I said to someone who asked me for specific details of what happened in the Spanish embassy, I can't invent my own personal version from my imagination. None of our *compañeros* can know exactly. This event marked my life personally as much as it did the lives of many of my *compañeros*. We moved on to a new stage of the struggle.

XXVI

RIGOBERTA TALKS
ABOUT HER FATHER

*'Remember us after we have gone. Don't forget us. Conjure
up our faces and our words. Our image will be as dew in the
hearts of those who want to remember us.'*

—Popol Vuh

My father was our community's elected leader, and so was
my mother. My father used to say: 'We don't do this so that
our neighbours can say, "What good people they are!" We
do it for our ancestors.' So anything we did that our neighbours might take as a bad example, my father would correct
us at once. But he didn't chastise us, because he considered
that the things we did, we'd learned from the times we live
in. He blamed the times we were passing through, but he
also said that we had to prevail over these times through the
living memory of our ancestors. He would give us many examples from our grandparents: 'Your grandparents used to
do this, your grandparents used to say that.' And then when
they were hunting my father and he had to be away from the
village often, the responsibility fell on my eldest brother. But
he didn't talk about himself, he'd say: 'This is what my father
did.' And they knew the whole of our grandparents' lives like
a film. My father used to say: 'There are many secrets we
must not tell. We must keep our secrets.' He said that no

rich man, no landowner, no priest or nun, must ever know our secrets. If we don't protect our ancestors' secrets, we'll be responsible for killing them. And this is something which has restricted us a bit, because everything we'd do, we'd do thinking of others: would they like this? or wouldn't they like that? – and even more so because of my father, since everyone loved him and considered him a very important man. So, we, his children, must follow his example.

We also had the example of my grandfather. My grandfather is still alive, I think. He's one hundred and six years old. He's my mother's father. That grandfather used to tell us many bits of his life: he said that years ago, he'd lived when there was slavery. He was the eldest of his brothers and sisters and in those days, the eldest of a family was forced to work as a slave for white men. At whatever time the landowner came to get him, he had to go, because, well, he was their slave. It happened to my grandfather because he was the eldest. He told us about many parts of his life. And it was like an education for us. My father used to tell us: 'My children, whenever you have time, go and talk to your grandfather. He knows what our ancestors said.' It was like a political discussion every time we talked to him, whereby he'd tell us about his life, his own grandparents' lives, and something of the lives of those who'd lived before them. He'd explain why our people didn't live as long now as our ancestors did. He said that when he was a boy, he saw people of a hundred and fifteen, a hundred and seventeen, still alive. And women of a hundred and ten too. He said: 'It's not you children's fault. The modern machines which have come to our land are to blame.' You have to remember, of course, that my grandfather never went to school. But he'd say: 'It's that you eat these chemical things today and that stops you living as long as you should. It's not your fault but that's how it is.'

My grandfather used to curse the Spaniards. The Spaniards were at the root of our plight. They began taking so many things out of our lands, they began stealing from us. Our ancestors' finest sons were those who were dishonoured. They even raped the queens elected by our community. That's how the *ladinos* came into being. The *caxlans*, that is, of two bloods, Indian and Spanish. *Caxlan* means a bit of a mixture. My grandfather used to say: 'The *caxlans* are thieves. Have nothing to do with them. You keep all our ancestors' things.' And he'd be continually talking about his life, about himself. And this helped us preserve our things very much; the majority of our people still keep many things. But many things have been lost too. Now they're not done in exactly the same way as they were before. We have our secrets. My mother had many little secrets that she taught us, just small things. For instance, what to do when a lot of dogs are barking or biting someone. My mother has never been bitten by a dog because she had a secret way of quietening them. And I think this is part of nature, because it has its effect.

My father was a very simple man, like my mother. My mother had a round face and I look rather like her. My father was a very patient man. He wasn't at all bad tempered. He was very kind. Whenever he corrected us, he'd talk to us about it. Unfortunately he wasn't at home a great deal because he was often in the *finca* or in the capital; working for a few *centavos* for us, or dealing with papers. He often came home only once a month, or once every three months; we'd all be together and then he'd have to leave again right away. There were very few times he was with us, but however short a time it was, we learned many things through his teaching. The whole village did. I feel very proud of my father. He was an orphan with no father of his own to teach him or educate him, and even less a mother: he only had people teaching him bad things – hate and rejection. But in spite of this, he made his life himself and I'd say he was a complete man in human terms. He endured real suffering, and had huge problems to resolve, but he never lost his calm way of doing things. And this is the important thing for me. I often can't do things even though I know they are very important, but he did everything with all the serenity this work needs. If he'd been a nervous man, he'd never have been able to do anything, with all that happened to him in life.

I didn't have enough time with my father, but I spent more time near him than my brothers and sisters, because I began going to the capital with him when I was very little. Sometimes I left the work in the *finca* to accompany my father to the capital and other places. And he'd talk to me and explain things to me. When we had nothing to eat, I'd have to go hungry with him, and he'd explain to me why this was so. It was when I still wasn't earning, so my father told me that to earn a *centavo*, something we all knew very well, we had to make a few sacrifices. When I was older, my father regretted my not going to school, as I was a girl able to learn many things. But he always said: 'Unfortunately, if I put you in a school, they'll make you forget your class, they'll turn you into a *ladino*. I don't want that for you and that's why I don't send you.' He might have had the chance to put me in a school when I was about fourteen or fifteen but he couldn't do it because he knew what the consequences would be: the ideas that they would give me.

I remember that we once went to work in a region to the north of El Quiché, in Ixcán. It's the region they call the Zona Reina. It's very well known in Guatemala. There are high, high mountains. No buses or lorries, not even bicycles or anything, can get there. You have to walk over high mountains to reach the area. We went there because we had no more maize. We'd been told that there was work in the Zona Reina at that time, because a certain priest had been there for a long time helping the people with money so they could cultivate their own plots. We'd been told that there was a lot of fruit there: all the fruit, maize, vegetables, beans, that people want to sow. It's a hot region. So when our maize finished, my father said: 'Let's go and work there, and perhaps it will be better than going to the *finca*, if we get maize in exchange for our work.'

We went with all the things we needed for the week or month we'd be there. We took little *tamales* already cooked, so we wouldn't have to waste time making food. We left home all loaded down: my elder brothers, my father and myself. It took us three days to reach the Zona Reina. And on the way I discovered that there were many people, Indians like myself, who'd never seen other people. They were so isolated in the mountains that they didn't know any other people in the world. The first night we were in a town whose name I don't know in Spanish, but we call it 'Amaí'. The people hid and wouldn't let us into their homes. We were thirsty and wanted to rest for a while but the people did not welcome us. We stayed in the yard of an abandoned house there, and carried on our way the next day. We reached the next town. My father had a friend there who later became an undesirable person in the government. He asked him for hospitality for the night and we stayed there. Then we carried on walking.

During the journey my father told us all about the marvellous things there were in our land (and thinking of our ancestors of course), and the closeness of the peasant to nature. We kept quiet and listened to the silence of the mountains. It's a pleasant silence. And in that silence, birds and animals were singing. It is a beautiful region. After a third day's walking we reached the village. This village was wonderful, because everybody had bananas in their gardens. Everyone had a lot of crops: bananas, plantains, *yuca*, maize, beans, *ayote*, *chilacayote*, all the things that grew there. There were so many things, there were things to spare. But the problem was that it was three days' journey through the mountains, and another day from my village to the town – in fact four days in all – so it was difficult to transport the produce. They couldn't get their produce out themselves because horses didn't come as far as these areas. There were some horses but they belonged to the landowners who lived not far away, although they didn't own the whole area.

So the people there received us but they were all afraid. They'd had bad experiences with people who'd taken advantage of this natural wealth. The people said: 'We don't go hungry but we don't have any other things. We buy our clothes every three or four years.' Most of the children were naked, with swollen bellies. They ate hardly any of their maize because they took it to a man who lived nearby. He was a landowner but he didn't own the land where we were yet. They sold him the maize for a little money. They *did* have a pharmacy. They had a *cantina*. That was all they had. What they earned, they spent straight away. The people ate baked or grilled banana every day. They ate almost no *tortillas* because there was no market to buy lime. And lime was very expensive there. The few little traders hardly even carried soap. These people, isolated in the jungle, didn't even have salt.

We stayed there for a month. It was a very good time. We worked every day. There were beautiful rivers: rivers of crystal where you could see the stones at the bottom. They were white or grey and made the river look white or grey. That's what I liked most about being there. But there were a lot of snakes and the people were constantly being bitten by snakes. The snakes used to bask in the sun at midday. It was incredibly hot. So my father said: 'We must get to know what time it is here, otherwise the animals will bite us. We have to know when the snakes are out, because the snakes come out into the sun and then go into the rivers when they are hot. And they could give us scurvy, one of those diseases snakes have.' We liked catching little fish in the waters of the big rivers which ran through there. Four rivers flow through there. The people there call them the Four Torrents. They are four rivers which join together and form one big one. The noise it makes is the noise of a plane taking off. We worked there for a month because there wasn't much food. We had to eat plantains, bananas, *camotes*, and *yucas*, because there was no maize for the people to eat. And there wasn't any lime either. What does all that fruit do? The children all have worms, and little animals in their stomachs. They all have really swollen bellies. I said to my father: 'These children are very fat.' I'd had worms, I'd had them in the *finca*. And my father said: 'It's because they only eat bananas. These children won't live, they're going to die.' And we realized the value of our maize, the value of our lime. That is why, as our ancestors said, it is so sacred. It is true that without maize, without lime, a man has no strength. And perhaps that's why many of us Indians have survived, eating only maize and lime which is in the maize.

Then we went home. On the way – we'd been walking for two days – my father fainted on the path. It was because he was very weak. I was thirteen at the time. I was carrying fifty pounds of maize. My father was carrying a hundred pounds and so were my brothers. With a *mecapal*, as we say in Guatemala – that's the rope we carry the maize with. Then suddenly, my father fainted. We didn't know what to do with him. We were right up in the mountains. I was terrified, really very frightened. It was the first time in my life I'd been really frightened. I'd been afraid when I got lost in the mountains that other time, afraid that a lion or another animal would eat me. But I wasn't too afraid, because I thought, if the animals come I'll talk to them and they'll understand me. But this time, perhaps because I was older, it was a fear which I couldn't express. I just said: 'Oh God! So few of us here in the mountains.' Just my two elder brothers and my father, and my father had fainted. After a while we managed to lift him up, and we shared out his load between the three of us, leaving him with just a little because we couldn't manage all of it.

It was the first time that I felt how much I'd miss my father if he died. My father used to say: 'Don't be afraid, because this is our life, and if we didn't feel this pain, perhaps our life would be different, perhaps we wouldn't think of it as life. This is our life: we must suffer it but we must also enjoy it.' My father loved my brothers too, but for me he felt the same love I did for him. I loved him very much. If anything was wrong, if my stomach ached, I'd go to him rather than to my mother. He discussed everything with me. When we went off to work, for instance, he'd have a conversation with me just as if he were talking to a neighbour. He had a lot of confidence in me and he explained a whole lot of things to me. Me . . . always behind my father. What I liked was that my father never stopped to rest. Sometimes he'd get home, and some trees near the house had to be arranged so that the hens could go and sleep there at night, so my father would climb the trees. He'd say to me: 'Come with me if you want,' and I'd give him my hand for him to help me up the tree. And every time my father opened up a path to go up into the mountains, I'd go behind him to see how he did it. Any single little thing and I'd go with him. But most of all I'd accompany him when he went round doing his work, because although my elder sister worked in the fields and in the *fincas* like I did, when she grew up it was up to her to look after our house in the *Altiplano*. We'd go off to work and she'd stay. So my work was almost the same as my father's and I was very fond of the work we did.

My father always sorted out my problems: that's why I missed him so much when he died, even though we hadn't seen each other for a long time. I was still dependent on him in so many ways. He helped dispel my doubts. Whatever I asked him, he'd explain my doubts exactly. He also defended me a lot. From my brothers and sisters, and from my mother. From anything. However, if justice had to fall on me, if they were my mistakes, well, then I would feel his hand too. But he always defended me. The thing was that when I was a little girl, I was very shy. I was very timid. Sometimes I didn't even complain when my brothers hit me. And so when I grew up, I felt very insecure about many things. I had a lot of doubts. My father tried to get me out of that and always backed me up. Many of the things I found difficult, my father would explain to me. He said: 'Learning is difficult, but you do it and you learn.' When he had meetings with people, he'd choose me first, so I'd stop keeping my opinions to myself. I didn't like intruding when all the others were giving their views. So my father taught me how to speak. 'You must speak here,' he'd say. I hardly ever fought with any of the boys in my village, because I've got more or less the same attitudes as they have, getting mixed up in different things in just the same ways as my brothers. Take darkness, for example – my elder sister is terrified of the dark. Sometimes we'd be sent off to work at night, at three in the morning, to another village and we'd go through the mountains with a small *ocote*. My sister always thought that lions were coming out from all sides. But I wasn't frightened. If I thought there was something there, I'd stop, and if there wasn't anything, I'd carry on walking.

XXVII

KIDNAPPING AND DEATH
OF RIGOBERTA'S MOTHER

'We must prevail over the times we are living in with the help
of our ancestors.'

—Rigoberta Menchú

'He bragged that he would burn up my borders, and kill my
young men with his sword, and dash the suckling children
against the ground, and make mine infants as a prey, and my
virgins as a spoil. But the Almighty Lord hath disappointed
them by the hand of a woman.'

—Book of Judith 16:5–6

And so my mother went back to our village, and was going secretly to buy things for the community when they kidnapped her on the 19th of April, 1980.

I knew that after they'd killed my father, my mother was
on her way back to my village. It made me very sad for her
because she told me that she had a lot to do with other ethnic groups, in other regions, getting people organized. If my
mother went back to the *Altiplano* it was certainly because
eight *compañeros* from my village were killed in the Spanish embassy. These eight *compañeros* were our village's best,
most active *compañeros*. Well, my mother said: 'I'll go back
to my home because my community needs me now.' And she

went back. The priests and nuns who were in my village at the time offered to help her leave the country, but my mother had never thought of being a refugee. She said: 'No, I can't, my people need me and here is where I have to be.' She went home and, in fact, it was true that the community was dying of hunger, because they couldn't go down to any town or anywhere. Nobody dared risk their lives just to go and buy something to eat.

I sometimes used to hear that my mother was in other provinces because, just by chance, people would tell me about this woman who'd had such and such an experience. And I'd say: 'That's my mother. Thank goodness she's not in the *Altiplano*.' But I was extremely uneasy because I didn't know where she was and what could be happening to her. We know very well, we're quite clear about it, that if the time comes for our parents to die, they die knowing it's for our cause. And I always hoped to see them again. If only we could all be together again one day. My mother used to say that through her life, through her living testimony, she tried to tell women that they too had to participate, so that when the repression comes and with it a lot of suffering, it's not only the men who suffer. Women must join the struggle in their own way. My mother's words told them that any evolution, any change, in which women had not participated, would not be a change, and there would be no victory. She was as clear about this as if she were a woman with all sorts of theories and a lot of practice. My mother spoke almost no Spanish, but she spoke two languages – Quiché, and a bit of Kekchi. She took all that courage and all that knowledge she had, and went to organize her people. But it was, oh, so painful for me, when I'd hear that my mother was in Sololá, and then I'd hear from someone else that she was in Chimaltenango, or that she was going around El Quiché.

My mother travelled through many provinces organizing. She actually went to the women and said that when a woman sees her son tortured and burned to death, she is incapable of forgiving anyone or ridding herself of that hatred, that bitterness. 'I can't forgive my enemies,' she said. She took this important message and was very influential in many places. Many people respected her. She even went into the shanty towns round the cities. My mother was very active. She worked alongside other women and she talked to them. That is, you didn't have to go to a meeting to talk to my mother because she'd go to houses and recount her experiences while they all made *tortillas*. That was how she worked. She talked about her experiences while she helped them with their work.

I remember when my little brother disappeared, our whole community united and joined together in a protest, after my mother had gone to enquire after him at the police, and the army, and had received no reply. So, they all went, all of them. The community acted together for the first time; the majority of them were women. We knew that if the men went, they'd be kidnapped and tortured. So my mother said it would be better to hold a demonstration of women and children to see if the enemies, the army, were so shameless, so cowardly, that they would massacre women and children. We knew they were capable of it. That is, we all came knowing full well that there could be a massacre in the town. They reached the town, occupied the administrative offices, and took the mayor prisoner. If he saw justice was done, they would respect him, but if he turned his back on justice, he would be executed. It was the first time women had acted this way. Everyone admired them. First, because they'd come a long way, and second, because they came with their children to protest to the authorities against the kidnapping, and demonstrate their revulsion.

Some days later, they occupied the Guatemalan Congress. My mother was there, and my father, and the peasants. It was on the Guatemalan National Day. All the deputies were there. Indians from all over El Quiché joined those from Uspantán in the march and, with the help of the unions and of the CUC, took over the Congress building. When the deputies realised what had happened, it was too late to get us out. We were helped by the unions, other peasants and students as well. So what would they do? Were they going to massacre us? That was the first danger we faced. Something rather amusing happened. When they entered the Congress, the soldiers immediately raised their rifles. The person at the head of the demonstration was one of my brothers. When my eldest brother began to speak, they raised their rifles and took aim. Then my little sister came with a white flower. This is very meaningful for us. I think I said before, we only cut flowers when we really need to or when it's for something important. Well, all the people on the demonstration held bunches of flowers to mean that they appealed for respect for human life and also for a solution to their plight. My little sister put herself in front of the rifle with her flower, and they didn't dare shoot my brother. We occupied the Congress to plead for my little brother who'd been kidnapped, and for the hundreds of catechists who'd been taken away in different villages. We also demanded the withdrawal of the army from our communities and that they cease massacring us and raping our women. It was a protest to ask the president to stop the repression, and we did it peacefully. But nothing.

Their immediate reply was to burn my brother. And they went on massacring more villages, like before. Well, because of this, we had to act more quickly. What they told us was that Congress wasn't a building for Indians, and that Indians had no right to enter Congress. It was a respectable building, because it was for members of the government. But the peasants said, we're here and it's here you can kill us . . . That is, they'd gone ready to die, knowing that if there was a massacre, it would not be in vain but would be a protest against our situation. And after that, we went on organising continually, we did it joyfully because ours was a just cause and we were motivated by something, something real.

My mother was kidnapped. And from the very beginning she was raped by the town's high-ranking army officers. And I want to say in advance that I have in my hands details of every step of the rape and torture suffered by my mother. I don't want to reveal too many things because it will implicate some *compañeros* who are still doing their work very well. My mother was raped by her kidnappers, and after that they took her down to the camp – a camp called Chajup which means 'under the cliff'. They have a lot of pits there where they punish the people they have kidnapped and where my little brother was tortured as well. They took my mother to the same place. There she was raped by the officers commanding the troops. After that she was subjected to terrible tortures. The first day they shaved her head, put a uniform on her and then they said: 'If you're a guerrilla why don't you fight us here.' But my mother said nothing. While they beat her, they asked her where we were, and said that if she made a confession, they'd let her go. But my mother knew very well that they did that so that they could torture her other children and would never let her go. She pretended she knew nothing. She defended every one of us until the end. On the third day of her torture, they cut off her ears. They cut her whole body bit by bit. They began with small tortures, small beatings and worked up to terrible tortures. The first tortures she'd received became infected. It was her turn to suffer the terrible pain her son had suffered too. They tortured her the whole time and didn't give her any food for many days. From the pain, from the torture all over her body, disfigured and starving, my mother began to lose consciousness and was in her death throes. Then the officer in charge sent for the medical team they have in the army and they gave her injections and enough serum to revive her, to bring her back to life again. They gave her medicine, they looked after her well, and found a place for her where she was treated well. When she was a little better, well, of course, she asked for food. They gave her food. Then they started raping her again. She was disfigured by those same officers. She endured a great deal, but she didn't die.

When my mother was on the point of dying again, they sent us messages by all sorts of methods. They took my mother's clothes to the town hall in Uspantán. They exhibited it to prove to us that she was in their hands. We sent certain people to investigate what was happening to her and they said that we should go, that my mother was still alive, that she was in their hands and they were torturing her. She needed to see one of her children. It was like that, the whole time. We'd lost my little brother, but I didn't know if my little sister had been captured with my mother or if she was doing other things. No-one knew. It was very painful for me to accept that my mother was being tortured and not to know anything about the rest of the family. None of us presented ourselves. Least of all my brothers. I was able to contact one of my brothers and he told me not to put my life in danger, that they were going to kill my mother anyway and would kill us too. We have to keep this grief as a testimony to them because they never exposed their lives even when their grief was great too. And so we had to accept that my mother was going to die anyway.

When they saw that none of her children were coming down to collect my mother's clothes, the army took her to a place near the town where it was very hilly. It was my hope that my mother would die surrounded by the nature she so loved. They put her under a tree and left her there, alive but dying. They didn't let my mother turn over, and her face was so disfigured, cut and infected; she could barely make any movement by herself. They left her there dying for four or five days, enduring the sun, the rain and the night. My mother was covered in worms, because in the mountains there is a fly which gets straight into any wound, and if the wound isn't tended in two days, there are worms where the fly has been. Since all my mother's wounds were open, there were worms in all of them. She was still alive. My mother died in terrible agony. When my mother died, the soldiers stood over her and urinated in her mouth; even after she was dead! Then they left a permanent sentry there to guard her body so that no-one could take it away, not even what was left of it. The soldiers were there right by her body, and they could smell my mother when she started to smell very strongly. They were there right by her; they ate near her, and, if the animals will excuse me, I believe not even animals act like that, like those savages in the army. After that, my mother was eaten by animals; by dogs, by all the *zopilotes* there are round there, and other animals helped too. They stayed for four months, until they saw that not a bit of my mother was left, not even her bones, and then they went away.

Of course, it was dreadful for us when we knew my mother was dying in agony. But, afterwards, when she was dead . . . naturally we weren't pleased because no human being is happy about that . . . but all the same, we were relieved to know my mother wasn't suffering any longer. She'd gone through so much torment that the one thing we wanted most was for them to kill her quickly, that she should live no longer.

XXVIII

DEATH

*'They began slowly to descend the side of the setting sun.
Then a cloud like rain hid them.'*

—Popol Vuh

Among Indians, the phenomenon of death is something that
we prepare ourselves for. It's not something unknown that
happens, it's more like a preparation. For instance, the coffin
is built a long time beforehand so that the person who is going to die, the old person, gets to know his coffin. And, at the
moment he is going to die, the moment he feels he will die, he
calls to him the person he loves most, the person he is closest
to (it can be a daughter, or a granddaughter in the case of a
grandmother, or a son or a grandson if it's a grandfather, or
any person close to them). He makes his last recommendations to them and at the same time gives them the secret of
their ancestors, their own experiences, their reflections. He
tells them his secrets, and advises them how to act in life,
towards the Indian community, and towards the *ladino*. That
is, everything which is handed down through the generations
to preserve Indian culture. The person who receives these recommendations keeps the secrets, and passes them on before
he dies, and so on, from generation to generation. Then after that the family gathers, and he talks to them as well. He
repeats his recommendations, and goes through his life for

them. This is not like the secrets. Those are only given to one person, the recommendations are made for everyone. Then he dies peacefully. He dies feeling he has done his duty, completed his life, as he had to.

The death ceremony is performed in the house of the dead person. Everyone comes, the whole village pays its respects to the dead person and visits the family. The community takes care of all the expenses. That is, the family bears none of the expense. They sit with the dead man through the night and prepare food for the people present. One very important thing is the drink, what they serve to drink, and it's one occasion that we can eat a little better. We can eat meat and other things. There's also a sort of ceremony, which is a bit like the ceremony we perform for the maize, when we sow our maize. We put candles in the four cardinal points, and cut flowers – one of the few occasions we do that. We cut flowers for the dead person and put them round his coffin. Then we talk about the dead person. Everyone recounts something about him. The family speak, and if he hasn't any family, the village representative speaks because he is like his family. We talk about him and recount the things he did during his life, but we don't only praise him – we can criticize him too. We spend the whole night talking about the dead person, about his life, remembering him.

We don't leave the body in the house for long. Respects are paid quickly and the body is buried within twenty-four hours. He is left as short a time as possible; just one night for the ceremony and then he's buried. The actual burial is very important. One detail is that, when he's buried, all the objects he most loved in his lifetime are put in his coffin. The objects are not to be used by his heirs but stay with him. We bury all the things he liked: the machete he'd had all his life; the cup he drank from; all the things he used every day. When he dies, his clothes are put in a place and not used again, unless they are used by a very dear friend, someone he loved very much. When he's about to die everyone is attentive to what he's going to say and recommend. We say that a person, on his deathbed, makes an inventory of his life, and his mind passes over all the places he has lived. That is, if he's lived in a *finca*, he returns to it again in his spirit, in his mind.

As for killing someone: death lived by others – be it death through an accident or any other kind – is something we feel very deeply, we feel it in our own flesh. For example, the way my little brother died: murdered. We don't even like killing animals. Because we don't like killing. There is no violence in the Indian community. Take the death of a child. If a child dies of malnutrition, it is not the fault of the father but the fault of the conditions imposed on us by the *ladino*. It is the system which abuses us. In the past especially, everything was the fault of the *ladino*. Now we've thought a lot about many of the things our grandparents used to tell us again and again. That now they want to destroy us with medicines and other things. Now they want to make us live differently to the way we want to live. For us, killing is something monstrous. And that's why we feel so angered by all the repression. Even more than that: our dedication to the struggle is a reaction against it, against all the suffering we endure.

We have put our trust in the *compañeros* in the mountains. They saw our plight. They go through what we go through, and they have adapted to the conditions we live in. We can only love a person who eats what we eat. Once the Indian opens his heart to them, all those in the mountains will be his brothers. We didn't feel deceived as we did with the army, when the army takes away the sons of Indians. That means a break with their culture, with their past. We felt abused when they came and took our men, our boys, because we knew that although we might see them again, they would no longer be the same. And for the soldiers, it's something much more serious than that. It's not only that they might lose their culture, but that the Indian soldier can kill other Indians. When Indians decide to go to fight in the mountains, they know that anything can happen to them. They can die in combat at any time. Since those rituals cannot be performed for a dying person in the mountains where conditions make it difficult, the ceremony of recommendations is performed in the village. The same ceremony that the dead person performs with his family, before dying, an Indian does before going off to fight in the mountains, in case anything happens to him. In this way he passes on his secrets before joining the guerrilla army. They get together one night. A family which is leaving the next day, for instance, gets together and performs the ceremony to make their recommendations. After that they leave. It's to fulfil your duty in case something happens to you.

XXIX

FIESTAS AND INDIAN QUEENS

'What hurts Indians most is that our costumes are considered
beautiful, but it's as if the person wearing it didn't exist.'
—Rigoberta Menchú

The fiestas which take place in the towns are more than anything a mixture. The actual fiestas that our ancestors celebrated probably no longer exist, and they are being replaced now
by celebrations of some saints' days, some famous people's
days. In the schools they often celebrate the day of Tecún
Umán. Tecún Umán is the Quiché hero who is said to have
fought the Spanish and then been killed by them. Well, there
is a fiesta each year in the schools. They commemorate the
day of Tecún Umán as the national hero of the Quichés. But
we don't celebrate it, primarily because our parents say that
this hero is not dead. So we don't celebrate. It's the *ladinos* in
the schools who celebrate it. For us it would be rejecting him
to say that he *was* a hero, that he fought and died, because
that is talking about him in the past. His birthday is commemorated as something which represented the struggle of
those times. But for us the struggle still goes on today, and
our suffering more than ever. We don't want it said that all
that happened in the past, but that it exists today, and so our
parents don't let us celebrate it. We know this is our reality
even though the *ladinos* tell it as if it were history.

'Tecún Umán' means the grandfather of everyone. '*Mán*' means something like father, or grandfather, someone respected. He was actually the leader of all the Indians, like their king or their president. Well, when the Spaniards arrived, there were great battles and many kings like him died. He was the last one to die in the struggle against the Spaniards. The story we tell about Tecún Umán is different to the one the *ladinos* tell. We don't celebrate Guatemalan Independence Day either because, in fact, it isn't a celebration for us. We consider it a *ladino* celebration because, well, Independence as they call it means nothing to us. It only means more grief and greater efforts not to lose our culture. Other than that it has no meaning for us at all. It is only celebrated in the schools and the people with access to schools are above all people with money. The majority of Indians have no access to primary or secondary schools. The bourgeoisie, middle-class people, celebrate it but lower down there's none of that. When teachers come into the villages, they bring with them the ideas of capitalism and getting on in life. They try and impose these ideas on us. I remember that in my village there were two teachers for a while and they began teaching the people, but the children told their parents everything they were being taught at school and the parents said: 'We don't want our children to become like *ladinos*.' And they made the teachers leave. What the teacher wanted was for them to celebrate the 15th of September. They had to wear school uniform and buy shoes. We never buy those things for children. They told them to put on a uniform, to disguise themselves by taking off their own clothes, their costumes, and putting on clothes of all one colour. Well, the parents didn't want their children to be turned into *ladinos* and chased the teachers out. For the Indian, it is better not to study than to become like *ladinos*.

As I was saying, the fiestas in the towns are always held for a saint or for any image. This happened more and more after Catholic Action started operating. At the same time, we began taking the Bible as a way of telling us about our ancestors. So our people identified with the Bible and with the Catholic religion a great deal. And that's how today in our towns we have fiestas for our patrons, for saints and images, because the people absorbed all this and made it their own. Indians regard all fiestas as a rest from work. But it's a rest which harms them as well, because instead of actually resting for two or three days, he has to spend the whole day of the fiesta in the town. He doesn't go to the fiesta only if he's ill, or very, very busy, or has nothing to eat. For music, they play the *marimba*. I remember *marimbas* years ago, but they were *marimbas* without other instruments and the people of the town played them themselves. There are dances in which the Indian represents how he repelled the Spaniards. We call it the 'Dance of the Conquest'. The Indians put on white or red masks to represent the Spaniards. The Spaniards have horses and the Indians fight them with the weapons of the people – machetes, stones. So they have a battle. And they do it as a dance. I liked everything but I like the 'Dance of the Conquest' very much because it gives an exact meaning to what Indians think about the 'Conquest'. There are other dances too: the 'Dance of the Bull,' the 'Dance of the Deer'. They are performed in the towns too, and men dress up and use masks like a bull or a deer. It's usually the people over thirty-five who do the dances.

My town is called San Miguel Uspantán. We commemorate Miguel Uspantán twice a year. One fiesta is dedicated to the town on the day of San Miguel, but since the people are very fond of the Virgin, the Virgin's fiesta is also dedicated to San Miguel de Uspantán. It starts on the 5th or 6th of May and doesn't finish until the 9th of May. The people are on their feet for all those days. People come down from even the furthest away villages and it's like a meeting for all the different communities which live outside the town. They come down and sell their things. For instance, if they've got an animal to sell, they sell it in the fiesta because a lot of tradesmen come too. Some of them are big tradesmen. There are also lotteries, and there, that's where you lose everything. They hold masses as well, and first communions. And there are *cantinas*. People come out of mass and into the *cantina*. Women drink as well. That is something incredible in these towns because it's not only the men who want to let themselves go and forget their problems for a while, but the women too. The thing is that very often a mother hasn't had a moment's relief, so she takes advantage of the fiesta to rest a bit. As I said, I see this as a rest for the people. My mother used to drink as well. My father, now, his personality was such that when he drank, and then couldn't drink any more, he'd give in and go to bed or sleep. Sometimes they'd go and drink together and sometimes my mother would be drunk and my father not. It's not unusual to see our women drinking. In fact, many women drink. And even more so in the fiestas. There have been cases of women sleeping on their children. And this is scandalous. Everyone, everyone, gets drunk, and after the fiesta there's not a *centavo* left. The *ladinos* are there too. Since not all *ladinos* live well, many poor *ladinos* get mixed up in all this drunkenness too. But many other *ladinos* take advantage of the fiesta to sell, to do business, and make money. For them every fiesta is for making money.

I remember the time I had my first communion. My parents had bought me a little piece of *corte* and a little blouse and a little apron. They also had to buy flowers and candles for me and all the other things I needed. So even before the fiesta they were in debt. My father was happy because I was alive, since it's already a miracle when a child reaches five years old. We think he'll survive then. So it was probably from happiness that my father went drinking and spent all his money. This meant that we had to go down to the *finca* for a long time, as after the fiesta we had to pay all the debts. I remember that I didn't see or do much in that fiesta because we were only walking around on our own, or in one of the bars. I didn't enjoy it.

Once a year there is a fair as well and that's when they choose the town's queen. There has to be an Indian queen and a *ladino* queen. The days for the parade of the Indian queen are decided and after that come the days for the parade of the *ladino* queen. I don't know the origin of this sort of parade. They choose an Indian girl, perhaps the most humble, to be the queen of all the town's Indians. This is done in most of the towns in Guatemala, even in the smallest towns. But we should really look at who is behind it all. This is the incredible bit for me, because they'd talk about an Indian queen but I never knew anything about it because I lived in the mountains and never went to town for the fiestas when I was a child. People talked about it but I never knew anything about it. I was in the town in 1977 when they were choosing the queen. I saw that a lot of *ladinos* were voting for the Indian queen. There were three Indian girls as candidates. I remember that they had a *ladino* friend who put up a lot of money so that the one he liked best won. It wasn't a competition because the votes were bought. And they also take a collection to buy the things for the queen. The municipality, that is, the authorities in the town, give a lot of money for the queen to appear in public and so on. This is some 'folklore' that I imagine has been imposed recently. It doesn't come from years ago.

The girl for whom most votes are bought becomes the queen. The votes are sold by groups of people interested in each girl. The candidates are chosen mainly by the young people in the town, either by friends, or some committee or organisation in the town itself, or by the municipality, that is, the authorities. So it's not the ordinary people, not the Indian people, who choose. As most *ladinos* are found in the towns in Guatemala, the majority of Indians go and live outside the towns, leaving the towns for the *ladinos*. That's what has happened in my town, Uspantán. Very few Indians live in the town itself. I saw that they began voting and then so-and-so won and everyone went to congratulate her. But these are only very small groups. I asked another friend, an Indian, and he told me that the mayor's office promoted all these events and paid for and financed the Indian queen. It was something that made me very sad, mainly because they choose the prettiest girl in the town and then it's like making this Indian girl into a business. After the queens are chosen, they appear in cars or carriages on the day of the fiesta. The Indian queen always appears first, on the 4th or 5th of May, and on the 8th they bring out the *ladino* queen. Or else they bring out the *ladino* first and then the Indian queen. They don't appear together. Well, all this gave me a lot to think about.

Later on they hold a big folklore festival in August at the fair in Cobán with the Indian queens from all the different areas. This fiesta is organised by the president in power, and important people like senators, foreign personalities, and ambassadors are invited. They all take part in the presidential fiesta. Well, the queen who was chosen by each town has to be there. It is obligatory, she has to be there by law. All the queens go with the costumes from the different regions but they have to get to Cobán by their own means. The president (he's always a general) is there in Cobán, so are all the principal deputies, all the important guests and a lot of tourists. There are always a lot of tourists in our communities, in all the tourist spots in Guatemala. And they take all the photos they want. But for an Indian, taking a photo of him in the street is abusing his dignity, abusing him.

Well, they make these Indian girls parade around, throw kisses, and wave to everyone. They take photos of them and make them behave like the stars of the rich. In Guatemala there are no stars among the poor. Then they parade so that the public will come and see them, more than anything because of their costumes. There are a whole lot of presentations. I remember that in the months before the fiesta, they fuss over the queens, teaching them how to present themselves because they assume that Indians don't know. Well, they teach them and they arrive at Cobán all prepared. A friend who was a queen told me that they taught her how to present herself. This *compañera* couldn't speak Spanish very well, so she had to learn the boring little speech she was going to give: greetings for the president, greetings for the most important guests, greetings for the army officers. They made her learn what she was to say. After she'd learned all the movements she had to make, they took her to a cheap hotel, not even to the hotel where the guests were. After the fiesta they told them: 'You've played your part, now go home.' So they asked to be given a place to stay and they gave them something for a cheap hotel: in Guatemala these are places where just anybody goes, where the drunks go. Well, the *compañeras* had to go to a cheap hotel after the presentation. This is what hurts Indians most. It means that, yes, they think our costumes are beautiful because it brings in money, but it's as if the person wearing it doesn't exist. Then they charge the people who go to the festival a lot for their tickets and get a lot of money from the presentation of the queens. Everyone has to pay to go in. Only people with money can go.

XXX

LESSONS TAUGHT HER BY HER MOTHER: INDIAN WOMEN AND LADINO WOMEN

'My mother said: "I don't want to make you stop feeling a woman, but your participation in the struggle must be equal to that of your brothers." '

—Rigoberta Menchú

Indian women are not coquettish. They don't have time for new hairstyles, and arranging their hair, and all those things. But *ladino* women do. Even if they've nothing to eat, they'd rather put pins in their hair, and have a waistline, and at all costs wear shoes. There are many differences between us. I remember my mother telling me: 'My child, you don't need to paint your face because make-up abuses the wonders God has given us. Don't you learn these things.' But there came a time when I began to move away from my mother and this worried her very much. It isn't that I didn't love my mother, but I felt slightly more love for my father. It's probably because of all his work, because of all the threats made against him. I never thought my mother would meet a worse death than my father. I always thought it would be worse for my father than for my mother.

But when I was ten I was closer to my mother. That's the age she told me about the facts of life. She taught me by talking about the experiences of her grandmother: she told me about when her grandmother was pregnant. She didn't pass on her own experiences, not that she hadn't had them, but because she felt more comfortable teaching me through the experiences of others. Well, my mother told me that an Indian woman is only respected if she's wearing her full costume. If she forgets her shawl, the community starts losing respect for her and a woman needs their respect. 'Never forget to wear your apron, my child,' my mother used to say.

Our tenth year actually marks the stage when we enter womanhood. It's when parents buy their daughters everything they need: two aprons; two *cortes*; two *perrajes*; so that when one is being washed she can wear the other. Whenever we go out to do an errand, we must wear our complete costume. My mother told me not to cut my hair: 'If you cut your hair, people notice and say that that woman is breaking with many of our things, and they won't respect you as they ought to.' My mother often used to scold us when we'd run off without our aprons: 'You must dress as you're always going to dress. You mustn't change the way you dress, because you're the same person and you're not going to change from now on.' My mother also explained what maize meant for us. She said that a pregnant woman mustn't carry maize which has been cut in her apron because the cuttings are what give the maize life. It's the womb of the maize which nourishes us. But you can't liken it to a child either. The child will eat maize when he grows up. The child deserves as much respect as the maize cuttings. You can't compare the two, then. They mustn't be mixed. That was the significance my mother saw in it. Our aprons are also something very important: women use them all the time, in the market, in the street, in all her work. It's something sacred for a woman and she must always have it with her.

Later my mother explained many other little things. For instance, about birds, about medicines. She'd say: 'Don't ever eat this or that plant, or take it as medicine,' and she'd explain why not. A pregnant woman can't take just any kind of medicine, or any old concoctions from trees either. She went on to explain that I'd have to have periods. I asked her a lot of questions out loud while we'd cut plants at the foot of the mountains but, as I said, she usually told me about my grandparents, not about herself. But when I had stomach ache, I didn't tell my mother, I'd usually look for my father because of that very trust I had in him. And there were many little things I could have asked my mother, but I asked my father. My mother told me that she'd been rather abandoned when she was a little girl. No-one looked after her so she'd had to learn everything alone. She said: 'When I got my period, I didn't even know what it was.' Mamá used to get very angry. She taught us to do all our jobs well, and if we didn't do them right, she'd punish us. She said: 'If it's not put right now, who'll teach you later on? This is for your own good, not mine.' I remember beginning to make *tortillas* when I was three. I could wash the *nixtamal*. She taught me to wash it and to make it. When I was older she explained that there were certain things you mustn't walk over – a plate or a cup, for instance – and not to walk over the maize since maize is our food. Well, just details we had to learn!

I also remember going to sow our crops in the fields. Mamá explained the days which were fertile for sowing. She always dreamed about nature. I think it was just her own imagination working. But when someone believes, things that you imagine often happen. I've proved this many times with medicines. I'd say: 'This is sure to make me better,' and logically I'd get better even though it's not the medicine that had the effect. I think that my mother was like that. She said that when she was little she used to climb on tree trunks and up trees and look after animals and things like that. She used to talk to animals a lot. When she hit an animal, for instance, she'd say: 'I hit you for this reason, so don't be angry.' And this way she gets on good terms with it again. And she also told me that, once, when she was little, she'd found a little pig in the mountains and she knew it didn't belong to anyone because we had no neighbours then, we were the only families living there. There were other families a few kilometres away from where we were. She picked the pig up and carried it home. By my grandfather was a very honest man and was capable of beating any of his children if they stole anything, even a fruit or something small. Among Indians, it's forbidden to steal from a neighbour's house. Nobody can abuse his neighbour's work. So my mother took the little pig home but she didn't know how to explain to my grandfather because he'd probably throw her and her pig out of the house. So she hid it in the *temascal* and left it there. My grandfather had two cows and the cows gave milk, and they made cheese to take to market to sell to rich people. Well, my mamá took part of the milk and gave it to the little pig so that he'd grow without my grandfather seeing. But after fifteen days – it's incredible that the little pig was alive – it had grown and got bigger and bigger even though it didn't have a mamá. And my grandfather noticed that my mother had a little pig.

He almost killed her. He said: 'Go and take that pig away. I don't want stolen pigs in my house.' There was a terrible row. But afterwards the little pig was allowed to grow up, although my grandfather told my mother that she had to find food for it herself. Well, my mother made sacrifices, and the pig was soon big, about five or six months old. My mama was very worried and discussed it with the pig. She said: 'My papá doesn't love you, but I do.' Then, one night some *coyotes* came in and took the pig away. There were about three or four *coyotes*. And the pig started screaming and my mamá went running out. She was resolute and went into the mountains running after them to try and catch the pig, but when they got further into the mountains, my mother felt a breeze and said: 'Ah, it's obvious that the pig belongs to the world, not to me.' So she left the animal and went back. But she used to dream about her little pig all the time. She'd see it in the *coyote*'s mouth as they were taking it away.

It was about that time that she said she was going to learn from a *chimán*. That's what we call a man who tells the Indians' fortunes. He's like a doctor for the Indians, or like a priest. My mother said: 'I'm going to be a *chimán* and I'll learn with one of these men.' And she went to the *chimán* and he taught her many things out of his imagination connected with animals, with plants, with water, with the sun. My mamá learned a great deal, but who knows, perhaps that wasn't to be her role in life. Nevertheless, it helped her a lot to learn and dedicate herself to other things. My mother loved the natural world very much. In Guatemala the sky is nearly always blue, so when clouds begin to gather on the sides of the mountains, it means it is going to rain. My mother could tell the days it was going to rain; what kind of rain was going to fall; if it was going to be heavy or not. When a whole line of clouds passed in a certain direction, my mother would say: 'Hurry up, children, because it's going to rain.' And it was true. It rained exactly as if she'd planned it herself. She enjoyed life very much, in spite of the sad life we had and even though she suffered very much when we were ill. I remember that sometimes I couldn't walk because the soles of my feet split. When it rained, it was the mud which split them and it went septic between my toes. One thing I remember is that my mother knew a lot about natural country medicine and whatever illness we had, she'd go looking for leaves of plants and cured us immediately.

Another of the special things about my mother was that she loved giving little presents. Even if we didn't have very much, she said that any person who comes to a house must always be given something, even if it's only a little *pinol* or at mealtimes a *tortilla* with salt or whatever there is. 'You must always know how to give,' my mamá would say, 'because a person who gives will also receive when the time comes. When you're in a difficult situation, you won't have to face your troubles alone. You'll always receive help, even if it isn't from the same person you gave to. There will always be people who will hold you in high esteem.' She always made us have some hot water on the fire so there would always be something for anyone who came to the house, even if it was only a little *atol*.

She also taught us to look after and preserve our household things. Our cooking pots, for example. She had a lot of earthenware pots that she'd had for many years and they hadn't broken or been ruined because she knew how to look after her things. Well, she told us that if you are poor, you can't buy things all the time, nor must you only expect things from your husband. You yourself have to do your part to keep your little things too. And she gave us examples of people whom she knew or that she'd helped to improve themselves: 'That's what happens with women who don't look after their pots and then when they don't have them any more, they have to go and buy more.' She was like that with everything. Another of our customs she taught us was that you mustn't mix women's clothes with men's clothes. She told us to put our brothers' clothes on one side when we wash them. First you wash the men's clothes and then, at the end, our own. In our culture we often treat the man as something different – the woman is valued too, of course – and if we do things we must do them well. First, because they are our men, and second, because it's a way of encouraging them, in the same way our ancestors did for their men. Not mixing the clothes was, I think, the order they respected. My mother said that we women have certain things that a man doesn't have, like our period for instance. So we keep all our clothes separate. It's the same for everything: we don't mix them, but most of all with our clothes. However, with kitchen utensils and all the things for the house, there isn't one for each.

There's something else I used to see my mother do. My father would often come home from work tired, and my mother liked to give him the largest portion of the food and keep a little for herself. And I used to ask her: 'Why did papá have to eat a lot?' My mother would say that my father used a lot of energy in his work and that if we didn't look after him, he could become ill and get weaker. She gave him food to encourage him. That's how she was with everything. One of the important things, my mother used to say, is that it depends on the woman how little money is spent. In the country we buy things for a whole week and it's up to the woman how she manages her household expenses. She's the one who keeps the money. If it's the woman's turn to go to market, she buys the things, but if it's not, she has to show the man what they need so that he can buy it. My mother hardly ever went to market. My father used to go and he'd buy all the things my mother told him to, even if it were only a pot, or a broom. The other thing was that since my mother was a midwife for a long time and knew most of the medicinal plants, or any remedies for adults or children, she'd often be called out at three or four in the morning to go and see someone who was ill. She was hardly ever at home. She, therefore, had to give us a lot of advice and from when we were very little she taught us how to look after the house, and how to care for our things so that they didn't get ruined. My mother was very happy because I have a sister who copies my mother in every way. She learned all the small things, all of them, from my mother and acted like her in the house. She's married, but I don't know where she is now.

My mother didn't have to show us our food, because we had to go and look for food for ourselves. We had to look for new things to eat because it's tedious always eating the same sort of plants. And more so at harvest time, when there's only one woman at home while the others are all working in the harvest. So, the one who stays at home has to find food for the midday meal. My mother liked always being busy. She could make mats, weave cloth, plait straw for hats, make earthenware pots and *comales*. She knew how to do all these things. Sometimes, on a Sunday for instance, when she wasn't doing the washing (we all did it when we were older), my mother would make some things for the house. She'd have time to make one or two *comales*, or some cooking pots. Or people used to ask her to make things for them. During our last days in the village, she had a cow which she loved very much, really very much. When we were older, and when my sisters-in-law were there, my mother didn't have to do so many of the chores in the house, so she'd get up in

the morning and go straight away to see the animals, or take
them to places where they'd be for the whole day. And when
the men went off to work, she'd go to work in the fields as
well. People thought a lot of her because she was the woman
who was all over the place, even though we sometimes didn't
like my mother going off so much because we missed her
at home. There were times when she didn't come home for
two or three days because she had to look after people who
were ill. We used to get annoyed, my brothers especially. We
wanted our mother to be at home. Later on, she started going
to other villages and became a militant. She'd go and visit the
sick but at the same time she worked in the organization. She
organized the women.

There was something my mother used to say concerning
machismo. You have to remember that my mother couldn't
read or write and didn't know any theories either. What
she said was that men weren't to blame for *machismo*, and
women weren't to blame for *machismo*, but that it was part
of the whole society. To fight *machismo*, you shouldn't attack men and you shouldn't attack women, because that is
either the man being *machista*, or it's the woman. Because
very often we go to two extremes whereby the woman says
she is free and becomes radicalized in that sense. And instead of solving the problem, it just makes it bigger. My
mother said: 'We women have a very important role to play
in this sense, because we are better at expressing affection.'
And she'd point to my father as an example. When they
were young, my father always liked to be served. He was
also very jealous. But my mother told us that they began to
discuss these things because they had to learn to be adults.
When she got married, it was difficult for them to understand that they had to start a new life, and that married life
would not be like before. Well, anyway, I can't say because
I'm not married; but my mother used to say that where
there's a couple, there will always be. problems. However
good the marriage is, there will be problems. But it will be
up to the two of them to solve those problems, and to solve

them they must make a life for the two of them, an adult life. Perhaps that's what my mother was referring to when she talked about the problem of jealousy my father had. It was only when they started discussing that they both understood the problem and solved it. Because no matter how aware the woman is or how aware the man is, if they don't discuss things they can't understand. She said: 'The thing is that nobody, not even other women, are going to solve the problem if you yourself don't think about how you're going to do it.' It's the same with men.

Another example my mother gave us was that, when my father was really angry, my mother never answered him back. Then afterwards, when they were getting on well and were in their senses, that was when they'd discuss it. That's how the defects of both of them were sorted out and how they managed to have a happy family. Of course there were problems and they did argue sometimes, but that didn't mean that it was a bad marriage, no, it meant they understood each other and got on together. And it was mainly because of that that my mother had so much freedom to do her work and go out, because among Indians, it's often very difficult for a woman to go out alone. In fact, as I was saying before, when we were young girls, we were only allowed out with our mother or one of our brothers. And it's still like that today. A married woman is not free to go out, to go alone or visit her neighbours. Perhaps it's because her husband is jealous, since we always have to take into account our life in a community, and behave so society does not disapprove of us. It's the image we have to give to everyone. That's how this way of life emerges, often dependent on others. But my mother had absolute freedom to go out because she represented our community. We'd managed to have a relatively communal life in my village. Sometimes the women went to market or went together to town to buy some things. I remember that whenever we went down to the town, a whole troupe of women would go, all from our village, and we always had plenty to discuss with our neighbours. And sometimes men, women and children

would all go down the path together. We'd split up to buy
our things and then all go back again.

My mother also had a lot of patience with her children,
and her daughters-in-law. There were lots of problems because we grew up in a very big household. There were my
grandparents, all our children and my sister-in-law and her
three children who lived with us. This meant a lot of work,
looking after the house, the food and the dishes. Well, most
of us went off to work and my sister-in-law stayed at home
or sometimes she went with us to work. It was nice when we
all went off to work. We liked it best of all when we were
picking the beans and bringing in the maize harvest. Sometimes the beans are picked before the maize and sometimes
afterwards. My brothers and sisters and I always got on well
together. But the time came for some of them to get married
and my mother had to cope with big problems because, first,
her son's wives weren't used to the kind of work we did, and
second, because they didn't want to live on their own since
they came from big families as well and they'd feel bad being
in a house alone with their husbands. So they stayed with
us. It is an obligation that every community has; to let the
wife live with her husband's parents. We began having problems because my sister was very bad-tempered and she didn't
like things being left half finished – she liked things done and
done quickly. My sister was hardly ever still. She was always
working, always busy, and, of course, it was difficult for my
sisters-in-law to adapt to this sort of work. We were forced
to find somewhere separate for my sisters-in-law because
there was no way they could go on living in our house. So my
mamá faced a lot of problems because she had to share her
affection between her children and her daughters-in-law as
well. We felt very hard done by. There was a bit of jealousy
on our part when my other brothers got their houses and my
mother would go over there and still look after them as if
they were little boys. We began to be jealous and scolded my
mother when she got home. We quarrelled with my brothers
because of my sisters-in-law. But my mother shared herself

with all of us and said that if she loved one she had to love all. Or she'd have to reject all of us!

My mother couldn't express her views about political things; but she was very politicized through her work and thought that we should learn to be women, but women who were useful to the community. And so from when we were very small, we had to go with her to learn from her example and copy all the little things she taught us about politics. She was the first to decide to join the struggle, before I did, because I didn't really know anything, or what anything meant. My mother was a woman who already had a political vision and was already working in organizations before I knew anything. She didn't belong to any specific organization. She received information from the CUC, but when she got to know the *compañeros* in the mountains, the guerrillas, she loved them like her sons too. She'd known them first in other areas because my mother used to travel a lot tending the sick, and she was often called to assist pregnant women in other areas. That's how she got to know them. When she worked with the CUC, she represented the CUC, but she didn't belong to any specific organization. She said what was important was doing something for our people. She said it would be sad to die without doing anything, without grasping reality in your hands. When she talked to me, before I had any specific work for the CUC (because at the beginning I only helped them with any work they wanted done, I wasn't an organizer), she said: 'My child, we must organize. It's not something I demand of you because I'm your mother. It's your duty to put into practice what you know. The days of paternalism, of saying "poor girl, she doesn't know anything," are over.' My mother made no distinction between the men's struggle and the women's struggle. She said: 'I don't want to make you stop feeling a woman, but your participation in the struggle must be equal to that of your brothers. But you mustn't join as just another number, you must carry out important tasks, analyze your position as a woman and demand a share. A child is only given food when he demands it. A child who makes no noise gets nothing to eat.' And that is why I felt that I had to participate more actively. My mother was also very courageous. On Sundays, she'd leave for the town at three in the morning with only her horse for company. As I said, my mother was brave but, nonetheless, I learned more from my father. I regret this very much now because my mother knew many things that I don't know, things like medicines and what she knew about nature. I know this as well, of course, but only on a general level, not at all profoundly. My mother had the same idea of women as our women had had in the past. They were very strict and believed a woman should learn her womanly occupation so that she could live and face many things. And she was right. Because we can see a difference. My father was very tender and always protected me, but it was my mother who coped with the big problems in our family. She was capable of seeing her son even as he was dying and doing everything she could to save him. But my father, for instance, he'd see my little brother ill or nearly dying and he'd escape from it. For him it was better to get drunk and forget everything, while my mother didn't allow herself the luxury of getting drunk when she had to do something to save my little brother whose life was in danger. There were many estimable things in my father; many things which he could face but also many things he couldn't face. And my mother too. She could face many things, but there were other things she couldn't do. So I love them both the same. I love them both but I have to say that I grew up more at my father's side. My mother taught many people many things, but I didn't learn as much from her as I should have learned.

XXXI

WOMEN AND POLITICAL COMMITMENT. RIGOBERTA RENOUNCES MARRIAGE AND MOTHERHOOD

'We have kept our identity hidden because we have resisted.'
—Rigoberta Menchú

I still haven't approached the subject – and it's perhaps a very long subject – of women in Guatemala. We have to put them into categories, anyway: working-class women, peasant women, poor *ladino* women, and bourgeois women, middle-class women. There is something important about women in Guatemala, especially Indian women, and that something is her relationship with the earth – between the earth and the mother. The earth gives food and the woman gives life. Because of this closeness the woman must keep this respect for the earth as a secret of her own. The relationship between the mother and the earth is like the relationship between husband and wife. There is a constant dialogue between the earth and the woman. This feeling is born in women because of the responsibilities they have, which men do not have.

That is how I've been able to analyze my specific task in the organization. I realize that many *compañeros*, who are revolutionaries and good *compañeros*, never lose the feeling that their views are better than those of any women in charge of them. Of course, we mustn't dismiss the great value of those *compañeros*, but we can't let them do just whatever they like. I have a responsibility, I am in charge, and they must accept me for what I am. But in this respect I've met serious problems when handing out tasks to those *compañeros*, and I've often found it upsetting having to assume this role. But I really believed that I could contribute, and that they should respect me. All the same, it was difficult for me to say: 'Listen, *compañero*, these tasks are for you; and you, *compañero*, these are your defects, what are we going to do about them?' It doesn't mean you dominate a man, and you mustn't get any sense of satisfaction out of it. It's simply a question of principle. I have my job to do just like any other *compañero*. I found all this very difficult and, as I was saying, I came up against revolutionary *compañeros, compañeros* who had many ideas about making a revolution, but who had trouble accepting that a woman could participate in the struggle, not only in superficial things but in fundamental things. I've also had to punish many *compañeros* who try to prevent their women taking part in the struggle or carrying out any task. They're sometimes willing to let them participate but only within certain limits. They start saying: 'Oh no, not that. No, not here. No.' Well, we've had to talk seriously with these *companeros* to solve that problem.

My mother, of course, didn't know all these ideas, all these theories about the position of women. But she knew all these things in practice. I learned a lot from my mother but I also learned a lot from other people, especially when I had the opportunity of talking to women who aren't from our country. We discussed the organization of women and we came to the conclusion that many women so often take other people's problems upon themselves and push their own to one side. This doesn't do us any good. It shows us that we must solve our problems ourselves and not ask someone else to come and solve them, otherwise it's dishonest. No-one will solve our problems for us.

The Indian women who have a clear political vision and participate in the leadership of the organization are realizing this. We're seeing change, revolution, taking power, but this isn't the profound change within society. We women *compañeras* came to the conclusion (because for a time we thought of creating an organization for women) that it was paternalistic to say there should be an organization for women when in practice women work and are exploited as well. Women work picking coffee and cotton, and on top of that, many women have taken up arms and even elderly women are fighting day and night; so it isn't possible to say that now we're setting up an organization so that women can rebel, work or study women's problems. It won't always be like this, of course. That is just the situation we're facing at the moment. Perhaps in the future, when there's a need for it, there will be a women's organization in Guatemala. For the time being, though, we think that it would be feeding *machismo* to set up an organization for women only, since it would mean separating women's work from men's work. Also we've found that when we discuss women's problems, we need the men to be present, so that they can contribute by giving their opinions of what to do about the problem. And so that they can learn as well. If they don't learn, they don't progress. Our struggle has shown us that many *compañeros* have clear ideas, but if they don't follow in the footsteps of their woman, they'll never have the clarity that she has, and they'll be left behind. What is the point of educating women if men aren't there to contribute to the apprenticeship and learn as well? By creating an organization for women we would be presenting the system which oppresses us with another weapon. We don't want that. We must fight as equals. If a *compañero* is asked a question about *machismo*, he must be able to give a wide, balanced view of women, and a woman must be able to do the same for men, because the two have been studying the problem together.

That has been my experience anyway. I'm not married, but I've taken part in important discussions where we've talked about the problem of men and women, in a mixed group. We think that this is the right path to follow. Naturally, we can't say that this alone will do away with *machismo*, because it wouldn't be true. In all revolutionary countries, socialist countries, wherever you care to name, *machismo* still exists. The whole world is afflicted with this sickness. It's part of society. Part of it we can improve, and part of it we can wipe out. But perhaps it's not possible to solve the problem entirely. There is something else we are discovering in Guatemala to do with intellectuals and illiterate people. We've learned that we haven't all got the ability of an intellectual: an intellectual is perhaps quicker and able to make finer syntheses. But nevertheless, others of us have perhaps the same ability for other things. Before, everyone used to think that a leader had to be someone who knew how to read, write and prepare documents. And our leaders fell into that trap for a time, and said: 'I am a leader, it's my job to lead and yours to fight.' Well, in every process there are certain exchanges which have to be made. That is not unusual. I think that every movement has gone through the process whereby an opportunist arrives, feels that he is worth more than the others and abuses their confidence. At one time, many of our leaders would come from the capital to see us in the *finca* and say: 'You peasants are stupid, you don't read or study.' And the peasants told them: 'You can go to hell with your books. We know you don't make a revolution with books, you make it through struggle.'

And that was why we decided to learn many things, and rightly so, because, remember, that now everything was in our hands. We had to make big sacrifices. And so, we peasants have learned to direct our struggle ourselves, and *that* we owe to our understanding of our situation. A leader must be someone who's had practical experience. It's not so much that the hungrier you've been, the purer your ideas must be, but you can only have a real consciousness if you've really lived this life. I can say that in my organization most of the leaders are Indians. There are also some *ladinos* and some women in the leadership. But we have to erase the barriers which exist between ethnic groups, between Indians and *ladinos*, between men and women, between intellectuals and non-intellectuals, and between all the linguistic areas.

The situation we are in means that our women don't get married because they're expecting something happy, a lovely family, pleasure, or something different from what they already have. No, not at all. They know that a very hard life awaits them. Although for us marriage is something joyful (because the concept our ancestors had was that our race must not die out and we must follow our traditions and customs as they did), at the same time it is something very painful, knowing that when you get married you'll have the responsibility of bringing up your children, and not only of looking after them, but worrying, trying to make do, and hoping they live. In Guatemala, it's unusual for a family not to see some of their young children die.

Well, in my case, I analyzed my ideas about not getting married with some of my *compañeros*. I realized that what I said wasn't crazy, that it wasn't some personal mad idea, but that our whole situation makes women think very hard before getting married, because who will look after the children, who will feed them? As I was saying before, we're used to living in a community, among up to ten or eleven brothers or sisters. But there are also cases of women who are left alone because all their brothers and sisters go off and get married, so they're sometimes forced to get married because they know how hard it will be for them by themselves. But knowing that I had to multiply the seed of our ancestors and, at the same time, rejecting marriage . . . that was a crazy idea. I thought I was alone in feeling like this, but when I discussed it with other women, they saw the whole thing of getting married in the same way I did. It is terrible to know that such a hard life awaits you, with so much responsibility to make sure your children live. You can't think any other way in Guatemala: when you get engaged or married, you immediately think of the many children you're going to have. I've been in love many times but it was precisely because of that fear that I didn't jump into marriage. But the time came when I saw clearly – it was actually when I'd begun my life as a revolutionary – that I was fighting for a people and for many children who hadn't anything to eat. I could see how sad it would be for a revolutionary not to leave a seed, because the seed which was left behind would enjoy the fruits of this work in the future. But I thought of the risks of having a child. It would be much easier for me to die, at any time or place, if I weren't leaving anyone behind to suffer. That would be sad, because although my community would take care of my child, of my seed, no other person can give a child the love his mother can, however much that person looks after and cares for the child. I was very confused about all this because so many dedicated *compañeros* said they would be there on the day of victory, but I knew that they could give their lives at any time and would no longer be there. All this horrified me and gave me a lot to think about.

I was engaged once but I wasn't sure, because, well, the idea our ancestors had – and it's ours too – is that you don't only look for happiness for yourself but also for your family. I was very confused. Society and so many other things wouldn't leave me alone, I always had a heavy heart.

And then when my parents died, I felt what a daughter feels for a father and mother when they die, and even more so because of the way they died. That's when I decided, although I can't say that it's a final decision because I am open to life. My idea is, though, that there will be time enough after our victory; but at the moment I wouldn't feel happy having a *compañero* and giving myself to him while so many of our people are not thinking of their own personal happiness and haven't a single moment to rest. This gave me a lot to think about. As I said, I am human and I am a woman so I can't say that I reject marriage altogether, but I think my primary duty is to my people and then to my personal happiness. I know many *compañeros* who have devoted themselves without reservation to the struggle, without thinking of personal happiness. And I know *compañeros* who've gone through bitter moments, who have troubles and worries, but who, nevertheless, are in the struggle and carry on. It could be that I renounced marriage because of the harsh experience of having seen so many friends die. This not only frightens me, it puts me in a panic, because I don't want to be a widow, or a tortured mother. I'm restricted by so many things. It's not just not wanting a child. Many little things have made me think about renouncing all this. I know that our men have suffered too, because many *compañeros* had to give their children away so they could carry on the struggle, or they've had to leave their women in other places – not because they don't want marriage but because they feel it is their duty to fight for their people.

The conclusion I came to was that, while we have so many problems, we shouldn't look for more. There are married women in the struggle, however, who contribute as much as I do, *compañeras* who have five or six children and do magnificent work. Being afraid of all that is a certain trauma I have. I'm even more afraid when I think that if I had a *compañero*, I'd probably love him very much and I wouldn't want it to be for only a week or two because after that he wouldn't be there. While I don't have this problem, I won't look for it. But, as I said, I'm open to life. It doesn't mean that I reject everything because I know that things come in their time and when you do things calmly, they work much better.

As I said, I was engaged once. At one time he wanted a lot of things in life; a nice house for his children and a peaceful life. But I didn't think like that. We'd known each other since we were children, but unfortunately he left our village and had to go to the city. He became a factory worker, and then really turned into a *compañero* with good work prospects who thought differently from the way I and my village thought. So, when I became a revolutionary I had to choose between two things – the struggle or my *compañero*. I came to all sorts of conclusions because I loved this *compañero* and I could see the sacrifices he made for me. It was a more open engagement than was usual for people of my culture.

Well, there I was between these two things – choosing him or my people's struggle. And that's what I chose, and I left my *compañero* with much sadness and a heavy heart. But I told myself that I had a lot to do for my people and I didn't need a pretty house while they lived in horrific conditions like those I was born and grew up in. Well, that's when we went our separate ways. I told him that it wasn't right for me to stay with him because he had other ideas and we'd never understand each other, since he wanted one thing and I'd always go on wanting another. Then I went on with our struggle and now I'm on my own. But, as I said, there'll be a time when things will be different, when we'll all be happy, perhaps not with nice houses, but at least we won't see our lands running with blood and sweat.

XXXII

STRIKE OF AGRICULTURAL WORKERS AND THE FIRST OF MAY IN THE CAPITAL

'Our commitment made us realize that we now had to find new forms of struggle.'

—Rigoberta Menchú

After the occupation of the Spanish embassy, all the sectors whose leaders had died there began to unite. We began to talk. I took part as a leader of the CUC. While we had very close relations with the other sectors, there was no one organization which cemented us all together. Our *compañeros* keep silent about a lot of things and this had helped strengthen our organization. But our commitment made us realize that we now had to find new forms of struggle. So in February of 1980, the last peasants' strike in Guatemala took place. It was a strike of eighty thousand peasants, sugar and cotton workers in the south of the country and in the Boca Costa, on the coastal strip where the sugar and cotton plantations are. The workers stopped work. We began with eight thousand peasants; then, little by little, the number grew and we finally managed to paralyze the work of between seventy and eighty thousand peasants for fifteen days. Yes, and in this strike we used the weapons of the people, the weapons we'd learned in each of our various sectors, in the various ethnic groups of the *Altiplano*, in all our different communities. Many different methods were used. In the sugar plantations, the owners had introduced a modern machine which strips the cane and collects it up, although the workers still cut it. It was found that this machine didn't pick up one ton, it picked up more. So they're stealing from the workers because they are only paid per ton. So the *compañeros* decided to sabotage these machines, to burn them so that the peasant would be paid for his work. The peasants also took a more violent attitude towards the army. The result was that we were surrounded by troops on land and in the air, but they couldn't do anything because there were just too many peasants for them to massacre. We decided that not one of our *compañeros* would be massacred there and that it was our duty to look after every life and help each other. When the army began to move in against the strikers, in many places in the *Altiplano* people began building barricades on several of the roads leading down to the coast. This was to prevent the army from passing. The peasants on the coast also set up big barricades so that we would have defences for when the army arrived. We fought with nothing more than machetes, stones and sticks, but we were concentrated in one spot. That's how we managed to paralyze the economy. We were on strike for fifteen days and, for a landowner, seventy or eighty thousand workers on strike for fifteen days is pretty tough. It was a pretty heavy blow. Many *compañeros* were shot during the strike but as they shot the first *compañeros*, the people became more determined. More people came forward and threw themselves at the army.

The strike was declared in February of 1980. I was working with the CUC but I was still a labourer in the *fincas* as well. I wasn't only a leader. We have learned that the role of a leader is as a coordinator more than anything, because the struggle is propelled forwards by the *compañeros* themselves. My work was mainly preparing new *compañeros* to take over the tasks that I or any of the other leaders do. In practice, the *compañeros* have to learn Spanish as I did, have to learn to read and write as I did, and assume all the responsibility for their work as I did. The reason behind this was that we're continually changing our roles, tasks, and our work. Our experience in Guatemala has always been to be told: 'Ah, poor Indians, they can't speak.' And many people have said, '*I'll* speak for them.' This hurt us very much. This is a kind of discrimination. But we have understood that each one of us is responsible for the struggle and we don't need leaders who only shuffle paper. We need leaders who are in danger, who run the same risks as the people. When there are many *compañeros* with equal abilities, they must all have the opportunity to lead their struggle.

We called the strike to demand a minimum wage of five *quetzals*. We didn't get the five *quetzals*. We only got three *quetzals* twenty. The landowners promised us a minimum wage of three-twenty but they didn't keep this agreement in many things. They increased the wage with one hand, and stole from us in different ways with the other. Before the strike we earned seventy-five *centavos* per day if we worked well, i.e. three-quarters of a *quetzal*. There were cases of only forty-five or fifty *centavos* being paid. We asked for five *quetzals*. Naturally, it was a heavy blow for the landowner, because to jump from seventy-five *centavos* to five *quetzals* is a lot. We began working again when the landowners signed an agreement giving us the three-twenty. It was a fair wage. At the same time, we demanded better treatment for the workers. That is, that they shouldn't give us hard *tortillas*, or rotten beans, but that the food should be fit for human beings.

When the strike began I was down on the coast, but afterwards I went up to the *Altiplano* to organise solidarity with the strikers on the coast. What we did in the *Altiplano* during that time was paint signs and make banners repudiating the landowners in various towns and villages. We also gave out leaflets calling on people to join their organization: the CUC. Well, that was when the government started getting more worried about the situation, because while they'd thought it was just a few of us risking our lives, they hadn't paid much attention to us. Not all the eighty thousand peasants were organized, of course. Many of them acted spontaneously. When they saw the others were on strike, they joined in too and demanded their rights. This helped heighten the political awareness of many of them. After the strike, there was a lot, really a lot, of work to be done, because all over the country our peasant *compañeros* were asking to be organized. They needed organizing because that's when the repression really began. This time it wasn't only in El Quiché, but our *compañeros* in Sololá, Chimaltenango and Huehuetenango were also suffering. This was the case in all the most militant Indian zones, in all the areas most inhabited by Indians. I remember that it was when I was working with *compañero* Romeo and others who are dead now, tortured by the government. The villages were very heavily repressed. What the army did was to put armoured cars in the parks and other places in the towns. They fired all kinds of ammunition at the houses, to make people hide inside their homes. Then they bombed the houses. What they wanted was to exterminate the population once and for all. They didn't want anyone to survive. During the bombing, my mother had to attend to many of the wounded, people who'd lost fingers, eyes. And the children were crying and crying. There was nothing that could be done about the crops because they were ready for harvesting, and the army set fire to them so that the whole lot would burn. The children who lost their parents had to take refuge in the mountains. People were looking for their children and couldn't find them. They were all concentrated in one place and were living almost like little guerrillas.

The way the priests behaved there was very beneficial, because they kept the people's spirits up. When the army bombed the village with a type of grenade which burns – napalm – many of them didn't explode and the children would pick them up and take them away. In Chimaltenango, the army put all the people they'd kidnapped – men, women and children – around the barracks, so that if the guerrilla groups attacked them, they would have to kill them first. All this hit the population very hard. The army didn't enter many of the villages. They stayed on the outskirts and marched over the mountain because they were afraid of being attacked by guerrillas. That's why they preferred bombing. They went through the region and rounded up many young men who didn't belong any organization because of how hard the work is in that region and the concentrated repression. They took them away and set up militias in the towns of Chimaltenango. They forced them to learn to kill, but many of them escaped because they didn't want to be there.

Our situation is very difficult. The army passes with its lorries along the main roads. Many of our people are living in camps after the bombing. But now the people have four politico-military armed organizations. The Ejército Guerrillero de los Pobres (EGP),* the Organización del Pueblo en Armas (ORPA)†, the Fuerzas Armadas Rebeldes (FAR)‡, and the Partido Guatemalteco del Trabajo (PGT)§. This is the nucleus of the national leadership. At the time of the Spanish embassy affair there was already a rapprochement between the people's organizations and the students, but the occupation of the embassy was the first operation they carried out together. When all those student, peasant and workers' leaders died together in the embassy, we knew we had an alliance and we looked at how we would confront the policies of the government together. The repression had spread out over the whole of the *Altiplano* and the coastal region. It had reached sectors which hadn't been touched in the beginning.

We came to the conclusion that we had to form a united front. We called it the 31st of January Popular Front, in honour of our *compañeros* who died on that day in the Spanish embassy. The people's organizations which make up this front are: the CUC, the Revolutionary Workers groups, the

---

*   Guerrilla Army of the Poor (GAP).
†   Organization of the People in Arms (OPA).
‡   Rebel Armed Forces (RAF).
§   Guatemalan Workers Party.

coordinating committee in the shanty towns,* the Vicente Menchú Revolutionary Christians, the Robin García Secondary Students Revolutionary Front, and the Robin García University Students Front. Robin García was a student *compañero* who was very concerned with the safety of others. He was a student leader and was killed after being kidnapped and tortured. For the students he is a hero. So at the beginning of 1981, we announced the creation of the 31st of January Popular Front, to combat the political repression. It organized numerous actions throughout the country under the slogan 'Out with the Political Clique'. Through the CUC, it incorporates nearly all the peasants. It includes the people who live in the shanty towns on the outskirts of the cities through their coordinating committee. The conditions in the shanty towns are tragic. The people live in houses made out of cardboard; they're not even houses. And the students are active in their circles. And the workers in the front are the ones for whom belonging to an officially recognized union would mean death. They work as individuals.

Our idea is to put into practice the methods initiated by the masses when they evolved their 'people's weapons': to be able to make Molotov cocktails to fight the army; to use their knowledge. What we use most in Guatemala are propaganda bombs. For the First of May, we carried out many actions and set up barricades. We wanted to weaken the government economically, politically and militarily. We weaken them economically by our actions in that, although the workers carry on working, they tamper with their machines or break parts. Small things that drain economic resources. This is a struggle for our rights, but it also weakens the landowner economically. We boycott anything we can, or destroy a coffee estate, or a cotton estate, depending on the attitude of the landowner. We have to do these things because we can't show our repudiation of the landowners by striking. Our ac-

---

* The Report of the Guatemalan Committee on Human Rights calls these 'The Revolutionary Workers' Nuclei' and the 'Committee of Slumdwellers'.

tions weaken the regime militarily too. We try to split up the armed forces so that not only do they have to attack our politico-military organizations, but they have to spread themselves to attack us as well.

The First of May this year was very important as well. It was the most important action we've carried out in Guatemala. The First of May is Labour Day in Guatemala. We'd been calling strikes and demonstrations on that day for some time. All the peasants used to come to the capital on foot from the interior. In 1980 the regime showed its repressive capacity by killing workers, industrial workers and peasants. The demonstration was held in the capital and the army opened fire on the people. There were many kidnappings after the demonstration too. That's why we commemorated the First of May, 1981, by more militant actions. Peasants, workers and Christians undertook actions in the capital and the interior. The police, the authorities, and the army were warned a week before that we were going to commemorate the First of May and they announced that they would be on the alert, controlling the situation. Well, on the 28th of April, we began our actions in the capital, and also in the interior. We set up barricades, threw 'propaganda bombs' and held lightning meetings. We had to complete each of these actions in a couple of minutes, or it would mean a massacre. And so, we were organized in such a way that the barricades would be opened, the propaganda given out, and the meeting held all at the same time. My part in this was in the Avenida Bolivar, in the capital. It's a very important street which cuts across part of the city centre and has many smaller streets running into it. There were barricades in various streets in the city and, remember, each of us had a specific part in the exercise. People would say: 'Come on, hurry up, hurry up!' We were so worried, so afraid, that the enemy would arrive. Many *compañeros* set off 'bombs' explaining these actions, while others gave out leaflets, or called the enemy (the police or the army). The idea was that this dispersed their resources, because we

knew we wouldn't be there when they arrived. We'd finish
with the barricade, call the enemy and when they arrived,
we weren't there any more. The First of May had arrived
and we managed to do everything we wanted to.
The government and the factory owners had to give the
workers the day off. On the 2nd of May, we started fresh actions. We telephoned all the factories and told them that we'd
placed high explosives there and that they were responsible
for the lives of all those people. They had to get all the workers out and they let them leave. Many workers had a week's
rest because we threatened them every day. This was one way
to get rest for the workers. But above all, what we achieved
was that the government had to recognize that our strength
lies in the strength of the people themselves, who step by step
are learning to do things better. A *compañero* placed a box
with an aerial which looked like high explosives near a building where people could see it. The police arrived and made
a tremendous fuss. They called the army. They even came in
tanks. They called high explosive experts to disconnect it very
delicately with special pincers. They were furious when they
discovered that it had nothing in it. The soldiers began firing
in the air. They were livid. The 31st of January Popular Front
has gone on doing this type of actions on all the commemo-
rative days. And on other occasions too. For instance, when
ex-Somoza officers in Honduran territory attacked Nicaragua, we repudiated this action by burning the offices of the
Honduran airline. The important thing is that we were using
all our resources.

Women have played an incredible role in the revolutionary struggle. Perhaps after the victory, we'll have time to
tell our story. It is unbelievable. Mothers with their children
would be putting up barricades, and then placing 'propaganda bombs', or carrying documents. Women have had a great
history. They've all experienced terrible things, whether they
be working-class women, peasant women, or teachers. This
same situation has led us to do all those things. We don't do
them because we want power, but so that something will be

left for human beings. And this gives us the courage to be steadfast in the struggle, in spite of the danger.

The government has many, many spies in different places. It might be on a bus, in a restaurant, in a market, on any corner. They're everywhere. They've got people who ride around in respectable bullet-proof cars, but they've also got poor people who sell brooms from door to door. But in spite of everything, this control hasn't been able to stop the will of the people.

After the events of the Spanish embassy, revolutionary Christians decided to set up an organization and give it my father's name. It's called the 'Vicente Menchú Revolutionary Christians'. The Christians took my father's name because he is a national hero for them: a man who despite his terrible experiences never lost his faith. He never confused what Heaven is with what Earth is. He chose to fight with his people, a people which through its faith came to denounce terror and exploitation. As a Christian, he fought against this. And this was because of the different churches which exist in Guatemala. There is the Church of the poor which is at war. We opted for the just war. In El Quiché many priests left the Church because they saw that this wasn't 'communism', it was the people's just war. Christians realized that they needed an organization, not only for the sake of having an organization in the struggle, but also because it actually reflects the attitudes of the Christians who are fighting in the mountains today, motivated by their Christian faith. The Christian hierarchy is not able to join the people's struggle and this means that it will disappear in Guatemala. It does not understand the situation despite all the massacres. It doesn't want to understand. It says we must forgive, but it doesn't see that the government does not ask *our* forgiveness when it kills our brothers. The Church has actually divided into two: the Church of the rich, in which there are many priests who don't want problems; and the Church of the poor which has joined us.

The Church has always talked of love and freedom, but there is no freedom in Guatemala. Not for us at least. And we're not going to wait until we see the kingdom of God in the sky either. I must also say that, although the majority of the Bishops conserve their church of privilege, there are some who have realized that their duty is not to defend a building, a structure. They've understood that their commitment is to their own people, so they've been persecuted and forced to abandon the Church. The ecclesiastical hierarchy has made its position very clear. For five or six years now they've been going around with bodyguards. This makes us think a lot about the attitudes of these men. At the beginning of the electoral campaign in 1981, Archbishop Casariego blessed the campaign. The cardinal and his priests were involved in it. To make all the priests clarify their positions, the government decided, in July of 1981, to send them telegrams with their complete names and addresses, calling them to the capital to attend a meeting with deputies and government ministers. Priests and nuns all had to attend; they had no choice. Before entering the Congress building they were asked their exact names and addresses, and had their photographs taken. At this meeting, that assassin Lucas called on them to initiate a literacy campaign. Many priests preferred not to say anything for fear of reprisals. The most militant were some nuns who said that they hadn't waited for this meeting to teach people to read and write but had been doing it for a long time. They said that they had nothing to do with the government.

After this, many priests had to go into hiding. Those who didn't respond to the government's invitation were attacked on radio and television. The government announced that there would be tighter control of religion in Guatemala, and that convents and churches would be searched. Well, they began raiding the houses of nuns who'd taken the side of the people. They kidnapped the Jesuit Luis Pellecer, and made him talk after torturing him badly. All that happened because the Church did not respond as it should have done to the death of hundreds of catechists and twelve priests. There was the case of a priest who handed over a group of forty peasants who'd taken refuge in his church. He then handed over his own niece because the girl's mother was a union leader who organized a campaign for the reappearance of the forty peasants. This sixteen-year-old girl was raped by many of the G2 troops. Her mother was a union leader so a lot of pressure was applied, and the girl was saved but went out of her mind. She couldn't talk or move her body because of the repeated rape. They gave her three hours to leave the country and now she is out of the country, but she still can't speak or move.

XXXIII

IN HIDING IN THE CAPITAL.
HUNTED BY THE ARMY

*'My commitment to our struggle recognizes neither bounda-
ries nor limits: only those of us who carry our cause in our
hearts are willing to run the risks.'*

—Rigoberta Menchú

Well, after all that, I was a hunted woman. They were out
looking for me and I couldn't do anything. I couldn't live with
any of the *compañeros* because it would put the family in
danger. The army were looking for me in various places; and
they were looking for my brothers too. For a time I stayed in
the house of some people who gave me a lot of affection and
all the moral support I needed at that time. All these memories are painful because those were very bitter times. Nevertheless, I knew I was a grown-up woman, a strong woman,
who could face this situation. I told myself: 'Rigoberta, you'll
have to grow up a bit more.' Of course my experience had
been very painful, but I thought a lot about things, especially
all the other orphaned children who couldn't speak and tell
their story as I could. I tried to forget so many things, but
at the same time, I had to face up to them as an adult, as a
woman with a certain level of consciousness. I told myself
that I wasn't the only orphan in Guatemala. There are many
others, and it's not my grief alone, it's the grief of a whole

people. It's the grief of a whole people, and all of us orphans who've been left must bear it.

Then afterwards, I had the opportunity of being with one of my little sisters. She told me that she was stronger than I was and had faced situations better, because there was one point when I was losing hope. I asked her: 'How is it possible for our parents to be no longer with us? They never killed any one, they never stole from their neighbours. And yet, this could happen to them.' Thinking about this made my life very difficult and I often couldn't believe it or stand it. I even wished that I had some vices. I said; 'If I had some vices, perhaps I could lose myself in depravity, so I didn't have to think or bear life.' Well, the meeting with my little sister was lovely. She was twelve years old. She said: 'What has happened is a sign of victory. It gives us reason for fighting. We must behave like revolutionary women.' 'A revolutionary isn't born out of something good,' said my sister, 'he is born out of wretchedness and bitterness. This just gives us one more reason. We have to fight without measuring our suffering, or what we experience, or thinking about the monstrous things we must bear in life.' And she made me renew my commitment completely and showed me how cowardly I'd been in not accepting all this. This encouraged me a great deal.

Since I couldn't live in one house, I had to change places all the time. Then I fell ill in the house of some people. I was in bed for fifteen days. I remember that that was when I got an ulcer. It was just after my mother died. I was very ill. I wanted to go out after that, but I told myself that I just could not do it. Then I dreamed about my mother and my father. My father said: 'What you are doing is not right, my child. You are a woman. That's enough of that!' And my father's words acted like a medicine and cured me straight away. So with my spirits raised, I left the house where I was staying. I went to a little town where the army spotted me. It was a little town in Huehuetenango. I was in the street. What happened was that by now I was fed up, tired of hiding in houses. There comes a moment when you just don't want to hide any more. I went out, and coming down the street was an army jeep. It came so close to me that it nearly took me with it and its occupants said my whole name. I knew what that meant for me. It meant that I'd be kidnapped or killed. I remember the feeling I had at that moment. I felt I didn't want to die, that I had a lot of things still to do, that it wasn't time for me to die yet. The army came back again. They said they wanted to talk to me. They passed by again. There was hardly anyone in the street. I didn't know what to do! I was with someone else. We thought of going into a shop but that was useless because they'd kill us there. So, we had to run and run, to the little church. We managed to reach the church but the army saw us go in. They went crazy looking for us. They came into the church. It was useless going into the priest's room because they'd get me out in any case. So I said to myself: 'Well, here it is then, my contribution.' I was sorry to die because I thought that my participation was still pretty valuable and there were many things to do. I remember that I had very very long hair which I wore tied up. I let my hair down, and it all fell loose. My hair covered the whole of my back and I kneeled down. There were only two people in the church, no-one else. My *compañera* went and knelt down beside one of the people and I stayed beside the other. I waited for the moment they'd catch me. They went through the church but they didn't see us. They were like madmen. The church adjoined the market and they thought that we'd managed to go through the church to the market. They didn't recognize us. We waited there for over an hour and a half. They looked all over the market. Then they left the town and surrounded it. But we escaped another way.

I wasn't afraid because I wasn't thinking. When you're in danger and you know you've only a minute of your life left, you don't remember what you did yesterday, or what you're going to do tomorrow. I remember that my head was empty, empty. The only thing I knew was that I didn't want to die, that I wanted to live longer. And that showed my real cowardice because I'd often wished for death. I'd felt that because of all that had happened, it was better not to be alive. But this strengthened my commitment again, and I said that, yes, I could give my life, but not like this. I'd give my life carrying out a task, a specific task. Of course. But not this way. Well, I was wrong then, but I was obviously suffering the consequences of contributing to the struggle of my people, suffering what they were suffering.

We managed to get out of the town. I remember having to walk a lot to get far away from that town. I couldn't stay anywhere. I couldn't stay with peasants, nor any of the nuns sympathetic to us. The *compañeros* didn't know what to do with me, or where to hide me. The trouble was that so many people knew me, many of them only because I'd worked in the *fincas*. And so had many young men before they'd been taken off for military service. So I'd be recognized in many different places. This was the situation I was faced with. The *compañeros* had to take me to Guatemala City; but what was I going to do when I got to the capital? Where was I going to stay? There wasn't the organization then that there is now. Now they have all kinds of ways of hiding any *compañero*, but in those days we didn't have those possibilities. Well, I went to work clandestinely as a maid in the house of some nuns. With all the horrors that I had inside me, it would have been comforting for me to be able to talk to all the *compañeros*, or people who understood me, people who were sympathetic. But I went to the house of these nuns and there I couldn't talk to anyone, because no-one knew my situation.

They set me to work straight away washing a pile of clothes and this made my problem worse, because as I washed the clothes, my mind was focused on the whole panorama of my past. There was no-one to tell, no-one in whom I could find some comfort. If I'd told them they wouldn't understand. Anyway, I stayed there because I had no alternative. I was there for about fifteen days. But the nuns began to be suspicious of me, even though I didn't say anything. I kept all my troubles, all my suffering, close to my heart. And the nuns, well, they were holy, they didn't allow a humble worker near them.

They had their own community, a house where they ate well. They had their own special bedrooms, and even their clothes had to be washed with great care because they were nuns. I found this intolerable. Just more misery. I told myself: 'What a terrible situation to be in! Not even suffering for something, but suffering just to save my life.' I stayed there. None of the nuns talked to me. They ignored me, but gave me a lot of work to do. As well as washing the clothes, I had to clean the house, and I also had a lot of extra things to do on top of my work. And frankly, I'd lost a lot of my energy with all the worries I'd had. I'd been ill in bed, I hadn't eaten for many days, and I had an ulcer. Everything was piling up together: it was all on top of me. Then, I became friendly with one of the nuns' maids. At least it was someone to listen to me. Of course, I didn't tell her about my situation or any of my problems; I told it in a different way, talking about my experiences in the *finca*. I found this a relief, there were less things on top of me.

I remember having to get up very early. At five o'clock I'd get washed ready to start work. At half past one or two in the afternoon I'd be called to eat, to eat all the scraps off the plates. It was a very hard and difficult time for me. At the same time, I was obliged to hold my tongue. There were some pupils in the house, but I was forbidden to speak to them. I don't know if it was because the nuns suspected something. And there was a young man who came to the house a lot. They'd put cake aside for him. He was the only man allowed into the community, into the nuns' dining room. The nuns liked him very much. Well, I thought he was a seminarist or a priest. But from the way he spoke, he was something different, you could tell he wasn't Guatemalan. Well, I asked myself: 'Who am I with here, then? What am I doing here? Who could this man be?' Every morning when he came, they'd said: 'Here's your coffee, and your plate, and your cake.' And they'd ask if his food was hot, and all that. So I plucked up courage to ask the cook who this young man was. But she told me that she couldn't say because the nuns would scold her if they found out. Well, then I became more suspicious. I had to find out who he was: because of all the danger I was in and the risks I was running, I had to know who the people were where I was living. So I took the cook to one side and asked her: 'Who *is* he?' And she told me he was Nicaraguan. 'He comes from Nicaragua and has no father, and he's poor.' That's what she said. I began suspecting many things. I told myself that I had to ask, even if it was indiscreet. I began getting to know one of the nuns and asking her things, and, finally, I said: 'Who's that young man?' This nun had begun to trust me, so she told me that he had worked for Somoza, that he was poor and had no-one to look after him, and that they were being kind to him by looking after him. The government wanted to give him a house, but, poor thing, it's awful to live alone. It just couldn't be. And that was why they had him there in their house. This was enough for me to imagine who he was. I found out afterwards that that young man worked for the *Judicial*, the secret police. That's the most criminal group in Guatemala, the ones who kidnap and torture. And I was living with the enemy! I didn't want to stay there one more night; I didn't want to spend any more time in that place because I knew I'd be discovered. The fact that they'd begun to be suspicious, that they told me not to talk to the pupils, was a sign that they were thinking something. I was very, very worried. I couldn't sleep at night thinking about what I was going to do.

Of course, other people were working to get me out of the country or to get me to another place. A lot of people loved me very much. But there was still a lot to do. One of these people came, and I told him: 'Look, I can't stay here a moment longer.' They thought I was in despair. But I kept all this in my heart because I was very worried for those people too, in case they made mistakes through not doing things properly. But my life was in danger. If they found me, they'd kill me.

XXXIV

EXILE

'We are the avengers of death. Our race will never be extinguished while there is light in the morning star.'
                                              —Popol Vuh

And so the time came for me to leave there. I was happy, but, at the same time, something happened that I would never have believed possible. The *compañeros* got me out on a plane to Mexico, and I felt a shattered, broken woman, because I'd never imagined that one day those criminals would force me to abandon my country. All the same, I also hoped to come back very soon and carry on working. I didn't want to interrupt my work for a single moment, because I know that I can only hold my parents' banner high if I dedicate myself to the struggle that they left half finished.

I went to different parts of Mexico, but I didn't know what to do there. Poor people never dream of travelling abroad, we don't even dream of travelling anywhere. Because we can't. But, well . . . I left, I went to other places, got to know other people. I was with many people who love me very much and I've received the same affection from them as from my loved ones. I remember that they asked for my testimony about the situation in Guatemala and I was very moved. I was invited to take part in a conference of church people from Latin America, Central America and Europe, where I was asked to describe the lives of our women, and with such great pleasure. I talked about my mother at that meeting. I often had to suppress the great grief I felt when I spoke of her, but I did it with love, remembering also that my mother wasn't the only woman to have suffered and that many women are as courageous as she was.

Later I was told that some people were coming to visit me and that I'd be together with *compañeros* coming out of Guatemala. I was happy. It didn't matter which *compañeros* they were, men or women, because I loved all my people, and for me they're all brothers and sisters whoever they are. And soon afterwards I had the wonderful surprise of seeing my little sisters, and I felt so happy. And it doesn't really matter that we (not only myself but all my brothers and sisters) don't know the whereabouts of the grave of my brothers who died in the *finca*, nor the grave of my little brother who was tortured, nor that of my father, nor my mother. But after my parents' death, I hadn't heard anything about my brothers and sisters, yet I hoped and hoped that they were alive. When we were separated, my littlest sister was helping my mother. The other one had gone into the mountains with our *compañeros*, the guerrillas. The two of them had left the country together simply because my sister who was in the mountains felt that she had to go and help the other one, to accompany her and see that everything went smoothly. My little sister had opted for the armed struggle; she was eight when she joined the guerrillas. She thought like an adult, she felt like a woman, especially when it came to defending her people. Well, anyway, she went into the mountains. It was perhaps because she'd got to know the guerrillas before I did. I'd begun leaving our community and going off to others, so I'd begun to move away from the mountains to other more populated towns where they don't have the wonderful mountains we have. It wasn't because the guerrillas came to our village, but because when my sister went down to work in the Brols' *finca*, she found that most of the Brols' labourers were guerrillas. So my sister had contact with them, but she knew how to keep all her secrets. She never told my parents that she had direct contact because she thought it could mean death for my parents. She'd be risking everything. She thought of my parents' lives and her own life, so she kept it all secret. When we realized that my sister had disappeared, we started investigating immediately and went looking for her. But people told us: 'Oh yes, she was in touch with the guerrilla army, so it's obvious she's gone off to the mountains.' But we weren't sure. We thought that perhaps she'd got lost, or been kidnapped, or anything, because they'd threatened that if they couldn't kill one of my parents, they'd kill one of us. I only knew for certain in 1979, when my sister came down from the mountains once and we met. She said: 'I'm happy. Don't worry about me. Even if I suffer hunger, pain and long marches through the mountains, I'm doing it with love and I'm doing it for you.' It was in a village where she'd been given permission to hear mass and go to communion. She'd come down to the village and by pure chance we were at the mass.

In Mexico I met people from Europe who had helped us. We'd met those same people when my parents were alive. They offered us help to go and live in Europe. They said it wasn't possible for a human being to bear so much. They told us, with the best of intentions, that we should go over there, that they'd give us a house and everything we needed. And my little sisters would have the opportunity to study. I couldn't decide for my sisters because I thought of them as women who could think for themselves and decide their own lives. So they talked to my sisters, but they rejected the proposition. They said: 'If you want to help us, send us help, but not for ourselves, for all the orphans who've been left.' These people couldn't understand why, despite all the risks we run, we still want to live in Guatemala. Of course, they couldn't understand, because only those of us who carry our cause in our hearts are willing to run the risks. After the army's furious urge to capture us had calmed down, our *compañeros* helped us to go back to Guatemala.

We went back to Guatemala and my sisters each chose an organization to work in. The *compañeros* told us to choose the best one for us, where we could contribute most. Well, me, I love the CUC. I love it because that's where I realized the importance of the people's revolutionary war, that we had to fight our enemies, and at the same time, fight for change, as a people. I'd no doubt about that. So I said: 'I want to work with the people, even though it means running a lot of risks.' I was very worried about my youngest sister because she grew up in the mountains, she grew up in our village which was very high up in the mountains, and she loved the mountains, the greenery, all the natural world, and I thought that she would opt for a task which was even harder than mine. And it was true. She said: 'I can only honour my mother's banner by taking up arms. For me, there's no other choice.' She made her decision clearly and responsibly. She said: 'I'm a grown-up woman. I am a *compañera*.' My other sister told her: 'Sister, from now on we are comrades in arms. I'm a *compañera* like you and you are a *compañera* like me.' Then they had to find ways of reaching their organizations because we were out of touch with everything.

My sisters went up to the mountains and I stayed to organize the people. I thought a lot about whether to go back to the CUC, but I decided that the CUC had enough leaders, enough peasant members, and also many women taking on responsibilities in the organization. So, because of my Christian background, I opted for the Vicente Menchú Revolutionary Christians. I didn't choose it because it bore my father's name, but because, as a Christian, it was my duty to work with the people. My task was to educate the Christian *compañeros* whose faith brings them into the organization. It's a bit like what I was talking about before, about being a catechist. Well, my work is just like being a catechist, except that I'm one who walks on the Earth, not one who thinks that the Kingdom of God only comes after death. Through all my experiences, through everything I'd seen, through so much pain and suffering, I learned what the role of a Christian in the struggle is, and what the role of a Christian on this Earth is. We all came to important conclusions by studying the Bible. All our *compañeros* did. We discovered that the Bible has been used as a way of making us accept our situation, and not to bring enlightenment to the poor. The work of revolutionary Christians is above all to condemn and denounce the injustices committed against the people. It is secret, but not a clandestine movement. We are the people and we can't hide completely. What we call 'clandestine' are the armed *compañeros* who live, not among the people, but up in the mountains. What we call 'secret' is all the work which we do secretly among the people. We also denounce the stance of the Church hierarchy because it is so often hand in glove with the government. This is actually something I have thought about a lot. Well, because they call themselves Christians, yet they are often deaf to the suffering of the people. This is what I really meant before when I asked Christians to put into practice what being a Christian really means. Many who call themselves Christians don't really deserve to be called Christians. They have no worries, and lovely houses. But that is all. That is why I say that the Church in Guatemala is divided in two. The Church of the poor (and many have taken this path) has the same beliefs as the poor. And the Church as a hierarchy, as an institution, is still a little clique. The majority of our people are Christian, but if our own shepherds (as they're called) teach us bad examples, and go hand in hand with the government, we are not going to follow them. This gave me a great deal to think about. For example, the nuns whom I lived with made me sad. With their comfortable lives, they were wasteful women who did nothing for others.

Well, my role is now that of a leader. This is mostly because the enemy knows me. My job is above all carrying papers into the interior or to the towns, and organizing the people, at the same time practising with them the light of the Gospel. My life does not belong to me. I've decided to offer it to a cause. They can kill me at any time, but let it be when I'm fulfilling a mission, so I'll know that my blood will not be shed in vain, but will serve as an example to my *compañeros*. The world I live in is so evil, so bloodthirsty, that it can take my life away from one moment to the next. So the only road open to me is our struggle, the just war. The Bible taught me that. I tried to explain this to a Marxist *compañera*, who asked me how could I pretend to fight for revolution being a

Christian. I told her that the whole truth is not found in the Bible, but neither is the whole truth in Marxism, and that she had to accept that. We have to defend ourselves against our enemy but, as Christians, we must also defend our faith within the revolutionary process. At the same time, we have to think about the important work we have to do, after our victory, in the new society. I know that no-one can take my Christian faith away from me. Not the government, not fear, not weapons. And this is what I have to teach my people: that together we can build the people's Church, a true Church. Not just a hierarchy, or a building, but a real change inside people. I chose this as my contribution to the people's war. I am convinced that the people, the masses, are the only ones capable of transforming society. It's not just another theory. I chose to stay in the city among the people, instead of choosing to take up arms, as I said. We all contribute in different ways, but we are all working for the same objective.

That is my cause. As I've already said, it wasn't born out of something good, it was born out of wretchedness and bitterness. It has been radicalized by the poverty in which my people live. It has been radicalized by the malnutrition which I, as an Indian, have seen and experienced. And by the exploitation and discrimination that I've felt in the flesh. And by the oppression which prevents us performing our ceremonies, and shows no respect for our way of life, the way we are. At the same time, they've killed the people dearest to me, and here I include my neighbours from my village among my loved ones. Therefore, my commitment to our struggle knows no boundaries nor limits. This is why I've travelled to many places where I've had the opportunity to talk about my people. Of course, I'd need a lot of time to tell you all about my people, because it's not easy to understand just like that. And I think I've given some idea of that in my account. Nevertheless, I'm still keeping my Indian identity a secret. I'm still keeping secret what I think no-one should know. Not even anthropologists or intellectuals, no matter how many books they have, can find out all our secrets.

Acknowledgements

Helena Araújo, Juan Ugné Karvelis, Carol Prunhuber, Jerónimo Pérez Rescanière, Francisca Ribas, Arturo Taracena, Nicole Revel-MacDonald, Marie Tremblay.

GLOSSARY

Altiplano	Name given to the mountainous region in the north-west of Guatemala where the majority of the Indian population live.
Antigua	Capital of the Captaincy General of Guatemala under Spanish rule (1542–1773), now capital of the province of Sacatépequez.
atol	Drink made out of maize dough, cooked with water, salt, sugar and milk.
ayote	Plant, the fruit of which is a type of gourd or pumpkin.
Boca Costa	Name given to the western slope of the Sierra Madre going down to the Pacific Ocean.
bojónes	Edible shoots of a variety of palm.
caballeria	Agrarian measurement equivalent to 64 *manzanas*, i.e. 45 hectares (= 2.471 acres).
caitios	Diminutive of *caite*, which is a leather sandal with a rubber sole.
cantina	Bar, where other types of groceries are sold.
cartucho	White flower (similar to arum lily) used in ceremonies.
caxlan	Quiché name for *ladino*.
centavo	Monetary unit. 100 *centavos* = 1 *quetzal*.
Chajul	Municipality and administrative centre of l Quiché. Centre of the Quiché people. The word also means '*ocote*' in the Quiché language.
chilacayote	Type of gourd.
chimán	Clairvoyant, sorceror.
Chimel	Village in the municipality of Canillá, in the province of El Quiché. In Quiché it means 'the place of rabbits'.

chirimía	Wind instrument.
Cobán	Administrative centre of the province of Alta Verapaz. Centre of the Kekchi people.
comal (pl.-es)	Earthenware disc on which tortillas are cooked.
compadre	No equivalent in English. Can mean a close friend, or relation, or godparent. Feminine is *comadre*.
compañero	Name widely used in Latin America to mean friend, companion, in general terms, and more specifically 'comrade' in political terms. Here it is used toward the beginning to refer to the inhabitants of the village who participate in the life of the community. Towards the end it becomes used in a more political sense for the militants of the CUC, the unions, or political organizations. The *compañeros* in the mountains are the guerrilla groups.
copal	Resin which is used as incense.
corte	Multicoloured material which Guatemalan women use as a skirt. It is part of their traditional costume.
Cotzal	Municipality and administrative centre of the province of El Quiché. Centre of the Ixil people.
despedida	Farewell, farewell party.
ejote	Tender pod of beans.
elate	Young corn cob when still green.
finca	Plantation, estate. Can be coffee, sugar, cotton, etc.
guaro	Type of *aguardiente*, i.e. brandy, liquor.
G2	Intelligence Division of the Armed Forces, Secret Police.
hueco	Homosexual.
Huehuetenango	Province, and provincial capital. Centre of the Mam people.
huipil	Embroidered or woven blouse used by Indian women. It is the top half of the traditional dress, used with the *corte*.
INAFOR	Instituto Nacional de Forestación de Guatemala: Guatemalan Forestry Commission.
INTA	Instituto Nacional de Transformación Agraria de Guatemala: Guatemalan National Institute for Agrarian Transformation.
jutes	Type of river snail.
Kaibil	Elite division of soldiers trained in counterinsurgency; means 'tiger' in the Ixil language.

ladino	Today, any Guatemalan – whatever his economic position – who rejects, either individually or through his cultural heritage, Indian values of Mayan origin. It also implies mixed blood.
manzana	Agrarian measure equal to 0.7 hectares: (1 hectare = 2.471 acres).
marimba	Percussion instrument generally composed of thirty slats of wood, and sound boxes of gourds or wood. These are then hit with sticks with rubber balls at the end (similar principle to a xylophone).
mazorca	Maize cob.
mecapàl	Wide belt or band of natural leather used to carry heavy loads on the shoulders by taking the weight round the head.
milpa	Field of maize.
mimbre	Type of willow, used for making cane baskets, furniture, etc.
morral	Little bag of woven wool.
nahual	The word given to the double, the alter-ego, be it an animal or any other living thing, which, according to Indian belief, all human beings possess. There is a relationship between the *nahual* and a person's personality. The designation of the *nahual* means the newborn child is recognized as a member of the community.
Nebaj	Municipality and administrative centre of the province of El Quiché. Centre of the Ixil people.
nixtamal	Cauldron where the maize is cooked. The name also applies to maize cooked with lime, which is the dough used to make *tortillas*.
ocote	Very resinous red pine. It also refers to a branch of the tree which is used as a torch because it flames.
Oriente	The eastern part of Guatemala which includes the provinces of Zacapa, Chiqimula, Jalapa, Jutiapa and Santa Rosa. It is mainly populated by *ladinos*.
pamac	Sort of palm used for roofs.
panela	Unrefined sugar. Brown sugar.
perraje	A coloured cotton cloak.
pinol	Grilled maize flour mixed with water, sugar and cocoa to make a refreshing drink.

pita	Fibre from the agave plant for making ropes.
pom	Incense.
quetzal	Guatemalan money. *Quetzal = 100 centavos.*
Sacapúlas	Municipality and administrative centre of the province of El Quiché. Means 'shredded fodder' in *Nahuatl.*
Santa Rosa Chucuyub	Hybrid Hispano-Quiché word meaning 'Santa Rosa before the Hill'.
sijolaj	Musical instrument, a whistle made of clay.
taltuza	Rodent, a kind of racoon.
tamal (pl.-es)	Maize paste wrapped in maize or banana leaves, and cooked. Can also be filled with meat or vegetables.
tapanco	Loft for storing crops.
tapizca	Harvest, especially of maize, cotton and beans.
Tecún Umán	Means 'grandson of the king' in Quiché. He was one of the four Lords of the Royal House of Cawek, and became commander of the Quiché forces. He died in February 1524 while fighting the troops of Pedro de Alvarado on the plains of Quetzaltenango. His *nahual* was the quetzal (bird) and, according to legend, it flew away the moment he died in combat.
temascal	Steam bath made of hot stones.
tortilla	Maize pancake which is the main food of the Central American peoples.
tún	Drum made from a hollow tree trunk.
Uspantán	Municipality and administrative centre of the province of El Quiché.
vara	Measurement. Approximately 83.5 centimetres.
yuca	Manioc.
zopilote	Buzzard.